Abstracts of the

DEBT BOOKS

of the

PROVINCIAL LAND OFFICE OF MARYLAND

Frederick County

Volume I

Calvert Papers: 1750
Liber 22: 1753, 1754, 1755

By

V. L. Skinner, Jr.

Printed for Clearfield Company by
Genealogical Publishing Company
Baltimore, Maryland
2014

ISBN 978-0-8063-5720-1

Introduction

The Provincial Land Office of Maryland was responsible for the dispensing of land from 1634 to 1777. Land was initially acquired by a warrant and was then patented. Information concerning these documents are found in the Warrants and Patents series of the Provincial Land Office located at the Maryland State Archives and are indexed by Peter Wilson Coldham in his five-volume series *Settlers of Maryland*, published by Genealogical Publishing Company.

Land was patented according to the desires of the patentee, and the name given to a patent was not necessarily unique within any particular jurisdiction.

The Lord Proprietor's personal hold on land affairs was much weakened during the royal period from 1689 to 1715. However, it was immediately revived when his proprietary rights were restored in 1715 (Hartsook and Skordas, *Land Office and Prerogative Court Records*). Both the Rent Rolls and the Debt Books date from this restoration period.

The Rent Rolls and the Debt Books are the means by which the Lord Proprietor kept track of the rents due him. Each piece of land granted to a person was subject to a yearly rent according to the terms of the patent.

A Rent Roll consists of entries for each tract of land patented, plus the name of the person for whom it was originally surveyed, the present owner, the acreage, and the rent. Alienations, or subsequent sales and leases of the piece of land, are also included.

A Debt Book consists of a list of persons owning land with the names and rents of each tract that he or she owned, all listed in one place under his or her name.

The Debt Books

The Debt Books are arranged by county, by year, and then by the name of the person paying the rent. There are a total of 54 libers, covering all of the counties. The extant Debt Books for the Western Shore counties are essentially annual, dating from 1753 to 1774. (The Debt Books for 1750 for five Western Shore counties–Anne Arundel, Baltimore, Charles, Prince George's, Frederick–are found in the Calvert Papers, located at the Maryland State Archives.) The extant Debt Books for the Eastern Shore counties are also essentially annual, dating from 1733 to 1775.

Each liber contains information for only one county, but for multiple years. For purposes of identification, each section (i.e., year) of any particular liber is given the denotation of the specific year.

Tracking land ownership over various years is particularly important for intestate estates, land inherited by women, and land that is not specified in a will.

The information in this series is presented in a tabular form:

- liber and folio citation, with any pertinent date.
- name of the person paying the taxes.
- name of the tract of land.
- acreage.

Notes to Reader

The following conventions are used in this book:

1. "The" at the beginning of any tract name has been omitted.
2. The index contains both tract names and surnames, sorted together.
3. "Crossed out" entries in the original libers have been included, as such.
4. Names have been transcribed as they are written; no attempt has been made to standardize any spelling.
5. Introduction and index pages of the original libers have been omitted.

Abbreviations

AA	Anne Arundel County	o/c	overcharged
ACC	Accomac County	p.	perches
a/s	alias	PA	Pennsylvania
BA	Baltimore County	PG	Prince George's County
CE	Cecil County	PW	Prince William County
CH	Charles County	pt	part of
cnp	name continued on next page	pts	parts of
cont	name continued from previous folio	QA	Queen Anne's County
		SM	St. Mary's County
CR	Caroline County	SO	Somerset County
CV	Calvert County	SU	Sussex County
DE	Delaware	s/o	son of
DO	Dorchester County	<t>	torn
FR	Frederick County	TA	Talbot County
h/o	heirs of	tbc	to be charged to
KE	Kent County MD	unr	unreadable
KEDE	Kent County DE	VA	Virginia
n/a	not available	WO	Worcester County
n/g	not given	w/o	widow of

Contents of this volume

This book is the first of six volumes for Frederick County, formed in 1748 primarily from Prince George's County. In the time period 1750-1773, Frederick County was the largest land mass county in the province. The debt books for Frederick County cover the following years: 1750, 1753, 1754, 1755, 1756/7, 1759, 1760, 1761, 1762, 1763, 1766, 1768, 1769, 1770, 1771, 1772, 1773.

From the Debt Books entries, two interesting facts are evident: (1) beginning in 1768, the Baptist Congregation, the Elders of the Kitocton Church, and the Elders of the Presbyterian Meeting House are taxed; and, (2) George Town, New London, Frederick Town, Sharpsburg, Tawney Town, and Winchester Town were established communities, with numerous lots already occupied. Charles Carroll (barrister) and Charles Carroll of Carrollton are the largest landowners. Some Frederick County landowners are cited as inhabiting the following jurisdictions: Prince George's County (MD), Charles County, St. Mary's County, Cecil County, Calvert County, Baltimore County, Anne Arundel County, Annapolis, London, New Jersey, Pennsylvania, Virginia, and Carolina.

CP:1750:1 ...		**Acres**
h/o Mr. Clement Craycroft	pt. "Brook Court"	375
	pt. "Joseph & Mary"	100
Mr. Thomas Letchworth	pt. "Brook Court"	142
	pt. "Joseph & Mary"	158
	pt. "Ridgeley"	75
	pt. "Beals Gift"	167
Mrs. Margrey Gant	"Hollydays Choice"	500
Mr. Mackall Skinner	pt. "Brook Court"	300
Mr. Samuel Roundall	"Hargrave"	210
Mr. Henry Grear	pt. "Ridge"	100
Mr. Ananias Grear	pt. "Ridge"	100
Mr. Richard Brightwell	pt. "Spinham"	45½
	"Padgets Rest" a/s "Marsh"	105
	"Runningaway"	50
	"Wilsons Lott"	70
Mr. John White	"Beals Inclosure"	456
Mr. Jonathan White	"Hopsons Choice"	220
	"Stepmothers Folly"	334
Mr. Alexander Magruder	pt. "Cox Hays"	300
	pt. "Exchange"	120
	pt. "Cox Hays"	249
	pt. "Anchovy Hills"	50
	pt. "Taytorton"	51
	1 lot in Mill Town	1
	pt. "Taylors Marsh"	21
Mr. Hezekiah Magruder	"Quicksale"	70
	pt. "Exchange"	80
	pt. "Anchovy Hills"	30
CP:1750:2 ...		
Mr. Benjamin Truman	pt. "Thomas & Anthonys Choice"	250
	"Taylors Cost"	37
Mrs. Elizabeth Lawson	pt. "Brook Court"	358½
	pt. "Joseph & Mary"	508
Mr. Thomas Baden	"Gore"	72
Mr. Robert Baden, Jr.	"Lawsons Lott"	100

Mr. Joseph Letchworth	pt. "Brook Court"	200
Mr. William Cox	pt. "Taylerton"	52
Rev. Mr. Samuel Clagett	pt. "Pitchcraft"	120
	pt. "Brock Hall"	200
Madam Jane Brooke	pt. "Poplar Neck"	244
	pt. "Dann"	250
Mr. John Johnson	pt. "Woodjoy"	100
Mr. John Boone	pt. "Brookwood"	400
	pt. "Hazard"	150
Mr. Henry Boone	pt. "Brookwood"	100
	pt. "Easycomeby"	200
Mr. William Watson	pt. "Trennent"	47
	pt. "Woodborough"	17
Mr. William Bright	pt. "Anchovy Hill"	220
	pt. "Levells"	33
Mr. George Magruder	pt. "Anchovy Hill"	72
CP:1750:3 ...		
Mr. Nathaniel Ranton	"Venture"	100
Madam Greenfield (SM)	"Taylors Hills" or "Trumans Hills"	200
Mr. Gerard Truman Greenfield	"Golden Race"	181
	pt. "Addition Retaliation & Barrens"	251
Mr. Paul Rawlings	pt. "Doves Nest"	27
	pt. "Doves Perch"	20
h/o Mr. Peter Brightwell	pt. "Spinham"	45½
	pt. "Colebrooke" & "Poplar Hill"	120
	"Nest Egg"	30
Mr. George Jones (CH)	"Quiksale"	170
	"Pasture"	144
	"Archers Pastured"	35
Mr. Thomas Gibbons	"Brookfield"	70
Mr. Henry Boteler	pt. "Ballington"	191
Mr. Richard Bean	"Digbeth"	100
Mr. Joseph Sarratt	"Thomas's Inheritance"	50
Dr. Thomas Hamilton	pt. "Mount Calvert Manor"	100
Mr. James Harvey	pt. "Mount Calvert Manor"	50
Mr. Thomas Addison	pt. "Discovery"	174

CP:1750:4 ...		
h/o Mr. John Deakins	pt. "Hazard"	50
	pt. "Brooks Discovery"	50
Mr. George Bigges	pt. "Ball"	126
h/o Col. Thomas Addison	"Locust Thickett"	1055
	"St. Elizabeth"	1430
	"Hart Park"	963
	"Barnaby"	543
	"Gleanings"	340
	"Discontent"	512
	"Force"	226
	"Content"	100
	"Maddox Folly"	340
	"North Britain"	300
	"Berwick upon Tweed"	209
	"Union"	393
	"Berry"	300
	"Pasture"	272
	"Addisons Choice"	2300
	"Addition"	287
	½ of "Whitehaven"	409
	"Philip & Jacob"	400
	"Gesborough"	850
	"Prevention"	336
	"Brothers Joynt Interest"	236
	"Nonsuch"	106
	"Chichester"	400
	"Friendship"	428
	"Long Point"	253
	pt. "Friendship"	1600
	pt. "Hunters Kindness"	65
	"Goodwill"	99
	pt. "Blue Plains"	135
Mr. Robert Bradley (cnp)	"Meadows"	7
	"Brook Grove"	320
	pt. "Mores Littleworth"	40

	pt. "Mores Craft"	58
	pt. "Four Hills"	230
	pt. "Sams Begining" & pt. "Bacon Hill"	150
	1 lot in Marlborough	1
	pt. "Croom"	2
	pt. "Morefields"	150
	"Berrys Fortune" pt. "Four Hills"	267
	"Pattenwick"	35
	"Addition to Morefields"	88
	"<t> Beals Chance"	21
CP:1750:5 ...		
Mr. James Thomas	pt. "Ball"	74
Mr. Allen Bowie	pt. "Mount Calvert Manor"	200
	pt. "Locust Thickett" a/s pt. "Brookridge"	300
	pt. "Leith"	200
Mrs. Henry	pt. "Alexandria"	100
Mr. Thomas Harris	pt. "Charles & William"	251
	pt. "Black Ash"	1
Mr. Robert Pottinger	pt. "Charles Purchase" a/s pt. "Charles & William"	297
	pt. "Fenwick"	35
	pt. "Majors Lott"	187½
	"Greens Delight"	200
	"Brothers Request"	500
	"Joys"	50
Mrs. Mary Thrasher	pt. "Benjamin"	100
Mr. Francis Piles	pt. "Advantage"	162½
	pt. "Buck Hill"	100
Mrs. Clagett	"Weston"	500
Mr. Charles Clagett	pt. "Clagetts Purchase"	286
Mr. Benjamin Berry	"Berrys Chance"	100
	"Berrys Fancy"	230
	"Long Lane"	77
	"Berrys Grove"	70
	½ lot in Marlborough	½
Mr. Jeremiah Berry (cnp)	pt. "Charles & Benjamin"	1090
	pt. "Levells"	340

	"Addition to Charles & Benjamin"	31
	"Marlborough Plains"	150
	"Swamp"	28
	pt. "Vale Benjamin"	109
CP:1750:6 ...		
Mr. Richard Burges	pt. "Westphalia"	300
h/o Mr. Thomas Lucas	"Largo"	250
	"Gradon"	20
Mr. Josias Towgood	"Halls Rest"	200
	"Bristole"	140
Mr. Meredith Davis	pt. "Beals Benevolence"	104
	"West Tract"	100
	"Merediths Hunting Quarter"	450
	pt. "Westphalia"	100
	"Good Luck"	400
	"Josiah"	200
	"New Park"	135
	"Lost Breeches"	100
	"Meredith"	118
	"Friends Goodwill"	57
Mr. Stephen Warman	pt. "Beals Benevolence"	49
	pt. "Duvalls Range"	100
Mr. John Wheat	"Friendship"	100
widow Blandford	pt. "Timberland"	154
	"Sailsburry Plain"	153
	pt. "Brook Plains" a/s "Widows Troubles"	1500
	"Brooks Chance"	209
Mr. Thomas Edlin 3rd	pt. "Thomas & Sarah"	250
Mr. John Eversfield, Jr.	"Eversfields Map Nally"	206
	"Hackthorn Heath"	363
	pt. "Brooke Reserve"	1½
	"Drury Lane"	27
	"Eversfields New Filgate" a/s "Sewal Addition"	88
CP:1750:7 ...		
Rev. Mr. John Eversfield (cnp)	"Glebe" being pt. "Brookfield"	100
	pt. "Deer Park" & "Bear Garden Enlarged"	200

	pt. "Brookfield"	30
	pt. "Brook Chance"	232
	pt. "Jacksons Necessity"	300
	pt. "Brookwood"	225
	"Eversfields Addition"	50
	pt. "Eversfields Necessity Enlarged"	50
	pt. "Friendship Enlarged" now "Upper Tract"	204
	pt. "Grove"	43
	pt. "Fathers Gift"	25
Mr. William Eversfield	pt. "Wedge Cross Cloath" & "Brookfield"	150
	pt. "Forrest Fancy"	92
Capt. Walter Smith	pt. "Swann Harbour"	172
	pt. "Batchellors Harbour"	420½
	"Brightwells Hunting Quarter"	1086
	pt. "Bradfords Rest"	4795
	3 lots in Nottingham	3
Mr. Nathaniel Offutt	pt. "Neighbourhood"	244
	"Gleanings"	77
	"Addition to Gleanings"	40
	pt. "Coverton"	206
	"Addition to Coverton"	498
	pt. "Coole Spring Levell"	230
	"Wilsons Venture"	37
	pt. "Younger Brother"	200
	"Goose Pond"	100
	"Bishops Island"	28
	"Addition to Goose Pond"	133
Mr. Robert Pearl	pt. "Archers Pasture"	56
CP:1750:8 ...		
Mr. Edward Willett	pt. "Gleanings"	150
	"Scotland"	100
	"Backland"	260
	"Addition to Scotland"	73
Mr. William Harper	"Bealington"	60
Mr. James Swan	pt. "Little Dan"	26
Mrs. Conden	pt. "Marlborough Plains"	156

Mr. John Ridle	pt. "Poplar Thickett"	50
	"Addition to Poplar Thickett"	63
Mr. Jeremiah Fowller	"Spreadax Forrest"	100
widow Culver	"Woodbridge"	120
	pt. "Pitchcraft"	156
Mr. Clement Hill	"Compton Bassit"	740
	"Spy Park"	309
	"Bread & Chease"	158
	pt. "Barralls Purchase" "Duvalls Hunting Quarter"	200
	"Range"	101
	"Trumans Choice"	375
	"Newcastle"	50
	"Giants Range"	100
	pt. "Timberland" & "Generals Gift"	308
	pt. "Chance"	128
	pt. "Partnership"	1000
	pt. "Addition to Partnership"	200
	"Turner"	200
Mr. John Hill	pt. "Baltimore"	731
	"Forrest"	612
widow Culver (Eastern Branch)	"Batchellors Forrest"	200
	"Chance"	100
	"Addition to Chance"	200
	"2nd Addition to Chance"	400
CP:1750:9 ...		
Mr. Richard Clagett	pt. "Croom"	750
	pt. "Croom"	433
Mr. John Clagett	"Greenland"	200
Mr. Thomas Claget	pt. "Dann"	250
Mr. Arnold Livers	pt. "Timberland" & pt. "Generals Gift"	375
	1 lot in Nottingham	1
	pt. "Dukers Wood"	521
	pt. "Ogles Goodwill"	105
	"Arnolds Chance"	600
	pt. "Backland" a/s "Arnolds Delight"	1074
Mr. John Carmack	pt. "Dukers Wood"	56

Mr. William Carmack	pt. "Dukers Wood"	56
	pt. "Luberland"	99
Mr. Samuel Busey	pt. "Charles Hills"	244½
Mr. John Contee	pt. "Neighbourhood"	244
	"Largo"	361
Mr. Jonas Lewis	"Jones Fields"	28
	"Addition to Bacon Hall"	100
Mr. Mareen Duvall	pt. "Poplar Ridge" a/s "Vale Benjamin"	212
Mr. John Cash	pt. "Turkey Thickett"	77½
	pt. "Milland"	50
Mr. Caleb Cash	pt. "Batsons Vineyard"	112
CP:1750:10 ...		
Mr. Dawson Cash	pt. "Turkey Thickett"	77½
h/o Mr. John Soper	pt. "Batsons Vineyard"	50
Mr. Thomas James	pt. "Vale Benjamin"	70
Mrs. Sarah Williams	pt. "Huckleberry Patch" a/s "Vale Benjamin"	156
Mr. John Summers	pt. "Moores Addition"	197
	pt. "Childs Portion"	35
Mr. Benjamin Becraft	"Becrafts Delight"	50
Mr. Thomas Blackloch, Jr.	pt. "Remains" & "Addition to Remains"	200
	pt. "Brook Plains" a/s "Widows Troubles"	220
Mr. Henry Wright	pt. "Essington"	205
	pt. "Brook Grove Reperation" & "Hearts Delight"	348
	pt. "Browns Chance"	19
	"No Name"	88
Mr. Thomas Snowden	pt. "Black Walnut Levells"	585
	pt. "Diamond"	35
	pt. "Bacon Hall"	154
	"Addition to Bacon Hall"	17½
	"2nd Addition to Bacon Hall"	25
	"Peter Point"	100
h/o Mr. Robert Taylor	pt. "Bowdles Choice"	187½
	pt. "Brazenthorp Hall"	10
	pt. "Brough"	548
	pt. "Chance"	25
	1 lot in Queen Ann	1

Mr. Reuben Roberts	pt. "Ryleys Lott"	100
CP:1750:11 ...		
Mr. Guy White	"Cool Spring Manor"	360
Mr. William Mulican	"William & Elizabeth"	110
Hon. Benedict Calvert, Esq.	pt. "Swansons Lott"	1000
	"Charles & Rebecca"	1172
	pt. "Cool Spring Manor"	315
	"Griffiths Purchase"	165
	pt. "Good Luck"	150
	"Cuckolds Delight"	86
	pt. "Elizabeths Delight"	100
	"Hogyard"	125
	pt. "Denmark"	355
	"No Name"	150
	"Gleanings"	53
	"Letchworth"	145
	1 lot in Marlborough	1
	pt. "Greens Purchase"	200
	pt. "St. Marks Place"	1100
	pt. "Charles Hills Defence", "Halls Adventure", & "Darnalls Delight"	400
	pt. "Timerly"	400
	"Generalls Gift"	400
	pt. "Hermitage"	873¼
	"Seamonds Delight"	504
	"Hoskinsons Folly"	100
	"Ryleys Landing"	75
Mr. James Wilson	pt. "Baltimore"	269
	pt. "Beals Pasture"	189
Mr. Humphry Hazeldine	pt. "Black Ash"	4
Mr. Richard Harwood	pt. "Snowden & Welshs Defiance of Williams & Clark"	288
	pt. "Black Ash"	1
widow Hyatt	pt. "Tewksberry"	300
CP:1750:12 ...		
Mr. Benjamin Boyd (cnp)	pt. "Ample Grange"	200

	"Turkey Thickett"	160
	"Castle Plains"	500
	"Frays Choice" & "Sway"	73
	"Rich Land"	200
	"Shelbys Addition"	50
Mr. John Boyd, Jr.	"Boyds Delight"	233
Mr. William Young, Jr.	"Noch"	500
Mr. Peter Young	"St. Davids", "Thorp Land" & "Perrys Hills"	300
Mr. Leonard Weyman	pt. "Sway"	100
	pt. "Ample Grange"	100
Mr. Abraham Boyd, Jr.	"Newsore"	79
Mr. John Hawkins	"Hawkins Lott"	184
	"Little Ease"	60
William Murdock, Esq.	"Padworth Farm"	600
	"Essington"	411
	"Perrywood"	800
	"Green Purchase"	200
	pt. "Bowdles Choice"	374
Mr. Thomas Fowller	"Wilsons Chance"	38
Mr. Benjamin Duvall	pt. "Darnalls Grove"	150
Mr. Benjamin Clancy	"Pindles Chance"	76
CP:1750:13 ...		
William Digges, Esq.	"Henrietta Maria"	500
	pt. "Warburton Manor"	1137
	pt. "Frankland"	700
	"Widows Purchase"	1120
	"Fellowship"	172
	"Kendalls Meadows"	550
Mr. Richard Isaac	"Ryleys Range"	150
	pt. "Isaacs Park"	215
	pt. "Isaacs Discovery"	45
	"Addition"	200
	"Beals Park"	100
	"Marys Delight" a/s pt. "Darnals Grove"	125
Henry Rozer, Esq.	pt. "Admorothia"	2211
	pt. "Elizabeths Delight"	100

Mr. George Sly (SM)	pt. "Elizabeths Delight"	100
Mr. Hyde Hoxton	"St. Elizabeth"	600
Mrs. Elizabeth Boyd	pt. "Ample Grange"	150
Mr. Thomas Allen	pt. "Dunkell"	150
Mr. George Hamilton	pt. "Gore"	200
	pt. "Meadows"	63
	pt. "Atwoods Purchase"	89
Mr. William Beal, Jr.	"Loving Acquaintance"	183
	"Plummers Purchase"	135
	"Addition to Plummers"	46
	"Lookout"	19
Dr. Samuel Preston Moore	pt. "Brough"	200
	"Bealls Reserve"	455
CP:1750:14 ...		
h/o Col. Gabriel Parker	pt. "Strife"	250
	pt. "Hazard"	74
	pt. "Partnership"	50
	"Langwore"	350
	"Pissimond"	220
	"Edelins Hogpen"	127
	pt. "Piscattaway Forrest"	346½
Mr. Francis King	pt. "Piscattaway Forrest"	346½
Mr. Thomas Wells	pt. "Strife"	50
	pt. "Ample Grange"	100
	pt. "Something"	4½
Mr. Thomas Lancaster	"Newcastle"	207
	"Queen Ann"	150
	"Moores Prosperity"	300
	pt. "Easy Purchase"	350
Mr. John Brashears	"Cucolds Delight"	62
	pt. "Gleaning"	8
	"Leavings"	19
	"Letchworth"	95
	pt. "Brahears Pocoson"	121
Mr. Alexander Falconer	pt. "Darnalls Grove"	100
Mr. Samuel Farmer (cnp)	"Ryleys Range" now called "Farmers Addition"	100

	"Molls Lott"	50
	"Farmers Purchase" & pt. "Dutchmans Enlargement"	50
	"Moores Cultivation"	57
	pt. "Strife"	20
Mrs. Mary Medcalf	pt. "Darnalls Grove"	206
Mr. Samuel Taylor	pt. "Taylerton"	240
	"Taylortons Pasture"	38½
Mr. Thomas Odell	"Marys Delight" a/s pt. "Darnalls Grove"	375
CP:1750:15 ...		
Mr. Rignall Odle	pt. "Darnalls Grove"	500
	pt. "Three Beals Manor"	216
Mr. Thomas Odle, Jr.	pt. "Darnalls Grove"	200
Mr. William Fowller	pt. "Ridge" & "Taylors Lott"	400
Mr. Thomas Foster	pt. "Evans Range"	100
Mr. Alexander Frazier (lawyer)	pt. "Lundee"	160
	pt. "Lundee"	13
Mr. John Beall, Jr.	pt. "Rovers Content", "Inclosure", "Fathers Gift", "Bread Cheese Hall", & pt. "Good Luck" lying on east side of the Cabbin Branch	753
	"No Name"	500
	"Sure Bind"	35
	"Bealls Chance"	290
	"Fife"	78
	pt. "Good Luck" on west side of Cabbin Branch	169
	pt. "Drumbledry"	152
	pt. "Beals Reserve"	253
	pt. "Allisons Park"	306
	"Cowpen"	76
	"Strife"	294
	pt. "Layhills"	649
Mr. Henry Darnall, Jr.	pt. "Brookfield"	330
widow Mullican	pt. "Levells"	240
Mr. James Mullican	pt. "Levells"	60
	pt. "Fellowship"	200
Mr. Nathan Smith	pt. "Somthing"	213
CP:1750:16 ...		

Mr. James Draine	pt. "Something"	109
	pt. "Brock Hall"	66
Mr. Joseph Ray (Backwoods)	"Lashmitts Folly"	50
Mr. Joseph Ray	"Bealls Hunting Quarter"	220
Mr. Joshua Busy	pt. "Charles & Thomas"	60
	"Jones Slipe"	50
Rev. Mr. John Orme	"Leith"	248
	"Collington"	104
widow Kirkwood	pt. "Quicksale"	100
	pt. "Archers Pasture"	50
Mrs. Elizabeth Turner	"Brashears Pocoson"	123
	pt. "Ralpho"	200
	"Beginning"	119
Mr. James Adams	pt. "Margaret Overton"	211
Mr. Morris Miles	pt. "Wickhams Purchase"	150
	"Skipping Camdenhouse" a/s pt. "St. Andrews"	100
Mr. Nathaniel Wickham	pt. "Berryston"	100
Mr. John Hallum	pt. "St. Andrews"	223
Joseph Evans	pt. "Belts Hunting Quarter"	200
Mrs. Ann Pottinger	"Pottingers Desire"	200
Mr. William Prather, Jr.	"Hogharbour"	583
CP:1750:17 ...		
Col. Joseph Belt	"Sinacor Hill"	200
	pt. "Good Luck"	165
	"Addition"	50
	"Belts Discovery"	200
	"Pacolts Rest"	100
	"Friendship"	200
	"Chevey Chace"	560
	pt. "Chelsea"	800
	"Arthurs Seat"	172
	pt. "Greenwood"	280
	1 lot in Marlborough	1
	"Thomsons Lott"	27
	"Darby"	60
	"Mount Araratt"	157

Mr. John Bowie, Jr.	"Thorpland"	110
	"Piney Thickett"	200
	"Piney Thickett Enlarged"	200
	"Ryleys Discovery"	210
	pt. "Brock Hall"	162
	pt. "Hermitage"	602¾
	"Allen & James"	34
Mr. John Prather, Jr.	"Turkey Thickett"	100
Mr. James Tanyhill	"Akinghead"	500
	"Attwood & Hamiltons Purchase"	112
Mr. Richard Weaver	"Ridge"	100
Mr. Walter Davis	"Weavers Prospect"	100
Mr. John Brice	"Wintersells Range"	400
Mr. Thomas Clayland	pt. "Hermitage"	100
	"Beersheba"	5½
	pt. "Dann"	250
Mr. Henry Ballenger	pt. "Henry"	280
	pt. "Mill Lott"	92
	"Ballengers Endeavour"	50
CP:1750:18 ...		
h/o Mr. Joseph Hatton	pt. "Thompsons Rest"	870
	pt. "Rich Hill"	219
Mr. John Goddart	pt. "Thomsons Rest"	80
	pt. "Rich Hill"	81
Mr. Edward Beane	pt. "Thomsons Rest"	50
Mr. Christopher Edelen	"Dublin"	200
	pt. "Majors Choice"	19
Mr. Richard Edelen s/o Christopher	pt. "Majors Choice"	23
	"Edelens Addition"	15
	"Edelens Folly"	100
widow Mason (VA)	"Barbadoes"	75
h/o Mr. William Mauduit	pt. "Scotland"	100
	"Pindles Addition"	76
	"Cattings Park"	73
Mr. Henry Hawkins	pt. "Archers Pasture"	125
	"Retaliation"	173

Mr. Richard Ball	"Brothers Delight"	165
Mr. John Ball	pt. "Sisters Delight"	166
Mr. Ralph Pickering	pt. "Chance"	100
Mr. Edward Marlow, Jr.	"Timothy & Sarah"	100
Mr. Thomas Waller Coffer	"Nonsuch"	125
Mr. Thomas Barnes	"Chance"	87
CP:1750:19 ...		
Mr. Edward Jones	"Philips Addition"	92
Mr. John Lanham 3rd	pt. "Huntersfield"	140
Mr. John Emmerson	pt. "Marburys Chance", "Land Kindness", & "Little Troy"	150
Mr. Peter Dent	"Whitehaven"	1330
	"Falling Spring"	50
Mr. William Talbut	"Gleanings & Pasture"	105
	pt. "Radfords Chance"	535
	"Charles Beals Discovery"	100
Mr. Samuel Mason	pt. "Prandon"	38
h/o Mr. John Talbutt	pt. "Langly"	88
	"Tanyard"	110
Mr. Edward Marlow	pt. "Westmoreland"	99
	"Small Hope"	141
Mr. Thomas Dyer	"Edelen"	250
	"Stone Hill"	300
	pt. "Edelens Hogpen"	919
	"Edelens Addition"	90
	"No Name"	400
Mr. Ignatius Gardner	"Dalkeith"	182
Visitors of the Free School	pt. "Ryleys Discovery" & pt. "Majors Lott"	215
Mr. Robert Goodwin	pt. "Markett Overton"	450
Mr. John Ward	pt. "Wards Wheele"	275
CP:1750:20 ...		
Mr. William Banson	pt. "Wards Wheele"	275
Mr. Edward Cole	"St. Anthony"	254
	"St. Dorothy"	334
Mr. Alexander Harbert (cnp)	"Leeds"	100
	pt. "Leeds Division"	60

	pt. "Exchange Enlarged"	250
Mr. William Harbert	pt. "Dunghill"	197
Mr. George Frasier	pt. "Blue Plains"	500
	pt. "St. James"	700
	pt. "Wades Adventure" & pt. "St. James"	235
	"Fox Hall"	150
	pt. "4½ Gallons of Rum"	350
Rev. Mr. Henry Addison	"Glebe" a/s "Little Hall"	75
Mr. John Winn	"Indianfield"	229
Mr. John Winn, Jr.	"Winns Chance"	66
	"Gardners Meadows"	266
Mr. John Thompson	"Thomsons Pasture"	227
	"Cooll Spring"	190
	"Small Island"	12
	"Thomsons Hopyard"	110
	"John & Youchanankey"	445
	"Dutch Folly"	105
	"Long Island"	20
	"Darby Island"	70
Mr. Thomas Stonestreet	pt. "Battersea"	275
Mr. John Perry	pt. "Beals Hunting Quarter"	80
CP:1750:21 ...		
Mr. Moses Orme	pt. "Twogood"	100
Col. George Dent	"Clarks Inheritance"	500
	"Clarks Purchase"	500
	"Dents Levells"	280
Mr. Thomas Sandsberry	"So So"	188
	pt. "Evans Range"	72
	pt. "Woodstock"	78
	"Poplar Neck"	336
	"Addition"	64
Mr. Peter Parker	"Hour Glass"	100
widow Welsh	pt. "Welchs Discovery"	464
	"Snowden & Welch Defiance"	310
	pt. "Bacon Hall"	54
Mr. Seth Hyatt	pt. "Maidens Fancy"	150

Rev. Mr. Thomas Digges	"Carrollsburgh"	1981
	"Taylors & Ridgleys Lott"	64
	"Cheneys Adventure"	151
	pt. "Essington"	18
	"Mounting Prospect"	600
	"Margery"	200
Mr. John Banks	"Quebeck"	134
	"Addition"	104
	"Adderton"	200
	pt. "Bacon Hall"	100
	"Littleworth"	16
	"Elizabeth"	40
Mr. George Scott	pt. "Darnalls Grove"	100
	"Fountain"	500
	"Friendship"	425
	pt. "Hermitage"	200
	"Friendship"	600
CP:1750:22 ...		
Mr. Charles Walker	"3rd Addition to Bacon Hall"	39
	pt. "Mistake"	25
	"Virgins Delight"	150
Mr. Joseph Walker	pt. "Bacon Hall"	154
	pt. "Addition to Bacon Hall"	17½
	pt. "2nd Addition to Bacon Hall"	28
	pt. "Mistake"	25
Mrs. Perry (cnp)	"Andersons Chance"	81
	"Perrys Addition"	22
	"Wood Joy"	113
	"Timber Neck"	250
	"Cole Brigade"	300
	pt. "Willards Purchase"	600
	"Willards Cattail"	30
	pt. "Popleton"	100
	"Bird" & "Make Heast"	180
	"Ludsfordshope"	200
	"Pasture" originally called "Woodjoy"	120

	"Perrys Purchase" – comprised of "Make Hast" & "Birdland"	216
	"Pea Patch" originally called "Ludfords Hope"	100
Mr. Edward Edelen	"St. Thomas's Chance"	200
	pt. "Little Ease"	140
	pt. "Little Worth"	28
	"No Name"	300
	"Neverfear"	15
Mrs. Jane Mockbee or Nathaniel Shaw (AA)	pt. "Nicholas Hunting Quarter"	150
Mr. Thomas Rawlie	pt. "Taylors Discovery"	104
Mr. Henry Allison	pt. "Allisons Adventure"	150
Mr. John Bond (SM)	pt. "Gleanings"	100
CP:1750:23 ...		
Mr. Thomas Gant	"Taylorton"	412
	pt. "Marshams Rest"	270
	"Gants Levells"	201
	"Marshams Range"	144
	"Bartonshope"	100
	"Nursland"	88
	pt. "Brook Grove Reparation" & "Hearts Delight"	391
	"Bullwick"	213
	pt. "Richland"	7½
	1 lot in Nottingham	1
	pt. "Covingtons Pond"	25
	pt. "Brooke Court"	274½
	pt. "Joseph & Mary"	120
	"Northampton"	120
	"Timberlane"	100
Mr. John Baker	pt. "Snowdens Mill"	273
Mr. John Jackson	"Jacksons Improvement" & pt. "Friendship Enlarged"	194
	pt. "Jacksons Necessity"	291
	pt. "Black Ash"	1
widow Acton	"Adventure"	270
widow Harris	"Harris's Pasture"	65
	pt. "Wedge"	170

Mr. William Thomas	pt. "2nd Addition to Snowdens Manor"	415
	"Thomas's Discovery"	1480
Mr. William Spicer	"Batchellors Adventure"	107
CP:1750:24 ...		
Mr. Richard Snowden	pt. "Snowden Manor"	451
	pt. "Addition to Snowden Manor"	573
	pt. "4th Addition to Snowden Manor"	5140
	pt. "3rd Addition to Snowden Manor"	109
	"John & Sarah"	200
	"Happy Choice"	279
	pt. "Addition to Clarks Grove"	350
	pt. "Snowdens Milland"	153
	"Josephs Neglect"	201
	pt. "Snowdens & Welch Defiance of Williams & Clark"	22
	"Moores Rest"	135
	"Linthcoms Lott"	1199
	"Clarks Grove"	200
	"Addition to Clarks Grove"	300
	"Clarks Fancy"	97
	"Williams Range"	412
	"Abrahams Fancy"	100
	"Williams Delight"	143
	"Locust Thickett"	225
	"Walnut Levells"	50
	pt. "Gunders Delight"	78
	"Richard & John"	517
	"John & Thomas"	300
	"Ryleys Plains"	172
	pt. "Snowdens 2nd Addition to his Manor"	1770
	"Addition to Wolf Harbour"	200
	"Woolf Harbour"	200
	"William & Mary"	100
	pt. "Batsons Vineyard"	287
	"John & Catherine"	76
Mr. John Moore	"Moores Industry"	212

Mr. John Adamson	"Clean Shaving"	277
	"Lucas Friend"	10
	pt. "Black Ash"	1
Mr. George Moore	"Cash"	150
	pt. "Barbadoes"	100
	"Gidon"	20
Mr. Thomas Lucas, Jr.	"Evans Range"	200
	"Plum Yard"	300
CP:1750:25 ...		
Mr. James Holmeard, Jr.	"Addition to James"	630
	"Discovery"	100
Mr. James Holmeard, Jr. [sic]	"James"	600
	"James Park"	52
	pt. "Token Love"	100
	pt. "Widows Mite"	206
	"No Name"	38
	"Beals Plains"	508
	"Outlett" a/s "Lammars Hills"	450
	"Millseat"	30
Mr. Walter Hanson (CH)	pt. "Inclosure"	250
Mr. Arthur Lee	pt. "Brook Reserve"	178
	pt. "Brookfield"	106
Mr. Hancock Lee	"Addition"	576
Mr. Joseph Chew	"Chews Chance"	9
	"Yarrowhead"	386
	"Yarrowhead"	500
Mr. John Child	"Spiteful" a/s "Newfoundland"	117
	pt. "Orphans Gift"	100
Mr. James Atchison	"Atchisons Pasture"	100
Mr. Thomas Wilcoxon	"Coxons Chance"	200
	pt. "Manchester"	50
	"Addition"	200
	pt. "Deer Park"	108
	pt. "Wilcoxons Underwood"	20
	pt. "Batchellors Hope"	20
Mr. Thomas Wilcoxon, Jr.	pt. "Deer Park"	112

Mr. Thomas Talbutt	pt. "Deer Park"	50
	"Talbutts Rest"	40
CP:1750:26 ...		
Mr. William Masters	pt. "Discovery"	156
	pt. "Progress"	49
John Darnall, Esq.	pt. "Hope"	2757
Mr. Thomas Dawson	pt. "Golden Ride"	90
	"Adventure"	44
	pt. "Chance"	100
Mr. Thomas Warring	"Warrings Lott"	200
	"Littleworth"	14
	"Fish Pond"	65
	"Troublesome"	325
	"Orphans Loss"	240
	"Reparation"	35
	"Offutts Adventure"	100
	"Beals Gift"	42
	pt. "Younger Brother"	200
h/o Mr. Samuel Warring	pt. "Warrings Gift"	60
	pt. "Bealls Pleasure"	193
Mr. Basil Warring, Jr.	pt. "Warrings Lott"	511
	pt. "Bealls Pleasure"	57
Maj. Jeremiah Belt	"Pigpen"	200
	"Jeremiah & Mary"	100
	"Addition to Good Luck"	150
	"Recovery"	400
	"Betts Tamhawk"	150
	"Brahears Neck"	86
Mr. David Cox	"Luberland"	50
Mr. John Wilcoxon	pt. "Accord"	200
	"Georgia"	36
	"Gleanings"	64
John Long	pt. "Poplerton"	100
CP:1750:27 ...		
Mr. William Nelson	"Moores Rest"	100
Mr. Caleb Letton (cnp)	"Oatory"	405

	"St. Mary"	67
Mr. Thomas Gant, Jr.	pt. "Batsons Vineyard"	287
	pt. "Grange"	166½
	pt. "St. Andrews"	33½
	pt. "Cranfords Adventure"	100
widow Markland	"Dann"	120
	"Beersheba"	47
Mr. Thomas Cattrill	pt. "James & Mary"	636
	pt. "Brothers Content"	360
	pt. "Bear Garden"	206
	pt. "Prevention"	281
MM Alexander & Robert Beall	pt. "Batchellorsforrest"	405
Mr. David Barnes	"Eleanor"	70
	pt. "Bealls Levells"	100
Mr. John Fleming	pt. "Hemsley"	100
Mr. James Green	pt. "Strife"	300
	"Greens Thickett"	15
	"Girls Delight"	40
	"Cowpen"	56
	pt. "Ax"	105½
	pt. "Strife"	151
Mr. John Dunn for h/o John Read	"James & Elizabeth"	174
Mr. James Hoskinson	pt. "Barbadoes"	50
Mr. Randell Brent	pt. "Greenage"	83½
Mr. Jeremiah Stimson	pt. "Hermitage"	100
CP:1750:28 ...		
Mr. Thomas Clark	"Craignight"	200
	pt. "Good Luck"	50
	"Battland"	300
	"Grooms Lott"	600
Mr. William Jenkins	"Kindericks Chance"	100
h/o Bryan Kelly	pt. "Brothers"	100
	"Advantage"	135
	pt. "Discontent"	100

Mr. Thomas Bowlling	pt. "Strife"	200
Osborn Sprigg, Esq.	pt. "Northampton"	400
	"Addition to Catterton"	125
	pt. "Stock Quarter"	160
	"Abels Lott"	100
	pt. "Ropers Range" a/s "Darnals Grove"	100
	pt. "Harts Delight"	22
	pt. "Forrest"	85
	"Hopsons Choice" a/s "Darnals Grove"	493½
	"Hogpen"	244
Mr. James Wallace	pt. "Brothers Industry"	929
	"Hopsons Choice"	134½
	"Discovery"	88
	"Weaversden"	200
	"Robersons Low Grounds"	10
Mr. William Wallace	pt. "Brothers Industry"	500
Capt. John Smith	pt. "Mansfield"	125
	pt. "Farm"	154½
	pt. "Collings Comfort"	125
Miss Martha Erickson	pt. "Mansfield"	125
	pt. "Farm"	154½
	pt. "Collings Comfort"	125
Mr. James Offutt	"William & James"	530
	"James Park"	200
	pt. "New Dumfrice"	200
	"Young Mans Folly"	100
CP:1750:29 ...		
Mr. James Offutt, Jr.	pt. "Cleverwill Enlarged"	1000
Mr. William Offutt	pt. "Cleverwill Enlarged"	400
	"Bears Denn"	200
Mr. Alexander Offutt	pt. "Cleverwill Enlarged"	600
Mr. Thomas Hollyday	pt. "Brookfield"	637
	"Hollydays Wild Goose Meadow"	227
	pt. "Chews Meadows"	100
	pt. "Mazoonscon" & "Retaliation"	252
	1 lot in Nottingham	1

h/o Mr. John Rogers	pt. "Bealls Manor"	280
	pt. "Snowdens Gift"	40
Mr. John Gather	pt. "Beals Manor"	200
Mrs. Crabb	"Deer Park"	470
	pt. "Essington"	390
	"Bowlling Green"	128
	pt. "Two Brothers"	28
	"Valentine Garden"	950
	pt. "Crabbs Purchase"	100
John Hepburn, Esq.	"Hannover"	1500
	"Outlett"	250
	"Weymouth"	517
	pt. "Maiden Dowry"	600
	pt. "Horse Race"	99
	"Gray Eagle"	236
	3 lots in Marlborough	3
	"Piles Grove"	566
Mr. John Philips	pt. "Rome"	14¼
	"Stone Hill"	98
	pt. "Littleworth" & pt. "Prevention"	102
	"Addition to Stone Hill"	30
CP:1750:30 ...		
Mr. Daniel Jenkins, Jr.	pt. "Prandon"	50
	"Pigmans Addition"	50
Mr. John Philips (Backwoods)	"Walnut Bottom"	50
Mr. Francis Jenkins	pt. "Gods Gift"	168
	"Range"	32
Mr. John Parmer, Jr.	pt. "Two Johns"	100
Mr. Milburn Sims (CH)	pt. "Easycomeby"	100
Mr. John Smoote	"Cranford"	100
	"Beals Design"	100
	pt. "Elizabeth"	25
Mr. John Flint (cnp)	"Flints Discovery"	138
	pt. "Vineyard"	29
	"Addition to Flints Discovery"	100
	"Newton"	300

	pt. "Elizabeth"	25
Mr. Robert Wheeler	pt. "Edelens Courtesy"	70
	"Addition to Edelens Courtesy"	30
	"Marlows Chance"	200
	pt. "Goodwill"	23
	pt. "Westmoreland"	49
	"St. Thomas"	97
	"Marlows Lott"	20
Mr. Thomas Athey	pt. "Atheys Chance"	200
CP:1750:31 ...		
Mr. William John Jackson	pt. "James & Mary"	54
	pt. "Bealls Lott"	100
Miss Bordley	pt. "Backland"	542
	"Bordleys Choice"	500
	pt. "Backland"	90
Mr. Beal Bordley	pt. "Bordleys Choice"	500
	"New Years Gift"	1143
Mr. Mathias Bordley	pt. "Backland"	2030
Mr. Richard Keene	pt. "Greenland"	300
	"Keens Addition to Greenland"	37
	"Little Addition"	33
	"Keens Purchase" a/s "Charles Hill"	100
	pt. "New Exchange Enlarged"	360
	"Cucolds Delight"	23
Mr. Thomas Tucker	pt. "Hogpen"	90
Mr. John Tucker	"Tuckers Addition"	60
	pt. "Hogpen"	40
Stephen Bordley, Esq.	pt. "Majors Lott"	90
Mr. John Daviss s/o Charles	"Charles & Jane"	100
	"Bealls Manor"	234
Mr. William Hall	"Girls Portion"	100
	"Isaacs Park"	150
Mr. John Bateman	pt. "Ample Grange"	129
Mr. John Beall (taylor) (cnp)	pt. "James & Mary"	54
	pt. "Grove"	219
	pt. "Bealls Seat"	100

	pt. "Black Ash"	1
	pt. "Grove"	126
CP:1750:32 ...		
h/o Mr. John Radford	"Sinacor Landing"	52
	pt. "Long Acre"	52
	pt. "Elizabeth"	50
	pt. "Henry"	105
Mr. George Parker	"Piles Addition"	90
	"Wheelers Addition"	76
	pt. "Hickory Hills"	375
	pt. "Carrick"	184
	pt. "Archers Purchase", pt. "Godding", & pt. "Wems Acre"	324
	pt. "Hazard"	¼
	"Chance"	241
Dr. Richard Piles	"Hogpen"	219
	"Coops Being" pt. "Scotts Lott"	40
	pt. "Beginning"	124
	pt. "Scotts Lott", pt. "Weston", pt. "Hughs Labour", & pt. "Ryleys Folly"	206
	"No Name"	3
Mr. William Piles	"Addition"	183
	pt. "Hickory Hills"	46
	pt. "Mistake"	84
	"Formlaine"	126
h/o Mr. Thomas Coleman	"Colemans Meadows"	50
Mr. Spicer Owen	pt. "Aaron"	50
Mr. Benjamin Harris	"Headake"	150
Mr. James Fry	"Friends Goodwill"	100
Mr. Edward Peirson	"Swancy"	61
	"Littleworth"	98
Mr. John Madding	"Stonepoint" a/s "pt. "Labryth"	100
	"Addition to Stonepoint"	50
Mr. James Young	pt. "Hickory Plains"	200
	pt. "Littleworth"	50
CP:1750:33 ...		

Mr. Smalwood Coghill	pt. "Hickory Plains"	100
Mr. James Plummer	"Wickhams Goodwill"	270
	"Tewsburry"	66
	"Harrisons Purchase" pt. "Tewsburry"	103
	"Batchellors Chance"	40
	"Good Luck"	72
Mr. Ninian Willett	"Beals Chance"	34½
	1 lot in Marlbro	1
	"Good Luck"	107
MM Wardrop & Russell	"Perry Folly"	111
	"Willetts Folly"	80
	pt. "Good Luck"	100
Mr. John Vennutree	"Pipe Meadows"	200
Mr. David Shepherd	"Pell Mell"	162
Mr. Thomas Palmer	pt. "Metre"	168
	"Palmers Choice"	58
Mr. Joseph Palmer	pt. "Metre"	142
h/o Mr. John Baldwin Adamson	"Adamsons Choice"	100
Mr. Edward Crabb	"Crabbs Purchase"	356
Mr. Thomas Butt	pt. "Darnalls Grove"	100
Mr. Peter Butler	"Paradice"	218
	"Magruders Hazard"	100
	"Locust Thickett"	100
	"Paradice Enlarged"	100
Mr. William Hughs	pt. "James & Mary"	130
CP:1750:34 ...		
Hon. Benjamin Young, Esq.	"Dudington"	1000
	"Pasture"	300
	"New Troy"	500
h/o Mr. Joseph Story	pt. "Vale Benjamin"	39
Mr. James Downing	"Foxes Denn"	50
	"Goodwill"	52
	pt. "Westmoreland"	108
h/o Mr. Thomas Stimson	pt. "Williams Portion"	50
h/o Mr. Thomas Lemar (cnp)	pt. "Joseph & James"	200

	pt. "Pines"	348½
	pt. "Two Brothers"	200
Mr. Thomas Lemar, Jr.	pt. "Buck Bottom"	120
	pt. "Joseph & James"	200
Mr. James Perry	pt. "Gideon"	80
	pt. "Gillard"	227
	"Stradan"	220
	"Stoneyhive"	200
Mr. Joseph Peach	"Search"	150
	pt. "Isaac's Discovery"	155
	pt. "Strife"	451
	"Peach Plains"	100
	"Peach Ballance"	100
	"Farmers Reserve"	177
	"Peaches Lott"	100
Mr. Michael Urin	"Smyrna"	400
	pt. "Yarrowhead"	120
h/o Mr. John Adams (CH)	"Naylors Range"	164
	1 lot in Mill Town	1
Mr. Thomas Beal 2nd	"Frozen Levell"	200
CP:1750:35 ...		
Mr. Richard Duckett	pt. "Spriggs Request"	389
	"Ducketts Misfortune"	200
Mr. Matthew Day	"Wodobridge"	100
Mr. Edward Boteler	"Ballington"	121
Mr. William Jones	pt. "Hatchett"	76
Mr. William Miles	"Geesing"	100
	pt. "Archers Pasture"	77
Mr. John Wood	pt. "Turkey Thickett"	100
Mr. Benjamin Belt	pt. "Lundee"	100
	pt. "Smithsfield"	138
	"Dunnall" & pt. "Dunnall"	190
	"Hope"	7
	"Love & A Bottle"	33
	"Belts Discovery"	18
Mr. John Low (cnp)	pt. "Batchellors Hope"	230

	"Deerspound"	129
	"Tryal"	92½
	pt. "Wilcoxons Underwood"	20
Mr. Robert Hooker	pt. "Twiver"	150
Mr. James Gordon	"Clyde"	76
Mr. Richard Holland	pt. "Jericho"	187
Mr. Edward Mobberly	pt. "Renchers Adventure"	100
Mr. Francis Mobberly	pt. "Renchers Adventure"	50
Mr. Thomas Lawson	"Stoke"	100
CP:1750:36 ...		
h/o Mr. Joseph Lovejoy	pt. "Renchers Adventure"	150
Mr. Jeremiah Perdue	pt. "Perdue" a/s pt. "Casteel"	50
Mr. Joseph Wheat	pt. "Perdue" a/s pt. "Casteel"	50
	"Wheats Choice"	53
h/o Mr. Joseph Newton	pt. "Plymouth"	210
	pt. "Apple Hill"	170
	pt. "Prevention" & pt. "Inclosure"	30
	"Joseph & Ann"	250
Mr. David Trayle	"Davids Industry"	170
Mr. David Trayle, Jr.	"Goodwill"	100
Mr. Jonathan Ellis	pt. "Craycrofts Purchase"	100
Mr. William Brashears	pt. "Majors Lott"	44
Mr. Joseph Ponett	pt. "Forrest"	265
Mr. Henry Hall	pt. "Ample Grange"	130
	pt. "Cool Spring"	110
	2 lots in Queen Ann	2
h/o Mr. John Mackonkey	pt. "Wheelers Purchase"	300
Mr. Benjamin Hall	"Eglinton"	300
Mr. Benjamin Hall (AA)	"Halls Choice"	100
h/o Mr. Edward Hall	"Parrott Thickett"	300
Philip Pindle	pt. "Sway"	118
CP:1750:37 ...		
Mr. John Levitt	pt. "Horses Race"	99
	6 lots in Marlborough	6
	"Hopes Addition"	152
Mr. John Orme (cnp)	pt. "Mount Calvert Manor"	70

	pt. "Leith"	10
h/o Mr. Edward Stoneberry	pt. "Chance"	100
Mr. Basil Warring	pt. "Hearts Delight"	311
	"Brookland"	38
Mr. Thomas Owen	"Jamaica"	500
	"Marshams Rest"	487
	"Barrenpoint"	50
	"Bowlling Neck"	200
	"Lordships Favour"	150
	"Mount Pleasant"	400
	1 lot in Marlborough	1
	"No Name"	50
	pt. "Exchange"	300
	pt. "Plymouth"	140
	"Haymmonds Addition"	75
	pt. "New Exchange Enlarged"	73¾
	"Mill Dam"	75
Mr. James Beal s/o Robert	"Enster"	225
	"Farm"	128
Mr. Pharoah Ryley	pt. "Dann"	100
Mr. Ninian Tanyhill	pt. "Fenwick"	263
Mr. Hugh Ryley	pt. "Dann"	250
Mr. Joseph Belt s/o John	"Gleanings"	100
Mr. Richard Jones, Jr.	pt. "Hogyard" now "Clarks Purchase"	100
	"Ryleys Neglect"	93
CP:1750:38 ...		
h/o Mr. John Watkins	pt. "Paschaham"	100
	"Watkins Range"	100
	"Addition"	320
Mr. John Aldridge	pt. "Paschaham"	100
	pt. "Tuckers Cultivation"	111
Mr. Robert White	"Mount Pleasure"	114
Mr. Mathew Roberson	"Josephs Goodwill"	150
Mr. John Mclane	"Cranfords Adventure"	100
Mr. John Leach	pt. "Rocky Spring"	100
Mr. William Pritchett (cnp)	pt. "Dunghill"	100

	"Harberts Chance"	100
	"Eleanors Green"	150
Mr. Isaac Jones	"Brazen Thorp Hall"	60
Mr. Turner Wootton	pt. "Essington"	302
	"Angle"	100
	"Burbidge"	208
	"Discovery"	119
	"Landover"	664
Mr. Philip Tennely	pt. "Radfords Chance"	170
	pt. "Hunters Kindness"	30
	pt. "Tennelys Chance"	50
Mr. William Tennely	pt. "Hunters Kindness"	100
Mr. William Williams or Sarah Williams – John Ellis living on land	pt. "Flints Grove"	150
	pt. "Smiths Pasture"	100
Mr. William West	pt. "Two Brothers"	300
	pt. "Joseph"	100
CP:1750:39 ...		
Dr. Andrew Scott	pt. "Goodwill"	91
	"Irvin"	150
	"Recovery"	200
	"Speedwell"	138
	"Whetworth"	700
	"Whitehaven"	350
	"Carrick Fergus"	100
	"Fancy"	144
	pt. "Addition"	48
	pt. "Saturdays Work"	280
	"Sallem"	200
	"Venus"	200
Mr. Robert Brashears	pt. "Brashears Meadows"	100
Mrs. Jane Contee (cnp)	pt. "Warburton Manor"	425
	pt. "Gore"	134
	pt. "Hargrove"	5
	"Vine Yard"	200
	"Brookfield"	650

	1 lot in Nottingham	1
Capt. Samuel Magruder	"Joys Fortune"	200
	"Forrest"	300
h/o Mr. Jonathan Wadham	pt. "Nelsons Pasture" & "Valentines Garden"	39
	pt. "Hickory Hills"	193
Mr. Daniel Clary	pt. "Bradfords Rest"	115
	"Bucks Bottom"	100
Mr. Benjamin Brown	pt. "Bradfords Rest"	115
Mr. John Duckett	pt. "Maiden Discovery"	100
Mr. Conrad Schomaker	"Charles"	50
CP:1750:40 ...		
Mr. James Edmonston	"Yarrow"	410
	pt. "Brothers Content"	360
	pt. "Black Ash"	1
	"Accord"	100
	"Bacon Hall"	54
	pt. "Preston March"	334
	pt. "Lubberland"	27
	"Batchellors Forrest"	405
	"Prevention"	281½
	pt. "Cool Spring Manor"	90
	"Beginning" of Samuel Beal	208
	"Westonfields"	82
	"Addition to Bacon Hall"	15
	pt. "Hermitage"	131
	pt. "Discovery"	41½
	"Land of Ease"	40
	"Georges Delight"	20
	pt. "Piles Delight"	500
	pt. "Piles Hall"	360
	pt. "Diamond"	200
	"Denby"	125
	pt. "Bally Crist"	200
	1 lot in Queen Ann	1
	"Silent Grove"	37

h/o Mr. Samuel Magruder	pt. "Magruders & Beals Honesty"	322
	pt. "Prevention"	140
	pt. "Good Luck"	7
Mr. Alexander Beall 3rd	pt. "Magruders & Bealls Honesty"	121
Mr. James Gibson	pt. "Bealls Chance"	70
	pt. "Bealls Chance"	424
Mr. William Young	pt. "Good Luck"	144
Mr. Clement Trigg	"Glovers Hall"	150
Mr. William Conden	pt. "Hermitage"	100
CP:1750:41 ...		
Mr. John Tolson	pt. "Long Point"	60
	"I Never See It"	400
	pt. "Manchester"	166
	pt. "Saturdays Work"	140
	pt. "Hunters Fields"	103
	pt. "Stock"	443
	"Hattons Lockrice"	110
Mr. William Magruder Selby	pt. "Chews Folly"	200
	"Grubby Thickett"	50
Mr. Samuel Selby for his sister	pt. "Chews Folly"	92
Mr. John Selby	pt. "Leith"	290
Mr. Charles Drury for h/o Nathan Shelby	pt. "Twogood"	200
Mr. Joseph Selby	pt. "Mount Calvert Manor"	75
Mr. Thomas Thomson (Rock Creek)	pt. "Rattle Snake Denn"	150
Mr. Thomas Miles	pt. "Spy Park"	91
	"Nannys Delight" a/s pt. "Lybrith"	150
	"Miles Pasture"	110
	pt. "Josephs Park"	100
Mr. Patrick Reading	pt. "Clagetts Purchase"	50
	"Green Spring"	100
Mr. Clement Mosely	pt. "Clagetts Purchase"	50
Mr. Peter Mills (SM)	pt. "Red Bird Thickett"	100
Mr. John West	pt. "Two Brothers"	200
	pt. "Joseph"	200

CP:1750:42 ...		
Mr. Stephen Hampton	"Bear Denn"	100
h/o Dr. John Haswell	"Brotherhood"	190
	"William & Mary Increased"	200
	pt. "Rovers Content", "Good Luck", "Fathers Gift", & "Bread & Chease Hall"	325
	pt. "Cowpen"	37
	"Drumaldry"	73
	"Beals Reserve"	127
	"Allisons Park"	143
Mr. Joseph Richardson	pt. "Charles & Benjamin"	100
	pt. "Brooke Reserve"	200
h/o Mr. John Browner	pt. "Hunters Kindness"	60
Mr. Benjamin Talbutt	pt. "Gleanings"	65
Mr. Grove Tomlinson	"Fletchalls Goodwill"	100
	"Good Luck"	200
	"Fellowship"	39
	"Addition to Fellowship"	20
	"Groves Hunting Lott"	136
Mr. George Wells	pt. "Swansons Lott"	100
Mr. William Hawkins	pt. "Long Point"	63
	pt. "Stones Delight"	143
Mr. John Cecill	"Twice Bought" lately called "Beals Manor"	135
Mr. Henry Hill	"Patowmack Landing"	250
	"Hills Second Thought"	217
	"Exchange"	229
	"Forrest"	200
Mr. Nathaniel Beall	pt. "Easy Purchase"	175
	"Addition to Easy Purchase"	153
CP:1750:43 ...		
Mr. Benjamin West	"Younger Brother"	370
	pt. "St. Andrews"	207
Mr. George Beckwith	"Beckwiths Range"	250
Mr. John Harris	pt. "Ridge"	200
Mr. Edward Swann (cnp)	pt. "Passam"	229
	"Wilderness"	48½

	"Addition to Brook Chance"	70
	"Brook Chance"	406
	"Brook Lane"	46
Mr. Thomas Turner	pt. "Jacobs Hope"	100
Mr. John Hatsell	pt. "Cucolds Delight"	100
Mr. John Norton	pt. "Grove Hurst"	100
William Cumming, Esq.	pt. "Accord"	100
	pt. "Amsterdam"	80
	pt. "Preston Marsh"	334
	pt. "Black Ash"	1
	pt. "Noraway"	630
	"Drummine"	668
	"Barbers Beginning"	100
	"Shue"	100
Mr. John Waters, Jr.	pt. "Jericho"	171
	pt. "Maiden Fancy"	430
	"Bear Neck"	151
	"Cherrywalk"	55
	"Mothers Gift"	400
Mrs. Dick	pt. "Cobrith Lott"	50
	pt. "Billingsleys Point"	50
	"Green Clifts" a/s "Lough Sterick"	100
Mr. John Welch	pt. "Welsh Discovery"	136
CP:1750:44 ...		
Mr. Brock Mockbee	pt. "Fellowship"	200
Mr. Richard Nevett	"Grammers Chance"	158
Mr. John Nelson	pt. "Chance"	25
	"Hopsons Chance"	615
Mr. John Delashmott	pt. "Sweeds Folly"	100
Mr. Elias Delashmott	pt. "Sweeds Folly"	100
	"Ramble"	100
Mr. Frederick Slunt Cunningham	pt. "Aarons Reserve"	75
Abraham Smith	pt. "Watsons Luck"	70
Mr. John Powel (Carolina)	pt. "St. Andrews"	165
Mr. Robert Wall (cnp)	"Walls Addition"	50

	"Smiths Green"	50
	"Wheats Pasture"	85
Mr. Francis Wheat	"Cool Spring"	100
	"Addition to Cool Spring"	100
Mr. Richard White	"Farm"	50
	pt. "Taylerton"	111
Mr. Weaver Barnes	"Moores Industry"	100
	pt. "Second Addition to Snowdens Manor"	200
Mr. John Cramphin	"Buck Lodge"	100
	"Grandmothers Goodwill"	150
	"Henry & Marry"	110
	"Kattingkin Bottom"	100
Mr. Edward Person for h/o (N) Clarvoe	pt. "Margaret Overton"	300
CP:1750:45 ...		
Mr. Francis Clarvo	"Addition"	10
	"London Pleasure"	79
	"Maiden Bradley"	69
	"Barrens"	15
Mr. Stephen Jullon	"Hedge Hog"	258
Rev. Mr. George Murdock	"Friends Goodwill"	150
	"Glebe of Rock Creek" a/s "Generosity"	100
	pt. "Mill Land"	2
	pt. "Charles & William"	248
Mr. Abraham Elting	"Abrahams Lott"	305
	pt. "Concord"	100
	"New Esopus"	100
Mr. Isaac Hite	pt. "Blackwalnut Tree Island"	142
Mr. Abraham Forre	"Eltings Right"	325
Mr. John Hite	pt. "Blackwalnut Tree Island"	142
	"Discord"	215
Mr. Thomas Richardson	"Marks Range"	400
	"Richards Addition"	50
h/o Dr. Samuel Stringer	"Joy Church"	1045
	pt. "Stringers Chance"	300
Mr. Robert Rideu	pt. "Advantage"	36

Mr. William Thomas	"Mistake"	227
Mr. William Thomas (Swansons Creek)	"Discovery"	41
Mr. Peter Moore	"Crouches Hall"	100
	"Childs Portion"	65
CP:1750:46 ...		
Mr. Cornelius Elting	pt. "Partnership"	100
	"Overplus"	170
	"Frog Island"	30
	"Forrest"	280
	"Melburn"	270
	pt. "Darby Island"	76
	"Fork of Grubby Hill"	305
	"Simacorford"	160
	"Fountain"	100
	"Cornelius Chance"	100
	pt. "Concord"	201
	pt. "Long Acre"	52
	"Fortune"	118
	"Eltings Rest"	60
	"Addition"	50
	"Mill Road"	240
	"Isaac Elting"	112
	"Fair Island"	172
	"Hills"	105
Mr. Henry Lee	"Goodwill"	100
Col. John Colvill (VA)	"Maryland"	6300
Mr. Daniel Hurley	pt. "Weavers Delight"	93
Mr. Thomas Hunter	pt. "Dicksons Lott" & "Foxhall"	100
Mr. John Dickson, Jr.	pt. "Charle Forrest"	100
Mr. Ephraim Gover	"Matsell Shell"	200
	"Dearbought"	100
	"Yarmouth"	70
	"Ladys Desire"	100
Francis Dorsett	"Plague Enough" & pt. "Girls Portion" a/s "Orphans Gift"	100

Mr. Thomas Hillary	pt. "Three Sisters" called "Thomas Lot"	300
	"Pick Ax"	58
	"Sugar Loaf"	80
	pt. "Stock Quarter"	100
CP:1750:47 ...		
Mr. Henry Hillary	"Hemp Lot" pt. "Three Sisters"	133
Mr. John Hillary	"Walnut Point"	100
Mr. Joseph Waters	pt. "Moores Industry"	30
	pt. "Batsons Vineyard"	113
Mr. James Magruder	pt. "Grubby Thickett"	200
	pt. "Alexandria"	300
h/o Mr. James Magruder, Jr.	pt. "Norway"	125
	"Lost Jacket"	200
Mr. Enock Magruder	pt. "Norway"	125
	pt. "Stones Harbour"	100
Mr. Ninian Magruder	pt. "Grubby Thickett"	333
	pt. "Alexandria"	300
	pt. "Magruder & Beals Honesty"	666
	"Friendship"	101
Mr. James Coleman	"Denmark"	100
Mr. Thomas Smallwood	"Moores Rest"	200
Mr. Francis Warring	pt. "Marthas Gift" & "Mazoons Cove & Addition"	246
	pt. "Westphalia"	100
Mr. Edward Reston	pt. "Chaffeys Delight"	157
Mr. Adam Miller	pt. "Turkey Thickett"	50
Mr. Robert Wade	"Stone Harbour"	400
Mr. Samuel Warren	pt. "Ludfords Gift"	100
widow of Leonard Brook	pt. "Brookwood"	350
CP:1750:48 ...		
Mr. Baker Brook	"Black Walnut Thickett"	300
	"Content"	300
	"St. Catherine"	50
Mr. William Magruder	pt. "Vale Benjamin"	192
Mr. Thomas Boteler	pt. "Wheelers Hope" & pt. "Apple Door"	232
Mr. Zachariah Magruder (cnp)	pt. "Friendship"	220
	"Zachariah"	100

	"Archibalds Lott"	100
Mr. Samuel Magruder 3rd	pt. "Friendship" & "Addition to Magruders & Bealls Purchase"	320
	"Mill Use"	25
	"As Good As We Could Get"	200
	"Samuels Delight"	200
	"Hemsley"	100
	"Addition to Hemsley"	50
Mr. John Magruder, Jr.	pt. "Friendship" & "Addition to Magruders & Beals Purchase"	316
h/o Mr. Robert Magruder	"T"	126
	"Lanhams Delight"	90
Mr. John Ray	pt. "Turkey Thickett" a/s pt. "John & Mary"	100
Mr. Samuel Queen	pt. "Inclosure"	297
Mr. Edward Pye	"Pinner"	200
	"Littleworth"	¾
Mr. Archibald Edmonston	pt. "Deer Park" & "Bear Garden Enlarged"	458
Mrs. Lydia Summers	"Coxens Rest"	100
CP:1750:49 ...		
Mr. John Saucer, Jr.	"Saucers Green"	300
Mr. William Davis	pt. "Hermitage"	197
Mr. Thomas Dowden	pt. "Hermitage"	70
Mr. William Davis s/o Griffith	"Hazard"	60
Mr. Charles Williams	"White Oak Valley"	100
Mr. Thomas Monrow	pt. "Markett Overton"	50
Mr. Griffith Daviss	pt. "Duvalls Range"	100
Mr. Benjamin Perry	pt. "Hermitage"	250
Mr. Robert Soper	pt. "Golden Rode"	110
	pt. "Warwick"	100
	"Sopers Rest"	74
h/o Mr. Thomas Clagett	pt. "Bealls Chance"	140
Mr. Leonard Piles	pt. "Croome"	150
	pt. Cucolds Point"	70
Mr. Thomas Kirk	"Longlane"	70
Mr. John Osborne	"Trundel Bad Cucold"	200
Mrs. Alice Hunter (cnp)	"Dunbar"	125

	"Angleser"	31
	"Essex Lodge"	100
h/o Mr. Thomas Mullican	pt. "Chelsea"	200
CP:1750:50 ...		
Mr. John James	"Chance"	75
Mr. John James (Pipe Creek)	"Dispute"	50
Mr. Philip Mason	pt. "Westmoreland" & "Dublin"	78¾
Mr. Christopher Beane	pt. "Grovehurst"	50
	pt. "Beanes Landing"	3
Mr. Edmund Casteel	pt. "Casteel"	100
	"Bormans Industry"	100
Mr. Edmund Offutt	pt. "Cool Spring Levells"	296
	"Out Lett"	600
Mr. Flayl Payne	"Paynes Delight"	100
	"Paynes Industry"	50
Mr. John Moore, Jr.	pt. "Bealls Pleasure"	125
Mr. Lingan Wilson	pt. "Bookhill" & "Kingsale"	250
	pt. "Beanes Landing"	84
Mr. Benjamin Jacobs	"Evans Range"	300
	"Jacobs Hope" a/s "Cheneys Adventure"	100
Mr. Mordecai Jacobs	pt. "Ryleys Range" now called "Widows Purchase"	137
	pt. "Darnalls"	56½
h/o Mr. George Noble	pt. "Welwork"	350
	pt. "Spring Garden"	170
	pt. "Elizabeth"	300
	pt. "Addition"	24
	pt. "Elizabeth" & "Piscattaway Manor"	500
	pt. "Drywork"	42½
Mr. Thomas Noble	pt. "Elizabeth"	300
	pt. "Elizabeth" & "Piscattaway Manor"	500
	pt. "Spring Garden"	170
	pt. "Welwork"	350
	pt. "Drywork"	42½
	pt. "Addition"	24
CP:1750:51 ...		
Mr. Richard Tubman	"Forrest"	500

Mr. John Lamar	pt. "Majors Lott"	116
	pt. "Ryleys Discovery"	260
	pt. "Howertons Range"	100
Mr. Edward Neale	"Grimes Ditch"	580
Mr. Edward Owen	"Shepherds Fortune"	200
	"What You Please"	120
Mr. Ninian Beale	pt. "Friendship Enlarged" now "Upper Tract"	232
	pt. "Enlargement"	90
	pt. "Black Ash"	1
Mr. Elipaz Ryley	pt. "Hopeyard"	250
Mr. Thomas Lucas	pt. "Hopyard"	250
	"Lucas Adventure"	100
Mr. Hillary Williams	"Figure of Eight"	205
Mr. John Smith Prather	pt. "Spriggs Request"	111
	"Hills Choice"	100
	pt. "Bear Garden Enlarged" & "Dear Park"	620
Mr. Thomas Claxton	pt. "Roziers Gift" a/s "Admorsther"	289
	pt. "Thomas & Sarah"	265
Mr. Nehemiah Wade	"Head Ake"	150
Capt. Alexander Magruder	"Friendship"	410
	pt. "Grubby Thickett"	333
	pt. "Elizabeth" & "Partnership"	12½
widow Page	"Killmore Neck"	100
	"Bealls Pleasure"	120
CP:1750:52 ...		
Mr. Roger John Sauser	pt. "Wards Pasture"	200
	"Long Looked for"	50
Mr. Charles Williams 3rd	pt. "Beals Manor"	200
Mr. William Robins	pt. "Hogpen"	100
Mr. Joseph Pickering	pt. "Lamster"	64
Dr. Andrews	"Keverton Edge"	500
	pt. "Charles & Thomas"	150
Mr. John Soper	"Good Luck"	100
	pt. "Levells"	200
widow Playfay (cnp)	pt. "Wades Adventure"	103
	pt. "Marburrys Schoolhouse"	66

	pt. "Marburrys Long Court"	88
	"Leith"	48
	pt. "Hazard"	5
	"Frazers Industry"	16
	"Rochester"	110
	"Rosscommon"	100
	"Craft"	37
	pt. "Hazard"	70¼
	pt. "Partnership"	3
Mr. James Moore	pt. "Allisons Park"	100
Mr. Charles Allison	pt. "Allisons Park"	50
Mr. George Gordon	"Prevention"	28
	"Pleasent Hills"	52
	"Freemans Hills"	334
	pt. "Bealls Gift"	164
	pt. "Knaves Disappointment"	236
	pt. "New Exchange"	700
	"Gordons Purchase"	150
	pt. "Friendship"	400
Mr. Henry Chapple	pt. "Allisons Park"	50
CP:1750:53 ...		
Mr. John Dowden	pt. "Addition to Fellowship"	119
	"John & Molly"	106
	"Jonnys Poplar Spring"	42
	pt. "John & Molly"	237
Mr. James Gore	pt. "Allisons Adventure"	150
Mr. John Jones (Piscattaway)	pt. "Hazard"	8¼
	pt. "Partnership"	22
Mr. Edward Clagett	pt. "Croome"	200
	pt. "Greenland"	205
	"Fowellers Delight"	100
Mr. William Webster	"Ridge"	675
Mr. William Clark	pt. "Clarks Fancy"	61
	"Hyams Choice"	100
Mr. Joseph Clark	pt. "Clarks Fancy"	73
Mr. Alexander Deal	pt. "Constant Friendship"	150

Mr. Nathan Wells	pt. "Strife"	163½
Mr. Robert Wells	"Cannew Bottom"	50
Mr. John Mitchell	pt. "Taylors Pasture"	50
Mr. John Mitchell, Jr.	pt. "Taylors Pasture"	51
	pt. "Mitchells Addition"	28
Mr. James Beck	"Becks Chance"	100
	"Penny Hedge"	88
	"Becks Addition"	300
	pt. "Darnalls Grove"	212½
Mr. Duncan Ferguson	"Hamiltons Addition"	128
	pt. "Hamiltons Adventure"	89
CP:1750:54 ...		
Mr. John Beall s/o Robert	pt. "Fathers Gift" a/s "James & Mary"	105
	"Chance"	100
	"Snowdens Mill Land"	120
	"Godfathers Gift"	123
	"Worse Than Nothing"	27
Mr. Samuel Lovejoy	pt. "Woodbridge"	84
	pt. "Tranent"	29
Mr. George Gibbins	"Bartons Hope"	100
	"Hickory Ford"	65
	"Brimmington"	100
Mr. John Bell, Jr.	pt. "Inclosure"	250
Mr. John Ferguson	"Bealls Plains"	113
Mr. Thomas Dryden	"Elizabeth & Thomas"	109
Mr. John Cecill 3rd	"Land Above"	100
Mr. Edward Betty	"Poplar Bottom"	52
	pt. "Dulanys Lott"	166
Mr. Benjamin Belt, Jr.	"Buck Lodge"	250
	pt. "Buck Lodge"	185
Mr. William Prather	"Poplar Bottom"	50
Mr. John Lackland	"Hope"	37
	"Addition to Hope"	100
Mr. Thomas Webb	"Prathers Grove"	100
	"Medium"	50

Mr. Thomas Ball (Backwoods)	pt. "Taken of Love"	97
CP:1750:55 ...		
Mr. Ignatius Wheeler	"Wheelers Desire"	200
	"No Name"	80
Mr. Leonard Wheeler	"Majors Choice"	70
Mr. Charles Boteler	"Harrys Lott"	200
	"Wilsons Adventure"	129
	pt. "London Derry"	149
	pt. "Renchers Adventure"	53
Mr. George Naylor	1 lot in Mill Town	1
Mr. John Buxton	"Buxtons Delight"	100
Mr. Thomas Johnson (Monococy)	"Johnson Delight"	50
	"Johnsons Levells"	50
Mr. David Weems	"Pork Hall"	300
Mr. John Thomson	pt. "Ax"	316½
h/o Mr. John Courts	pt. "Crouches Gift"	250
	"Clean Drinking"	700
Mr. Peter Murphy	"Bear Garden"	100
h/o Mr. John Smith (SM)	"Sharp"	431
Mr. Marsham Queen	pt. "Inclosure"	250
h/o Mr. Joseph White or James Wallace, Jr.	"Fletchalls Garden"	65
	"Reads Delight"	100
	"Roberts Lott"	50
Mr. Richard Deane	pt. "Hunting the Hare"	50
CP:1750:56 ...		
Mr. Moses Chaplin	"Mount Pleasant"	100
Mr. William Bowell	pt. "Forrest"	89
Mr. James Wilson (Mill Town)	pt. "Doves Nest"	73½
	pt. "Doves Perch"	100
	pt. "Tranent"	170
	"Haddington"	150
	"Dunbar"	100
	"Good Luck"	103
	pt. "Mount Calvert Manor"	375
Mr. Benjamin Moore	pt. "Childs Portion"	127

Mr. Clement Wheeler	"Middletons Lott"	96
Mr. William Goe	pt. "Ample Grange"	100
	"Pleasent Grove"	300
Mr. Francis Hudson	"Shoemakers End"	50
Mr. Thomas Willett	"Lickhill"	100
	"Little Dane"	26
Mr. Thomas Finch	pt. "Patowmack Forrest"	100
Mr. William Farquare	pt. "Rockland"	74
	"Kilfado"	200
	pt. "Mount Pleasent"	40
	"Swamp Miserable"	60
widow Franceway	pt. "Nannys Delight" a/s pt. "Labrinth"	100
Cornelius Vernoy	pt. "Concord"	226
	pt. "Forrest"	142
	½ of "New Esopus"	100
CP:1750:57 ...		
Mr. William Downes	"Queenforrest"	100
h/o Mr. Thomas Williams	"Williams Range"	100
	pt. "Three Sisters"	250
Mr. William Williams	"Fork"	400
	"Mill Land"	162
	"Addition to Fork"	80
Mr. Thomas Williams, Jr.	pt. "Three Sisters"	200
	pt. "Three Sisters" called "Johns Lott"	120
	pt. "Good Luck"	80
Mr. Thomas Stockett	pt. "Collington"	167
Mrs. Mary Frazer	2 lots in Marlbro	2
Mr. William Beanes	pt. "Brook Ridge"	288
	pt. "Grove Hurst"	350
	pt. "Beanes Landing"	50
	pt. "Mount Calvert Manor"	11½
Mr. William Beanes, Jr.	pt. "Brooke Ridge"	175
Mr. James Holland	pt. "Guttings Hah Hah"	117
	"Panthers Range"	50
Mr. Thomas Stump	pt. "Stumps Valley"	133½
Mr. William Ducker	"Cheneys Adventure"	100

Mrs. Elizabeth Steward	pt. "Hymans Choice" & pt. "Cheneys Adventure"	130
	"Woolf Bite"	25
Mr. Samuel Blackmore	pt. "Discovery"	100
Mr. James Lee, Jr.	pt. "Discovery" & "Labrinth"	100
CP:1750:58 ...		
Mr. William Beall	"William & Elizabeth"	134
	pt. "Friendship Enlarged"	290
	pt. "Discontent"	100
	"Hill Dale"	136
	"Prevention"	141
Mr. Samuel Beall	pt. "Laybrith"	240
Mr. Humphry Ball	"Jacob"	217
	pt. "Magruders & Beals Honesty"	233
	pt. "St. Elizabeth Manor"	100
	"Cuba"	3
	"Want Water"	35
	pt. "Partnership"	200
Mr. Ignatius Hardy	pt. "Casteel"	100
Mr. Samuel Young, Jr.	"Daviss Range"	100
h/o Col. Thomas Lee (VA)	"Morton"	165
	"Eden"	320
Henry Darnall, Esq.	"Addition"	948
	pt. "Twogood"	100
	pt. "Pitchcraft"	140
Mr. Thomas Plummer	pt. "Plummers Island"	100
	"Greenland"	37
Mr. Thomas Plummer, Jr.	"Saplin Hill"	63
Mr. John Wilson	pt. "Newfoundland"	79
	"Landabove"	132
Mr. John Holmes	pt. "Newfound Land"	71
	"Content"	50
Mr. Thomas Kinderick	pt. "Addition to Remains"	100
	pt. "Discovery of Scyth"	29
Mr. Isaac Downes	pt. "Bear Bacon"	223½
CP:1750:59 ...		
Mr. John Larkin	pt. "Bear Bacon"	200

Mr. Thomas Selby	pt. "Essex Lodge"	150
	pt. "Mount Calvert Manor"	75
Mr. Henry Boteler, Jr.	pt. "Chews Folly"	92
Mr. Samuel Evans	pt. "Evans Range"	200
h/o Charles Pye, Esq.	"Mattawoman Neck"	5000
Mr. Ninian Magruder, Jr.	pt. "Friendship" & "Addition to Magruders Purchase"	300
	pt. "Pritchets Purchase"	50
	"Magruders Lott"	100
	"Addition to Magruders Lott"	50
	"Black Oak Thickett"	150
	"Addition to Magruders Purchase"	18
Mr. William Head	"Redhouse"	412
Mr. John Brown (Eastern Branch)	pt. "Simmonds Lott"	107
Mr. Thomas Swann	"Quick Sale"	30
	"Forrest"	197
	"Bite"	25
h/o Mr. Thomas Sweringen	"Fellfoot"	115
	pt. "Hills Choice"	100
Mr. John Summers	pt. "Covert"	100
Mr. Abner Lewis, Jr.	pt. "Covert"	100
Mr. James Ranton	pt. "Forrest"	20
Mr. Jacob Foutt	pt. "Rocky Creek"	539
	pt. "Mill Lott"	50
CP:1750:60 ...		
Hon. Richard Lee, Esq. (cnp)	"Angle"	300
	"Cucolds Delight"	100
	"Scott Ordinary"	100
	pt. "Forrest Green"	170
	"Bowling Green"	86
	"Thomas Last Shift"	200
	"Meadows"	25
	"Reads Purchase"	40
	2 lots in Nottingham	2
	"Guests Pasture"	59

	pt. "Bealls Reserve"	400
	pt. "Woodbridge"	130
	"Reads Swamp"	580
	"Reads Pasture"	220
	pt. "Dann"	500
	pt. "Brookfield"	200
Hon. Thomas Bladen, Esq.	"Fairfax Beall"	200
	"Wakefield"	200
widow Crawford	pt. "Meadows"	99
	"Addition to Meadows"	100
	"Kingston"	250
	2 lots in Marlbro	2
	pt. "Bacon Hill"	148
Peter Apple	pt. "Rocky Creek"	150
	pt. "Arnolds Delight" a/s "Backland"	100
Mr. Henry Mayner	pt. "Rocky Creek"	250
Mr. Edward Tulley	"Hard Lodging"	322
Mr. Daniel Sing	"Breeches"	100
Mr. Samuel Brashears	"Brashears Industry"	169
	"Hog Harbour"	109
Mr. Thomas Brashears, Jr.	pt. "Cucolds Delight"	100
Mrs. Bridgett Clarvo	pt. "Maiden Bradly" & "London Pleasure"	75
Mr. Benjamin Norris s/o John	pt. "Hopewell"	125
	"Forrest"	100
CP:1750:61 ...		
Mr. William Norris s/o John	pt. "Hopewell"	125
Mr. John Norris	pt. "Hopewell"	50
Mr. Ezekiel Gosling	pt. "Discovery"	127
h/o Mr. Joseph Noble	pt. "Majors Choice"	80
	pt. "Littleworth"	3
Mr. William Holland	pt. "Charles & Benjamin"	187
	"Hollands Addition"	80
Mr. Francis Hall (cnp)	pt. "Partnership"	850
	pt. "Discovery"	98
	"Holloway" a/s pt. "Partnership"	250
	"Hope"	216

	"Brashears Meadows"	100
	"Cream" a/s "Ryleys Discovery"	110
	pt. "Partnership"	778
Mr. William Digges, Jr.	pt. "Mellwood Park"	500
Mr. Thomas Bowie	pt. "Ryleys Lott" & pt. "Concord"	300
	pt. "Cattail Meadows"	31
	"Craycrofts Right"	237
Mr. Greenberry Cheney	"Cheneys Delight"	100
Ignatius Digges	pt. "Craycrofts Purchase"	135
	pt. "Hatchett"	189
	"Little Addition"	122
	"Aquasca" a/s "Brook Court"	225
	"Free School Farm"	218
	"Cole Bridge"	250
	pt. "Mellwood Park"	500
	"Chittam Castle"	218
	1 lot in Marlbro	1
	"Clear Spring"	50
	"Collington Manor"	1000
Mr. Samuel Davis (Queen Ann)	"Forrest"	118
	"Ryleys Neglect"	50
CP:1750:62 ...		
Mrs. Mary Sim	pt. "Brook Discovery"	319
	pt. "Brook Point"	100
	pt. "Brook Reserve"	544
	2 lots in Nottingham	2
Mr. Peregrin Macaniss	pt. "Quick Sale"	90½
	"Sterling Park"	50
	pt. "Stock" a/s "Sarum"	105
Mr. Henry Moore (CH)	"Moores Chance"	200
	"Moores Rest"	100
Mr. Benjamin Fendall, Esq.	"Howards Park"	125
Mr. John Harvey	pt. "Dear Bought"	50
Mr. Daniel Page	"Cucolds Rest"	100
	"Bealls Good Luck"	100
Mr. Stephen Lewis (cnp)	"Strife"	500

	"Lewis Discovery"	60
Charles Carroll, Esq.	pt. "Enfield"	1350
	"Concord"	406
	"Carrolls Forrest"	500
	"Darnalls Goodwill"	206
	"Outlett"	919
	"Girls Portion"	1700
	"Bells Daft"	300
	"Betty Daft"	300
	"Clown Couse"	923
	"Beaver Dam Neck"	230
	pt. "Newfoundland"	195
	pt. "Stones Delight"	72
	"Carrolton"	10000
	"Stage"	228
	"Plaindealing"	500
	"Young Bloods Choice"	100
	"Addition to Carrolton" originally "Josephs Rest"	2700
	"Martinsfields"	100
	"Metchenfields"	153
	"Carrolls Delight"	5000
	"Carrollsburgh"	5000
CP:1750:63 ...		
Mr. Thomas Charters	pt. "Henry"	193
Mr. Daniel Carroll (cnp)	pt. "Fourhills" & "Polerwick"	268
	pt. "Darnalls Chance"	90
	pt. "Addition to Darnalls Chance"	100¼
	"Batchellors Chance"	100
	"Batchellors Content"	176
	"Killman"	1300
	"Partnership"	1000
	"John & Ann"	500
	"Henry"	100
	pt. "Refuse"	150
	pt. "Elizabeths Delight"	100
	pt. "Josephs Park"	3493¾

	pt. "Tunton"	25¼
Mr. James Gibbs	pt. "Rungfree" a/s pt. "Stoney Hill"	160
	"Philips Folly"	106
Mr. Holland Middleton	"Maidens Bower"	100
Mr. Thomas Conn	pt. "Labryth"	184
Mr. William Moore	"Spriggs Delight"	75
Mr. Higginson Belt	"Spriggs Garden"	250
	"Rogers Chance"	200
Mr. William Black (London)	"Black Acre"	435
Mr. William Park (VA)	"Park Hall"	1550
Mr. John Bowie	pt. "Brookfield"	350
	pt. "Brookwood"	225
	"Brook Reserve"	100
	1 lot in Nottingham	1
CP:1750:64 ...		
Mr. Robert Lazenby	pt. "Wolf Den"	217
Mr. Edward Sprigg 3rd	"Wickhams Chance"	300
Mr. Thomas Sprigg	pt. "Woodslock"	1000
	pt. "Chaffeys Delight"	250
	pt. "Thornland"	100
	pt. "Cobriths Lott"	100
Mr. Rodes (Cr. Branch)	pt. "Bealls Pasture"	48½
Dr. John Sprigg	pt. "Thorp Land"	380
Mary Beal (widow)	pt. "Bealls Adventure"	428
	pt. "Barren"	19
Mr. Charles Beall s/o Capt. Charles	"Pickletons Rest"	100
	"Conclusion"	473
Miss Rachel Beall	pt. "Grubby Thickett"	133¾
	pt. "Magruder & Bealls Honesty"	287
Mr. Joshua Beall	pt. "Barrens"	191
	pt. "Charles & Mary"	271
	pt. "Cranfords Adventure"	15
	pt. "Pritchalls Pleasure"	13
	"Charles & William"	80
	"Charles & Benjamin"	84
h/o Capt. Ninian Beall (cnp)	pt. "Charles & Mary"	30

	"Barrens"	262
	"Bealls Adventure"	72
Mrs. Jane Martin	pt. "Cranfords Adventure"	50
Mr. Samuel White	pt. "Charles & Benjamin"	170
Mr. Samuel White, Jr.	pt. "Charles & Benjamin"	250
CP:1750:65 ...		
Mr. Nicholas Maccubbins	pt. "Addition to Charles Forrest"	1470
Mr. Henry Watson	"Taylorsburgh"	38
Mr. Thomas Edelen, Jr.	pt. "Apple Door"	279
	pt. "Rome"	28¾
Mr. John Magruder	"Dunblane"	250
	pt. "Greenwood"	100
	"Knaves Dispute" & "Ridge"	180
	pt. "Charles & Benjamin"	50
	pt. "Good Luck"	200
	"Turkey Thickett"	350
	1 lot in Marlbro	1
	"Belfast"	200
	"Knaves Dispute"	40
	"Addition to Turkey Thickett"	44
	pt. "Chance"	106
	pt. "Bealls Benevolance"	126
	"Robert & Sarah"	100
	"Ridge"	78½
	"Bealls Purchase"	52
	pt. "Huckleberry Patch" a/s "Vale Benjamin"	36
	"Black Oak Thickett"	25
Mr. John Harbin	"Three Brothers"	200
Mr. John Peirce	pt. "Kittering"	80
	pt. "Northampton"	120
Mr. Robert Whitaker	pt. "Pentline Hills"	300
Mr. William Edeline	pt. "Vale Benjamin"	60
Mr. John Macklane, Jr.	pt. "Gleanings"	150
Mr. Daniel Jenkins	pt. "Port Royall"	50
	"Oxmontown"	219
CP:1750:66 ...		

Col. Edward Sprigg	"Spriggs Meadows"	183
	"Lane"	25
	"Gore"	48
	pt. "Northampton"	290
	"Kattering & Addition"	212
	"Three Partners"	75
	"Asdell"	100
	"Happy Choice"	1186
	"Addition to Piles Delight"	117
	pt. "Long Green"	28
	"Salisburry Plain"	200
	"Little Cave"	83
	"Ware Town"	360
Mr. Thomas Marshall	"Marshalls Adventure"	80
	pt. "Wheelers Hope"	160
	"Carrick"	128
	pt. "Pasture", "Mistake", & "Addition to Pasture"	390
	pt. "Mistake"	66
	pt. "Marburys Chance", "Little Troy", & "Carrolls Kindness"	225
Mr. Samuel Ryley	pt. "Chesnut Ridge"	182
h/o Mr. William Tannyhill	"Buckinghamhouse"	289
Mr. Thomas Brashears	"Wilsons Addition"	35
Mr. Butler Stonstreet	pt. "Wades Adventure"	115
	"Atheys Folly"	72
	pt. "Battersea"	125
	pt. "Littleworth"	90
	"Exeter"	216
Mr. Benoni Fowller	"Batchellors Hope"	200
Rev. Mr. Jacob Henderson	"Jacobs Addition"	125
	"Taylors Discovery" called "Ducketts Hope"	10
	pt. "Bowdells Choice"	187½
CP:1750:67 ...		
His Excellency Samuel Ogle, Esq.	"Beallecres"	1410
	"Woodcocks Range"	167
	pt. "Enfield Chace"	100

Mr. Robert Boyd Taylor	pt. "Duvalls Hunting Quarter"	100
Mr. John Coffee	pt. "Labryth" & "Discovery"	155
Mr. Richard Marshall	"Smiths Adventure"	200
Mr. Thomas Wall	"Walls Meadows"	220
	"Wards Pasture"	60
	"Smiths Pasture"	50
Mr. Robert Turner	"Nelsons Folly"	500
Mr. Thomas Pritchett	"Cucolds Delight"	140
Mr. Alexander Barrett	pt. "New Exchange"	200
Mr. Thomas King	"Good for Little"	188
Mrs. Sarah Toms	pt. "Valentine Garden" & pt. "Hickory Hills"	102
h/o Mr. Edward Prather	pt. "Darnalls Grove"	100
	"Addition to Darnalls Grove"	40
Mr. Charles Bussey	"Red Oak Bottom"	60
Mr. Charles Bevan	"Goodwill"	200
Mr. Zachariah Wade	"Wades Adventure"	100
	pt. "Stoney Harbour"	250
	"Wades Adventure"	100
CP:1750:68 ...		
Mr. William Smith	"One of Smiths Follys"	200
	pt. "Moores Plains"	517
	"Landing"	3
Mr. John Hook	pt. "Ketankin Bottom"	50
	"John & Sarah"	100
Mr. James Hook	pt. "Ketankin Bottom"	100
	"Hooks Hills"	55
Mr. Samuel Thomas	pt. "Winexberg"	493
	pt. "4th Addition to Snowdens Manor"	1029
Mr. John Walker	"Dormans Folly"	37
	"Addition to Dormans Folly"	31
Mr. Gerald Fitzgerald	pt. "Lundee"	50
Mrs. Mary Cramphin	"Cramphins Delight"	100
	pt. "Grandmothers Delight"	150
	pt. "Aaron"	250
Mr. Benjamin Musgrave	pt. "Locust Thickett"	250
Mr. Henry Truman (cnp)	"Blackwill"	200

	"Timber Neck"	15
	"Purchase"	100
	pt. "Ballington"	70
Mr. Samuel Beal, Jr.	pt. "Benjamin"	139
	pt. "Charles & William"	330
	pt. "Black Ash" & "Chittam Addition"	49½
	pt. "New Dumfrice"	270
	pt. "Longhead"	55
	pt. "Enlargement"	20
	pt. "Mill Seat"	3
Mr. William Brown	pt. "Mill Seat"	50
Mr. Abraham Davenport	pt. "Dann"	93
CP:1750:69 ...		
Mr. William Callioner	pt. "Dann"	67
h/o Mr. John Beall	pt. "Friends Delight"	100
	pt. "Poplar Thickett"	370
	"Dispute or Discontent"	200
Mr. Josiah Beall s/o John	"Easy Purchase"	300
	pt. "Longhead"	55
	pt. "New Dumfrice"	270
	pt. "Chittams Addition" & pt. "Black Ash"	49½
	pt. "Easy Purchase"	75
Edward Trafford, Esq.	pt. "Black Ash"	2
Mr. Levin Wales	pt. "Brook Court"	237
Mr. Charles Jones	pt. "Claggetts Purchase"	50
Mr. Thomas Draine	pt. "Swansons Lott"	75
	"Layford"	48
Mr. Micajah Plummer	"Simmonds Delight" & pt. "Swansons Lott"	25
	"Plummers Hunting Lott"	50
	"Plummers Delight"	50
Mr. Jacob Mathias Minches	pt. "No Name"	242
Mr. James Perry, Jr.	pt. "Wickhams Park"	200
	"Medcalfs Meadows"	100
Mr. Lancelot Wilson	pt. "Thomas & Mary" & "Williams Enlargement"	75
	"Lawcons Delight"	90
	"Wilsons Discovery"	53¾

Mr. Yate Plummer	pt. "Simonds Delight"	150
	pt. "Dundee"	15
CP:1750:70 ...		
Mr. George Plummer	pt. "Dundee"	91
h/o Mr. Edmund Carthage	"Hickory Tavorn"	200
Mr. James Watson	"Welshear"	100
	"Watsons Forrest"	166
	pt. "Forrest Fancy"	92
	pt. "Woodborough"	76
	pt. "Tranent"	11
	pt. "Poplar Hill"	308
	"Kemps Chance"	100
Mr. Matthew Wise	pt. "Cross Cloth"	109
	pt. "Taylerton"	20
Mr. Matthew Lodge	"Dear Stone"	150
Mr. George Buchanan	"Lanhams Delight"	100
	"Hopes Addition"	150
Mr. Philip Green	"Burges Delight"	200
	"Hickory Thickett"	78
Mr. Thomas Greenfield (SM)	pt. "Mazoonscon" pt. "Retaliation & Addition"	149
John Cook, Esq.	pt. "Northampton"	100
	"Gradon"	249
	pt. "Brook Grove" & "Reperation"	69
	"Addition to Gradon"	150
	"Reperation"	90
	"Mothers Delight"	200
	"Mothers Delight" & "Addition to Mothers Delight"	200
	pt. "Brook Grove"	50
	pt. "Reperation"	50
Mr. Richard Purnell	pt. "Wickham & Pottingers Discovery"	100
	"Newberry"	98
Mr. Jeremiah Plummer	"Batchellors Increase"	50
CP:1750:71 ...		
Mrs. Mary Whitehead	pt. "Brough"	150
Mr. George Wilson	pt. "Clagetts Purchase"	50

Mr. Richard Lanham	pt. "Oxmon Town"	225
	"Hap Hazard"	18
	pt. "Lanhams Addition"	200
	"Addition to Remains"	100
	"Pissimon Tree Branch"	121
	"Lanhams Folly"	20
	"Strife"	70
Mr. William Hardy	pt. "Addition to Remains"	100
	pt. "Refuse"	208
Mr. John Lanham, Jr.	pt. "Foxes Hall"	108
	"Foxes Hall" & "Dicksons Lott"	196
	"Lanhams Folly"	128½
Mr. Thomas Lanham, Jr.	pt. "Two Johns"	100
Rev. Mr. James Magill	"Mathias Choice" a/s pt. "Darnalls Grove"	300
	"Glebe" being pt. "Darnalls Grove"	96
Mr. William Waters	pt. "Charles & Benjamin"	152
Mr. Richard Waters	pt. "Charles & Benjamin"	152
Mr. Michael Dowden	pt. "Hermitage"	76
Mr. Clement Sims or John Jones	pt. "Markett Overton"	185
Mr. Joseph Belt, Jr.	pt. "Good Luck"	70
	pt. "Cobryths Lott"	150
	"Content" & pt. "Gleanings"	106
	1 lot in Marlbro	1
	pt. "Cobryths Lott"	100
CP:1750:72 ...		
Mr. Tobias Belt	"Lost Hatchett"	199
	"Oronoke"	290
	"Belts Delight"	120
Mr. Ignatius Mitchell	pt. "Remains & Addition"	100
	"Mitchells Fancy"	100
Mr. James Naylor	pt. "Cole Brook" a/s "Poplar Hill"	86
	"Vitles Range"	123
Mr. William Allyburton	pt. "Foxes Den" a/s pt. "Snowdens 2nd Addition to his Manor"	150
Mr. Joseph Lashear	pt. "Foxes Den" a/s pt. "Snowdens 2nd Addition to his Manor"	126

Mr. Murphy Ward or Robert Baden	pt. "Wards Pasture"	130
Mr. John Vertres	"John Mounting"	128
Mr. John Bayne	pt. "Hermitage"	100
Mr. John Martin	pt. "Dulanys Lott"	100
Mr. Joseph Bonnett	pt. "Dulanys Lott"	52½
Mrs. Pelly	"Bealls Gift"	16
	pt. "Mount Calvert Manor"	176
	"Mill Land"	10
Rev. Mr. Hugh Conn	pt. "Whittington"	100
	"Hudsons Range"	500
	pt. "Josephs Park"	300
	pt. "William & Ann"	95
Mr. Thomas Harwood	pt. "Brazen Thorpe Hall"	390
Mr. John Haggerty	"Sandy Thickett"	100
CP:1750:73 ...		
Hon. Daniel Dulany, Esq.	"Williamsburgh"	1400
	pt. "Conclusion"	956½
	pt. "Middle Plantation"	361
	pt. "Dulanys Lott"	2479½
	pt. "Spring Garden"	340
	pt. "Partnership"	100
	pt. "Taskers Chance"	850½
	"Good Hope"	132
	"Ocorsum"	100
	"Dispatch"	100
	"Addition to Spring Garden"	436
	"Long Meadow"	550
	"Addition to Long Meadow"	110
	"West Addition to Long Meadow"	100
	pt. "Taskers Chance"	320
	pt. "Dearbough"	200
Hon. Daniel Dulany, Esq. For h/o Samuel Chew	"No Name"	5000
Mr. John Hally	pt. "Exeter"	173
Mr. William Shaw	pt. "Whittington"	200

Luke Barnard	"Barnards Desire"	236
Mr. Ninian Beall, Jr.	"Nichols Hunting Quarter"	150
	pt. "Wilsons Park"	55
	"Wilsons Endeavour"	40
	"Uncles Goodwill"	116
Mr. Charles Hodges	pt. "Brook Hall"	232
Mr. Samuel Smith	pt. "Langly"	82
Mr. Thomas Evans	"Hazard"	156
	pt. "Dunghill"	100
	pt. "Island"	32½
	pt. "Attwoods Purchase"	193
	"Hogpen"	41
	"Chance"	414
CP:1750:74 ...		
Mr. Thomas Hamilton	pt. "Attwoods Purchase"	89
	pt. "William & Mary Increased"	94
Mr. Ninian Hamilton	"Aberdeen"	100
Mr. Andrew Hamilton	pt. "Attwoods Purchase"	89
Mr. William Plummer	pt. "Bealls Pleasure"	64
Mr. John Wivel	"Sugar Bottom"	37
Mr. Charles Friend	"Swads Delight"	260
	"Dear Bargain"	25
Mr. Nicholas Vannemore	"Vannemores Strugle"	100
Mr. William Boyde	"Pleasent Bottom"	164
Mr. John Jack	"Jacks Bottom"	175
Mr. Charles Cheney	pt. "Strife"	50
Mr. John Rutter	"Rutters Delight"	100
	"Cheneys Delight"	47
Mr. Thomas Gatterd	"Farr Well"	50
Mr. James Shaw	"Brothers Chance"	223
Capt. George Beall (cnp)	"Long Life to Lord Baltimore"	150
	"Rock Dunbarton"	795
	"Addition to Rock Dunbarton"	1380
	"Pens Disappointment"	86
	"Conjurers Disappointment"	46
	pt. "Lubberland"	27

	"Beals Chance"	100
Mr. Miles Foy	"Hunting Bottom"	80
Mr. Enock Enockson	"Enocksons Lott"	100
CP:1750:75 ...		
Mr. Edward Chalton	"Chaltons Forrest"	275
Mr. Evan Shelby	pt. "Maidens Choice"	268
	pt. "Hazard"	100
Mr. Hugh Gilliland	"Begg Spring"	150
	pt. "Hazard"	100
	"Bealls Fort"	50
Mr. Charles Dorecho	"Moldy Pond"	100
Mr. James Jack	pt. "Moldy Pond"	50
Mr. John Williams, Jr.	pt. "Maidens Choice"	100
Mr. John Darling	"Darlings Choice"	150
	"Deceit"	108
Mr. John Postlewhite	"Pleasent Bottom"	226
Mr. Michael Reysner	"Spring"	200
Mr. Peter Rench	"Hickmans Meadow"	150
	pt. "Springgs Delight"	75
	"Strife"	150
	"Four Springs"	200
Mr. John George Arnold	"Ramshorn"	494
	"Hogyard"	100
Mr. Jacob Foore	"Callachor Hall"	100
Mr. Thomas Cherry	pt. "Sky Thorn"	120
	"Chance"	138
h/o Mr. Peter Johnson	pt. "Sky Thorn"	180
	"Johnsons Lott"	139
	"Johnsons Desire"	67
CP:1750:76 ...		
Col. Thomas Cresap (cnp)	"Forrest of Needwood"	146
	pt. "Sky Thorn"	10
	"Indian Field"	250
	"Indian Purchase"	330
	"Linton"	155
	"Indian Field"	200

	"Conquest"	275
	"Three Fields"	165
	"Andersons Delight"	212
	pt. "Darlings Delight"	100
Mr. Joseph Perry	"Ash Swamp"	200
Mr. Joseph Tomlinson	"Water Sink"	150
Mr. John Fellingrah	"Fellingrah"	150
Mr. John Laman	"Lamans Choice"	200
	"Addition to Lamans Choice"	40
Capt. Joseph Ogle	"Peace"	250
	"Hunters Lott"	100
	"Peace & Plenty"	750
Mr. William Shaw	pt. "William & Elizabeth"	150
Mr. George Low	pt. "Chance"	75
Mr. William Luckett	pt. "Long Point"	75
	pt. "Thomas & Mary" & "Wilsons Enlargement"	95
Mr. John Marlow	pt. "Wheelershope"	80
Mr. George Dawson	"Addition to Golden Rode"	109
Hon. Benjamin Tasker, Esq.	pt. "St. Andrews"	67½
	pt. "Grange"	333
Mr. Samuel Waters	pt. "Jericho"	283
	pt. "Cherry Walk"	185
	pt. "Charles & Benjamin"	4
CP:1750:77 ...		
Mr. Jeremiah Mullican	pt. "Charles & Benjamin"	96
Visitors of Mr. Hendersons Chaple	pt. "Darnalls Grove"	4
Mr. Isaac Simmons	"Chalton Rackett"	100
	"Simmons Rackett"	200
	pt. "Simmons Rackett"	245
Mrs. Susannah Betty	pt. "Dulanys Lott" & pt. "Rocky Creek"	298
	pt. "Providence"	72
Mr. James Brook (cnp)	"Brooke Grove"	3154
	pt. "Brothers Content"	222
	pt. "Charley Forrest"	1080
	"Fork"	100

	"Brooke Chance"	20
	"Crows Content"	150
Mr. Thomas Betty	pt. "Dulanys Lott"	158
	"Wellwatered Bottom"	76
	"Bettys Venture"	100
	"Mackeys Choice"	50
Mr. William Betty	pt. "Dulanys Lott"	268
	pt. "Bettys Venture"	100
Mr. John Betty	pt. "Dulanys Lott"	166
	pt. "Rocky Creek"	85
Mr. James Betty	pt. "Dulanys Lott" & pt. "Rocky Creek"	245
Mr. Joannes Middagh	pt. "Dulanys Lott" & pt. "Rocky Creek"	251
Mrs. Agnes Betty	pt. "Dulanys Lott" & pt. "Rocky Creek"	300
Mr. Benjamin Stoddart	pt. "Friendship"	230
CP:1750:78 ...		
Mr. Zachariah Maccubbins	pt. "Friendship"	380
	pt. "Pritchetts Purchase"	81½
Mr. James Jones	pt. "Stoney Hill"	161
Mr. William Ray	pt. "Charles & Thomas"	140
Mr. Peter Hoggens	pt. "Solomons Purchase"	200
Mr. Robert Masters	"Through Fair"	100
Mr. Richard Simmons	pt. "Gettings Hah Hah"	200
	pt. "Wickham & Pottingers Discovery"	100
Mr. Robert Kenderick or John McDaniel	"Kendericks Hap"	50
Capt. Charles Higgenbottom	"Charlemount"	300
	"Neglect"	150
Mr. Samuel Plummer, Jr.	"Plummers Delight"	50
Mr. Baldus Foutt	"Foutts Delight"	150
Mr. John George Kerner	"Dutch Folly"	100
	"Addition to Dutch Folly"	100
Mr. Nicholas Smith	"Narrow Point"	50
Capt. John Charleton	"Darling Sail"	225
Mr. John William Smith	"Smithsfield"	150
h/o Mr. Edward Fottrell	"Colars Hall"	100
Mr. Isaac Plummer	"Trade Land"	40

Mr. William Spurgin	pt. "Anteatom Bottom"	50
CP:1750:79 ...		
Mr. John Shepherd	pt. "Anteatum Bottom"	50
Mr. John Vandever	pt. "Anteatom Bottom"	50
Mr. James Spurgin	pt. "Anteatom Bottom"	50
	"Trinting Spring"	120
	pt. "Stony Hill"	50
Mr. John Moore	pt. "Anteatom Bottom"	50
Mr. Richard Touchstone	"Anchor & Hope"	150
Mr. Amos Thatcher	"Johns Bottom"	100
Mr. Joseph Mayhew	"Chudleys Range"	50
Mr. Matthias Stallcop	"Mathias"	100
Mr. Butler Evans	"Evans Lookout"	20
Mr. Thomas Elder	"Elders Delight"	50
	pt. "Dann"	100
Mr. Samuel Elliss	"Chance"	150
Mr. John Keller	"Head of the Ash Spring"	150
Mr. Isaac Wells	"Lowland"	100
Mr. William Haywood	"Perrys Lott"	50
Mr. John Hanthorn	"St. Johns"	150
Mr. Charles Pocke	"Hanthdins Rest"	100
	"Pocke Meadow"	100
CP:1750:80 ...		
Mr. John Harding	pt. "Harding Choice"	126
	pt. "Hermitage"	117
Mr. John Harding, Jr.	pt. "Gunders Delight"	62½
Mr. James Wallings	"Dumhall"	50
Mr. James Warring	pt. "Weston"	222
Mr. George Moore	"Moores Delight"	50
Mr. John Lamar, Jr.	pt. "Charly"	130
	pt. "Ryleys Discovery"	80
Mr. William Elder	"Bever Dam Levell"	100
	"Black Walnut Bottom"	100
	pt. "Ogles Goodwill"	107
	pt. "Arnolds Delight"	300
	"Addition to Bever Dam Levels"	40

Mr. Jacob Mathies	"Slate Ridge"	123
Mr. Edward Pearce	pt. "Port Royall"	150
Mr. Thomas Pearce	pt. "Port Royall"	150
Mr. William Pearce	pt. "Port Royal"	(150)
Mr. Samuel Duvall (Ch Branch)	pt. "Pleasent Grove"	300
Mr. Lewis Duvall	pt. "Pleasent Grove"	250
	"Taylors Pasture"	74
	pt. "Sweeds Land"	35
Mr. Benjamin Duvall	"Pleasent Grove"	482
Mr. John Duvall	pt. "Pleasent Grove"	300
CP:1750:81 ...		
Mr. John Digges	pt. "Chance"	25
	"Charles Discovery"	100
	"Richards Hunting Ground"	366
	"Justices Delight"	250
	"Rich Levells"	352
	"Williams Intention"	246
	"Bear Garden"	568
	"Hazel Valley"	118
	"Spring Plain"	848
	"Digges Lott"	547
	"Meadows"	172
	"Disappointment"	182
	"Cedar Clift"	290
	"Brothers Agreement"	60
	"Brothers Tryall"	30
Mr. Joseph Green Simson	"Locust Thickett"	250
Mr. John Stevens	"Stevens Adventure" a/s "Chance"	225
Thomas Panuell, Esq.	"Fox Denn"	46
Mr. John Ramsay	"Labrynth"	100
MM John & Thomas Fletchell	"Two Brothers"	200
Mr. Charles Coots	"Flints Grove"	100
Mr. Richard Daviss (AA)	pt. "Dear Bought"	58
Mr. Edward Gillmore	"Owens Rest"	107

Mr. William Davis (Monococy)	"Stonhut"	50
Mr. Thomas Manners or William Turner	"Forrest"	66
	"Turners Promise"	50
h/o Mr. John Sittern	"Desire"	47
CP:1750:82 ...		
Mr. John Cook (Backwoods)	"Turleys Choice"	50
	"Cooks Choice"	87½
Mr. James Turley	pt. "Rattle Snake Denn"	100
Rev. Mr. William Williams	"Green Bottom"	250
	"Williams Project"	250
Mr. Robert Downey	"Downeys Lott"	150
	"Chester"	100
Mr. Evan Jones	"Jones Lott"	100
	"Evans Chance"	50
Capt. Henry Monday	"Truro"	844
Mr. George Read	"New Seat"	300
	"Earl Pearcy & Earl Douglas"	73
Mr. Mark Bigler	"Hulls Choice"	100
	"Hickory Bottom"	26
	"Marks Delight"	26
Mr. George Swineyard	pt. "Lost Spring"	255
MM Stephen & George Woolbery & Jacob Gripe	"Lafferdays Lott"	100
	"Marshhead"	100
	"Walnut Grove"	175
Mr. Edward Shippen	"Addition to Lafferdays Lott" .	186
	"Addition"	52
Mr. William Collier	"Stubb Hill"	100
Mr. Michael Taylor	"Good Neighbourhood"	50
Mr. Joseph Skidmore	"Monican"	50
CP:1750:83 ...		
Mr. John Friend	"Chesnut Levells"	50
Mr. Henry Abbey	"Scotts Lott"	150
Mr. Godfrey Mounga	"Delight"	100
Mr. Edmund Rutter	pt. "Strife"	50
Mr. Abraham Neighbours	"Abrahams Choice"	50

Mr. William Ford	"Wolfpit Neck"	200
	"Glassingbury"	93
	"Fords Delight"	32
h/o Mr. Henry Bevans	"Compass Hill"	50
	"Anchovy Hill"	28
Mr. David Jones	pt. "Bakers Purchase"	100
	"Addition to Bakers Purchase"	100
Mr. Battis Miller	pt. "Bakers Purchase"	100
Mr. John Clagett, Jr.	pt. "Clagetts Purchase"	286
	pt. "Pritchetts Purchase"	32½
Mr. John Mullican	"Bealls Gift"	300
Mr. Charles Brooke	pt. "Dann"	150
Mr. Joseph Beall	pt. "Layhill"	649½
Mr. James White	"Addition to Whites Lott"	40
	"Whites Lott"	50
	"Diamond"	10
Mr. Anthony Sim, Jr.	pt. "Stones Delight"	71
CP:1750:84 ...		
Mr. Peter Youngblood	"Cattail Marsh"	200
Mr. William Scott	pt. "Dann"	89
	pt. "William & Mary Increased"	170
Mr. Abel Hill (AA)	"Drurys Goodluck"	143
	"Good Luck"	85
Mr. John Pigman	pt. "Charley Forrest"	50
Mr. Henry Holland Hawkins, Jr.	"Grandfathers Gift"	305
Mr. Nicholas Ridgely (CE)	"Nelsons Rainbow"	100
Mr. Thomas Gordon	pt. "Bealls Pleasure"	61
	pt. "Wilsons Chance"	31
	"Widows Purchase"	10
	"Cranfords Adventure"	100
	"Judas Deceived"	50
	"Gordons Park"	37
Mr. William Gray	"Clarks Gift"	88
	"Rich Neck"	230
h/o Col. Thomas Lee (cnp)	3 lots in Marlbro	3¼

	"Backland"	350
	"Sweeds Land"	150
	"Wilsons Folly"	28
Capt. John Middleton	"Nothingworth"	30
h/o Mr. Hugh Ryley	pt. "Ryleys Range"	413
	"Hughs Labour"	112
Mr. Thomas Brooke	pt. "Prospect"	38
	"4½ Gallons Rum"	350
Mr. James Docker	"Docker Mile"	40
CP:1750:85 ...		
Mr. William Roberts (Pipe Creek)	"Broowood"	200
Madam Barbara Brooke	"Brookfield"	503
	"Brook Chance"	305
Madam Lucy Brooke	pt. "Brookfield"	322
	pt. "Forrest"	227
	"Vineyard"	258
	pt. "Dann"	1147
	1 lot in Marlbro	1
	2 lots in Nottingham	2
Mr. Edward Burch	pt. "Dann"	100
	pt. "Division of the Scyth"	29
	pt. "Dicksons Park"	90
	"Friends Advice"	15
~~Mr. William Flinthin or John McCoy~~	~~"Neglect"~~	~~50~~
Mr. George Gompe	"Chesnut Hill"	142
	"Four Springs"	50
Mr. Francis Burrell, Jr.	"Burrells Choice"	50
Mr. Francis Burrell	"Burrells Bower"	50
Mr. Daniel Vear	"Ram Punch"	60
Mr. Edward Purdey	"Jack of the Green"	100
Mr. Charles Trayl	"Trayls Choice"	50
Mr. James Dickson	"Matthews Lott"	100
	"Content"	112
Mr. William Field	"Bedfordshire Carrier"	108

CP:1750:86 ...		
Mr. William Juman	"Jumans Plains"	50
Mr. Christian Getslener	"Christian Choice"	100
	"Allamingle"	50
	"Frankford"	50
Mr. Joseph Foster	"Oxen Hill"	70
Mr. Nathaniel Alexander	pt. "Three Cousins"	300
Mr. Mendell Barrick	"Millplace"	100
Mr. Robert Birchfield	"Roberts Purchase"	50
Mr. Thomas McPherson	"Dann"	100
Mr. Arthur Charleton	"Charletons Purchase"	100
Mr. William Downey	"Walnutpoint"	164
	"Downeys Contrivance"	61
Mr. James Crouch	"Pleasent Valley"	84
	"Mount Pleasent"	122
Mr. Benjamin Warefield	"Walnut Ridge"	278
Mr. John Jones	"Linthecims Discovery"	84
	"Mill Race"	10
Mr. John Poole	"Pools Delight"	100
Mr. David Watson	"Henrys Grove"	50
Mr. Benjamin Berry	"Addition to Hensly"	50
Mr. George Cross, Jr.	pt. "Orphans Gift"	150
Mr. John Carrick	pt. "Moores Industry"	100
CP:1750:87 ...		
Dr. James Doule	"James's Field"	100
	"Finis Coronat Opus"	290
	"Douls Chance"	143
	"Douls Folly"	166
	"Twenty Acres"	20
	"Hay Park"	40
	"Hunting Park"	50
Mr. James Downey	"Nichols Contrivance"	75
Mr. George Dickson	"Dicksons Chance"	140
	pt. "Dicksons Chance"	110
Mr. William Forrest	pt. "Darnalls Grove"	100
Mr. John Needham (cnp)	pt. "Huntington"	308

	pt. "Pritchetts Purchase"	45
	pt. "Black Ash"	5
Mr. Charles Hedges	"Hedges Delight"	192
	pt. "Charles & Mary"	100
	"Whiskie"	100
Mr. John Warford	"William & John"	100
Mr. Thomas Wilson (Pipe Creek)	pt. "Rockland"	100
	"Addition to Rockland"	50
Mary Brook	pt. "Brookfield"	172
Mr. John Lewis	"Doe Little"	50
Mr. James Beall s/o Ninian	"Poplar Spring"	150
Mr. Charles Coggs	"Coggs Delight"	30
Mr. James Ford	"Turnup Patch"	60
Mr. George Lambert	"Lambert Park"	200
CP:1750:88 ...		
Mr. Isaac Baker	"Alloway"	150
Mr. Nathan Ward	"Wards Pleasure"	50
Mr. Nathan Wetsell	"Wine Garden"	150
Mr. Martin Wetsell	"Bonnetts Resolution"	150
Mr. Thomas Hargist	pt. "Darlings Delight"	125
Mr. Allen Farquare	pt. "Dulanys Lott"	100
	"Locust Thickett"	50
Mr. Philip Davis	"Save All"	50
Mr. Notley Thomas	"Hazard"	150
	"Strife"	328
Mr. James Alexander	"Wood Yard"	60
Mr. John Thompson	"Thompsons Adventure"	50
Mr. Andrew Hedge	"Mallingah"	100
Mr. Nicholas Rightenour	"Nicholas Rightenours Pound"	100
Mr. David Candler	"Swingabarker"	100
Mr. Matthias Risteau	"Bever Dam"	100
	pt. "Ogles Goodwill"	100
Mr. Henry Humphry	pt. "Radfords Chance"	200
Mr. John Davis	pt. "Forrest"	122
	"Davis Range"	100
CP:1750:89 ...		

Mr. Alexander Norton	"Lyons Hold"	100
Mr. William Wilkinson	pt. "Woodjoy"	200
	"Woods Prospect"	50
Mr. Richard Collyer	pt. "Token of Love"	96
Capt. Richard Williams	pt. "Darnalls Delight"	1600
	"Darnalls Last Addition"	262
	"Elizabeth"	310
Mr. John Hamilton (Backwoods)	"Upper Indian Bottom"	200
	"Hamiltons Recovery"	100
Mr. John Pritchett	pt. "Pritchetts Purchase"	38
Mr. Henry Child (AA)	"Wickham & Pottingers Discovery"	100
Capt. Alexander Jolly	"Wood Joy" & "Cross Gutt"	107
Mr. Joseph Noble, Jr.	"Addition to Levells"	100
	pt. "Levells"	67
	"Joseph & Marthas Delight"	200
Mr. Geust Cope	"Range"	420
Mr. Nathaniel Poach	"Round Knowll"	100
Mr. Columore Beans	"Colimores Ramble"	66
	pt. "Addition to James"	200
Mr. Henry Troutt	"Rich Bottom"	75
CP:1750:90 ...		
Mr. Christopher Lowndes	"Town Side"	100
	pt. "William & Mary Increased"	100
	pt. "Good Luck"	443
	pt. "Prevention"	180
	"Arthurs Swamp"	100
	"Whites Good Luck"	100
	pt. "Hermitage"	300
	"Simon & Jane"	107
	"Green Spring"	110
	"Expectation"	100
	pt. "Town Side"	612
	"Last Choice"	120
	"Matthews Goodwill"	176
	"Bear Denn"	100
	"Ranton"	100

Mr. Samuel Plummer	"Food Plenty"	167
	"Pleasent Meadow"	184
	"Rich Hill"	198
	"Hunting Lott"	226
	"Ross's Purchase" pt. "Scotts Lott"	106
	"Upgetting"	100
Mr. Peter Mire	"Cool Spring"	50
Mr. William Morgan	"Thomas's Forrest"	100
Mr. George Childen	"Longate Paugh"	100
Mr. George Huney	"Den of Wolves"	100
Mr. John Douthett	"Douthetts Chance"	50
Mr. Adam Spaugh	"Addition to the Sandy Elizabeth"	100
Mr. Basil Beckwith	"Garter Lost"	200
Mr. Peter Dent, Jr.	"Grubby Street"	100
Mr. Daniel Steagle	"Sinking Spring"	100
CP:1750:91 ...		
Mr. Joseph Wells	"Bocking Spring"	40
Mr. William Tracy	"Traceys Desire"	68
Mr. David Davis	"Cool Spring Addition"	63
	pt. "Cool Spring"	90
Mr. Robert Ward	"Grubby Hill"	50
Mr. Edward Brawner	"Elders Kindness"	100
Mr. James Trayle	"Rockhead"	60
Mr. Luke Ray	"Rays Venture"	150
Mr. Tader Lany	"Coopers Point"	200
Mr. Conrade Hawkersmith	"Low Mill"	100
	"Long Mill"	50
Mr. Thomas Lashare	"Square"	50
Mr. David Delantree	"Davids Choice"	100
Mr. John Restore	"Higgenbottoms Exchange"	100
Mr. Thomas Hunton	"Saplin Ridge"	100
Mr. Peter Stilley	"Saplin Ridge"	100
Mr. Robert Twigg	"Bear Range"	50
Mr. Thomas Hitchcraft	"Hannah Purchase"	55
Mr. William Hickman	"Three Springs"	100
CP:1750:92 ...		

Mr. John Smith	"New Germany"	50
	"Addition to New Germany"	50
Mr. Christian Kemp	"Kemps Delight"	100
	"Dispatch"	230
	"Good Luck"	150
Mr. John Thompson	"Griffith Park"	500
Mr. Henry Leeks	pt. "Gittings Ha Ha"	200
	"Leeks Lott"	50
	pt. "Leeks Lott"	<n/g>
Mr. John Vick	pt. "Progress"	83
	"Pleasent Nest"	100
Mr. William Gray (Backwoods)	"Grays Lott"	50
Mr. Thomas Taylor	"Little Grove"	91
Mr. Joseph Bell s/o Benjamin	pt. "Josephs Park"	326
Mr. Mareen Duvall, Jr.	"Wilsons Plains"	300
Mr. Samuel Galloway	1 lot in Queen Ann	1
Mr. John Young	"Backland" a/s "Arnolds Delight"	100
	"Switzerland"	50
Mr. William Murdock	pt. "Discovery"	268
Mr. John Row	pt. "Cranfords Adventure"	110
	"Lander Haughs"	20
Mr. John Hanson (CH)	"Clarksons Purchase"	192
	"Hansons Progress"	55
CP:1750:93 ...		
h/o Mr. John Masterson	pt. "Bare Bacon"	176
Mr. Thomas Lawson, Jr.	pt. "London Derry"	100
Mr. John Perrin	"Perrins Adventure"	222
Mr. Benjamin Rickett	pt. "Snowdens Addition to his Manor"	134
Mr. John Clark	"Prandon"	50
Mr. Michael Thomas	"Inlett"	60
Mr. Thomas Hodgkin	pt. "Brookfield"	199
	"Essex Lodge"	60
	pt. "Trower"	100
	pt. "Renchers Adventure"	664
	pt. "Renchers Adventure"	187

Mr. Daniel Pottinger	"Reyenton Plains"	261
Mr. Peter Studdenbaker	"Bakers Purchase"	100
	"Bakers Lott"	100
Mr. Daniel Ashcraft	pt. "Sky Thorn"	60
Mr. Thomas Whitaker	"Prevention"	50
Mr. Peter Bumgarner	pt. "Nazareth"	100
Mr. William Griffith	pt. "Dutch Folly"	66
	pt. "Nazareth"	100
widow Wilson	pt. "Forrest"	100
	"London"	100
	"Suburbs"	90
CP:1750:94 ...		
Mr. Absalom Wilson	"Forrest"	100
Mr. Wadsworth or Thomas Wilson	"St. Thomas"	150
Jacob Inglehert	"Swering Pasture"	96
Mr. James Summers	"Green Spring"	100
Mr. James Willett	pt. "Little Dane"	25
	pt. "Billington"	62
Mr. Richard Williams	"Wilsons Enlargement" & "Wilsons Fork"	119
	"Bealls Point"	40
Mr. James Bolding	pt. "Wickham & Pottingers Discovery"	100
Mr. John Hawkins, Jr. (cnp)	"Merry Thought"	40
	"Contention"	499
	pt. "Magruders & Beals Honesty"	101
	"Hawkins Lott"	88
	"Something"	49
	pt. "Never Fear"	15
	"Chance"	100
	pt. "Hazard"	1
	"Refuse"	137
	"Coxons Rest"	300
	pt. "Covington Pond"	24
	pt. "Brook Court"	316½
	pt. "Joseph & Mary"	120
	pt. "Ridgley"	75

	pt. "Bealls Gift"	167
	"Forrest of Needwood"	300
	"John & Priscilla"	125
	pt. "Comeby Chance"	88
	"Haw Meadow"	50
	"Hawkins Island"	125
	"Gods Gift"	117
MM George Fee & Richard Ancram	"Andrews Folly" & "Discontent"	50
Mr. William Piles	pt. "Hunters Fields"	187
CP:1750:95 ...		
h/o Mr. Samuel Pottinger	pt. "Wickham & Pottingers Discovery"	200
	"Addition to 1st Purchase" being pt. of "Wickham & Pottingers Discovery"	200
	pt. "Howertons Range"	100
	pt. "Majors Lott"	261
widow Massey	"Conveniency"	244
	pt. "Bealls Levells"	125
	"Bowling Green"	75
	"Doncaster"	93
	pt. "Hazard"	1
h/o Mr. John Piles	pt. "Hunters Folly"	334
	"Lanasley"	166
Mr. Richard Marlow	pt. "Edelens Courtsey"	70
	pt. "Addition to Edelens Courtsey"	30
Mr. John Piles	pt. "Hunters Field"	141
Capt. John Stoddart	pt. "Pasture" & "Pasture Enlargement"	1006
	pt. "Friendship"	300
	"Pastures Addition"	76
	"Southampton Enlarged"	1264
	"Mistake"	70
	pt. "Pasture"	500
Mr. Thomas Cramphin (cnp)	"Johns Delight"	100
	pt. "Black Ash" & "Dumfrice"	5
	pt. "Charles & Thomas"	69
	"Jacksons Necessity"	61

	"Addition to Jacksons Necessity"	100
	"Thomas & Mary"	450
	"Hermitage"	200
	pt. "Elizabeth Delight"	100
Mr. John Haymond	"Constent Friendship"	150
	"Haymonds Addition"	225
Mr. William Norris (Sugarloaf)	"Norris's Seal"	65
CP:1750:96 ...		
Mr. William Norris (schoolmaster)	"Ralpho"	65
	"Sarris Love"	100
Mr. Edward Wilson	"Wilsons Lott"	40
Mr. Thomas Johnson	"No Name" a/s "Sarahs Delight"	100
	pt. "Bares Desire"	100
	"Addition to Sarahs Delight" being pt. "New Exchange Enlarged"	24
Mr. Thomas Johnson (schoolmaster)	"Fork"	50
	"Thomas Johnsons Chance"	50
Mr. Alexander Beall s/o William	pt. "Jovial Ramble"	91
	pt. "Discovery"	268
	"Jacobs Cowpen"	50
Mr. William Beall s/o Ninian	pt. "Jovial Ramble"	109
Capt. Nathaniel Wickham	"Sailsburry"	50
	"Hope"	50
	pt. "Chance"	25
	"Pappaw Bottom"	160
	"Black Walnut Bottom"	15
	"Turkey Thickett"	100
	"Locust Thickett"	190
	"Wickhams Range"	50
Mr. Ninian Beal s/o Ninian	pt. "Dispute"	200
Mr. Richard Edelen	"No Name"	400
Mr. Richard Edelen, Jr.	"Longland" a/s "Frankland"	100
Mr. William Eilbeck (cnp)	"Cherry"	190
	"Addition to Cherry"	220
	pt. "Horsepen"	128

	"Long Acre"	100
	pt. "Dents Levells"	100
	pt. "Wheellers Purchase"	200
	pt. "Battersea"	100
CP:1750:97 ...		
Mr. Arthur Nelson	pt. "Nelsons Island"	56
	pt. "Broken Island"	45
	"Nelsons Adventure"	97
Mr. Arthur Nelson, Jr.	pt. "Nelsons Island"	150
Mr. John Nelson, Jr.	pt. "Nelsons Island"	150
Mr. Uril Virgin	pt. "Dickensons Delight"	133
Mr. Jeremiah Virgin	pt. "Dickensons Delight"	100
h/o Mr. John Dickenson	"Dickensons Chance"	30
Sarratt Dickenson	"John & James Choice"	150
Mr. Abel Brown	"Abells Levells"	400
Mr. Samuel Banks	"Strife"	30
	"Bell Tree"	25
Mr. Martin Houser	"Housers Choice"	110
Mr. Thomas Whitter	"Small Hope"	60
Mr. Jacob Brawner	"Inlet"	25
Mr. William Fee	"Batchellors Purchase"	150
Mr. Jacob Clount	"Hallow Spring"	100
Mr. Slafitt Shagh	"Half Moon"	108
Mr. John Patsall	"Blacksmiths Lott"	50
	"Smiths Lott"	50
Mr. James McCollom	"Ovall"	100
CP:1750:98 ...		
Mr. Lodwick Daviss	"Lodwicks Range"	150
	"Benjamins Squall"	50
Mr. John House	"Strife"	100
	pt. "Anteatum Bottom"	50
	"Two Wives"	33
	"Houses Addition"	70
	"Mill Place"	25
Mr. John Enockson, Jr.	"Enocksons Delight"	80
Mr. Samuel Waters, Jr. (cnp)	"Jericho"	254

	"Gleanings"	72
	pt. "Hog Yard"	177
	"Cherrywalk"	60
	"Addition to Hogyard"	34
	pt. "Hogyard"	280
Mr. James Smith	"Smiths Hills"	200
Mr. George Bond	"Law Pitt"	150
Mr. Adam Stull	"Chesnut Hill"	150
	pt. "Chesnut Hill"	100
Mr. Robert Owens	"Horse Shoe"	96
Mr. Thomas Harris, Jr.	"Pleasent Levells"	50
Mr. David Scott	"Charltons Victory"	50
Mr. Stephen Gattrell	"Gattrells Venture"	100
	pt. "Leeks Lott"	78
Mr. Jacob Stalley	"Switzerland"	150
Mr. Adam Meyner	"White Gravel Spring"	190
Mr. Matthew Pigman	"Rich Bottom"	15
Mr. Abraham Lakins	"James & Marocets Lott"	100
	pt. "Two Brothers"	52
CP:1750:99 ...		
Mr. Abraham Laking, Jr.	"Lackings Lott"	50
	pt. "Two Brothers"	50
Mr. Peter Shatter	"Palentine"	100
Mr. Felt Gran	"Felts Addition"	120
Mr. John Kennaday	"Dublin"	200
Mr. James Brown	"Browns Choice"	50
Mr. Nicholas Haile	"Mechacks Garden"	200
Mr. Robert Lamar	"Boys Lott"	100
	"Mill Tract"	93
	"Roberts Delight"	300
Mr. John Campbell	"Johns Good Luck"	130
	"Partnership"	300
	"Johns Delight"	59
Mr. John & Benjamin Mackingly	"Benjamins Inspection"	300
Mr. Jacob Weller (cnp)	"Taylors Lott"	200

	"Taylors Pighouse"	50
	"Taylors Shears"	50
Mr. John Willer	"Beauty"	50
Mr. Charles Davis s/o Griffith	"Davis's Forrest"	70
Mr. Charles Davis	"Davis's Delight"	100
Mr. William Hays	"Dove Harbour"	90
CP:1750:100 ...		
Mr. William Chambers	"Chambers's Desire"	44
Mr. Ignatius Perry	"Perrys Delight" a/s pt. "Wolf Den"	100
Mr. William Tyler	pt. "Dents Levells"	100
	pt. "Margaret Overton"	393
	"Tylers Discovery"	150
h/o Mr. John Perry	"Perrys Range"	100
	"Bushy Neck Hill"	100
Mr. Robert Constable	"Constables Range"	100
Mr. Jacob Hove	"Hoves Patconcon"	100
Mr. Lawrence Creger	"Cregers Delight"	100
	"Middle Choice"	100
Mr. William Willett	"Chaffeys Delight"	26½
	"Little Dane"	26½
	pt. "Bealington"	87
	pt. "Beals Craft"	43
Mr. Joseph Broner	pt. "Taskers Chance"	303
h/o Mr. Jacob Stoner	pt. "Taskers Chance"	571¾
	"Isaac's Inheritance"	200
	"Stoners Chance"	75
Mr. Francis Wise	pt. "Taskers Chance"	206
Mr. Casper Moyer	pt. "Taskers Chance"	202
Mr. Peter Hoveman	pt. "Taskers Chance"	225
CP:1750:101 ...		
Mr. Christian Thomas	pt. "Taskers Chance"	209¼
Mr. George Lay	pt. "Taskers Chance"	213
Mr. Henry Sinn	pt. "Taskers Chance"	145
Mr. Conrade Kemp	pt. "Taskers Chance"	335
Mr. Stephen Remsborough (cnp)	pt. "Taskers"	415
	"Shoemakers Choice"	100

	"Stoney Hill"	100
Mr. Henry Frought	pt. "Taskers Chance"	171
Mr. Henry Browner	pt. "Taskers Chance"	153
Mr. Thomas Stoddart	pt. "Taskers Chance"	340
Mr. Abraham Muller	pt. "Taskers Chance"	289¾
	"Mullers Chance"	100
Mr. Molock Wherfield	pt. "Taskers Chance"	355¾
Capt. Robert Debutts	pt. "Taskers Chance"	217½
	"Abins Choice"	300
	"Debutts Hunting Lott"	72
Mr. Unsold Land	pt. "Taskers Chance"	40
Mr. John Broner	pt. "Taskers Chance"	232
	"Good Luck"	100
CP:1750:102 ...		
Mr. Jacob Broner	pt. "Taskers Chance"	248
Mr. William Stevens	"Wheellers Folly"	116
Mr. Henry Stevens	pt. "Brook Plains"	100
Mr. Matthew Hopkins	"Stallop"	565
	pt. "Knaves Disappointment"	64
Mr. Christopher Ellis	"Beginning"	50
Mr. Thomas Marshall, Jr.	pt. "Charley"	100
	pt. "Carrick"	150
Mr. William Wells (AA)	pt. "Charly"	130
Dr. David Ross	pt. "Poplar Thickett"	100
Mr. William Ridgley	"Pocoson"	13
	"Hobsons Choice"	337
	"Boundabout Hill"	12
	"Jones's Addition"	40
	"Ridgleys Ridge"	50
Mr. Jacob Meller	"Meadows"	33
Mr. Jacob Meller (Monococy)	"Hazel Thickett"	100
	"Addition to Hazel Thickett"	105
Mr. Henry Fortney	"Dear Spring"	200
Mr. Alexander Warefield s/o Richard	"Warefields Vineyard"	270
Mrs. Jonna Croxall	"Brothers Generosity" a/s "Pork Hall"	587

CP:1750:103 ...		
Mr. Elisha Lansenee	"Good Luck"	163
Mr. George Hartman	"Hartman"	100
Mr. George Matthews	"Good Luck"	100
	"Good Luck"	212
Mr. Leonard Decouse	"Leonards Frolick"	50
Mr. Oliver Matthews	"Georges Discovery"	175
Mr. Moloher Staley	"Maswander"	30
Mr. Henry Sikes	"Piney Neck"	100
Mr. Edward Lamb	"Lambs Choice"	150
Mr. Conrade Kemp	"Wilber Sign"	30
	"Peace & Quietness"	50
Mr. Henry Coocus	"Shear Spring"	100
	pt. "Shear Spring"	135
Mr. Henry Karley	"Patricks Colt"	60
Mr. James Sharp	"Green Castle"	100
Mr. Valentine Mire	"Michaels Fancy"	50
Mr. Benjamin Bigge	"Benjamins Good Luck"	100
	pt. "Benjamins Good Luck"	43
Mr. Jacob Sly	"Addition to Wolfpit"	50
Mr. George Gue	"St. George That Slew the Wolfe"	50
CP:1750:104 ...		
Mr. William Summers	"Strawberry Patch"	50
Mr. Jacob Meek	"Inspection"	150
Mr. Jacob Peek	"Lambdon"	130
Mr. William Kersey	"Gravel Spring"	56
Mr. Thomas Adkey	"Lamster"	63
	"Youngs Direction"	100
	pt. "Fords Delight"	14
Mr. Nathaniel Tomlinson	pt. "Water Sink"	50
Mr. William Richardson	pt. "4th Addition to Snowdens Manor"	200
Mr. Matthew Ambrosier	pt. "Backland" a/s pt. "Arnolds Delight"	125
	"Sweed Land"	50
h/o Mr. Samuel Hyde (cnp)	pt. "Progress"	173
	pt. "Concord"	553
	pt. "Conclusion"	956½

	pt. "Middle Plantation"	361
	"Will Goodwill"	35
	pt. "Hadocks Hill"	150
	"Tanyard"	1
	pt. "Twiver"	150
	"Grange"	500
	"Chance"	200
	"Wallaces Chance"	500
	pt. "William & Elizabeth"	150
	pt. "Sinacor Landing"	52
Mrs. Elizabeth Jones	"Fletchalls Chance"	253
Mr. Joseph Mitchell	"Inclosure" & pt. "Prevention"	221
	pt. "Littleworth"	85
	pt. "Apple Door"	97
CP:1750:105 ...		
Mr. Luke Marbury	pt. "Apple Hill"	73
	pt. "Marburrys Long Court"	81
	pt. "Luke & Elizabeth"	100
	pt. "Hazard"	36
	pt. "Inclosure" & pt. "Prevention"	223
Mr. William Marburry	pt. "Apple Hill"	244
	pt. "Littleworth"	65
Mr. Leonard Marbury	pt. "Marburys Chance", "Carrols Kindness", & "Little Troy"	167
Mr. William Deacon	pt. "Twiver"	100
	pt. "Apple Hill"	65
	"Tewksberry"	35
Mr. James Lee (Ch Branch)	"Friends Goodwill"	53
Mr. Nicholas Baker	"Hazard"	300
	pt. "Knaves & Ridge Dispute"	133
Mr. William Head	pt. "Doves Nest"	48
	pt. "Doves Perch"	80
Mr. Thomas Grimes	"Taylors Cost"	113
Mr. Thomas Dorsett (cnp)	"Orchard"	190
	pt. "Trower"	228
	pt. "Largo"	70

	"Littleworth"	20
	"Good Luck"	100
	pt. "Farm"	100
	pt. "Mount Calvert Manor"	193½
Mr. John Brightwell	pt. "Spinham"	45½
	pt. "Colebrooke" a/s "Poplar Hill"	102
CP:1750:106 ...		
Mr. Philip Evans	pt. "Prevention" & "Littleworth"	88
Mrs. Mary Ryly	"Penny Choice"	200
Mr. Matthias Gray	"Grays Delight"	50
	"Grays Choice"	10
	"Grays Neck"	119
Dr. William Denune	"Denune Purchase" a/s pt. "Howerton"	200
Mrs. Rebecca Tilley	pt. "Black Ash"	4
	"Chittams Addition"	98
Mr. Nehemiah Ogden	pt. "Black Ash"	3
Miss Innocent White	pt. "Pascaham"	162
Mr. Moses Shelby	"Hunting Cabbin"	50
Mr. Basil Beal	"Industry"	163
Mr. John Huse	"William & John"	50
	"Retreat"	15
Mr. Joseph Wilson (CV)	"Exchange"	100
Mr. John Chalmers	pt. "Stumps Valley"	66½
Mr. Thomas Mills	"Lanes Fields"	175
	"Batchellors Hall"	100
Mr. Jacob Mills	"Beverdam Bottom"	138
CP:1750:107 ...		
h/o Mr. John Stutt	"Whiskie"	380
	"Stutts Addition to Whiskie"	160
	"2nd Addition to Whiskie"	40
	"Shole Spring"	150
	"Pleasent Hill"	90
Mr. Joseph Wood (Pipe Creek)	"Woods Lott"	126
Mr. Matthew Jones	"Jones Addition"	20
Mr. Benjamin Hiskitt	"Hiskitts Choice"	50

Mr. Evan McDonald	"Watsons Welfare"	100
Mr. Martin Carnell	"Martins Intention"	31
Mr. William Matthew	"Widows Rest"	100
Mr. John Mobberly	"Rich Levells"	120
Mr. William Dyall	"Dyalls Delight"	50
Mr. James Burgess	"Burgess Choice"	50
Mr. Richard Walls	"Susannah & Elizabeth"	50
Mr. Edward Mobberly (Backwoods)	"I Look'd Many Places Now I Like"	100
Mr. William Oneall	"Wheell of Fortune"	100
Mr. Michael Raynor	"Meadow"	150
CP:1750:108 ...		
Mr. John Owen	"Rich Plains"	100
Mr. Isaac Wood	"Come by Chance"	80
Mr. Mark Whitaker	pt. "Delight"	50
Mr. Thomas Swift	pt. "Delight"	50
Mr. Van Sweringen	"Piney Hills"	50
Mr. Robert French (CV)	pt. "Ridge & Knaves Dispute"	100
Mr. Thomas Wilson s/o Thomas	pt. "Ridge & Knaves Dispute"	66
Mr. Baruch Williams	"Addition to Bacon Hill"	100
	"Hopsons Choice" a/s pt. "Darnalls Grove"	200
Mr. Shadrack Hyatt	pt. "Hermitage"	101
Mr. John Nicholas	"Butter & Cheese"	80
	"Hickory Levells"	45
Mr. John Goodman	pt. "Batsons Vine Yard"	50
Mr. Jonathan Hagar	"Dicksons Rest"	100
	"Dicksons Fatiguing Journey"	100
Mr. Archibald Smith	"Edmonstons Pasture"	315
Mr. Edward Lanham	pt. "Stones Delight"	73
Mr. Joseph Fearis	"Harris Delight"	200
Mr. James Odell	pt. "Bally Christ"	303
CP:1750:109 ...		
Mr. William Bowie (cnp)	pt. "Brook Ridge"	162
	pt. "Brooke Point" & "Reserve"	350
	pt. "Brooke Point" & "Reserve"	77

	"Discovery"	8½
Mr. John Smith of the Farm	pt. "Forrest"	100
Mr. Joseph Robennet	pt. "Piles Delight"	129
Mr. William Allred	pt. "Piles Delight"	95
Mr. Samuel Wright	pt. "Forrest"	600
Mr. William Williams	"Williams Range"	132
	"Neds Quarter"	21
	pt. "Conclusion"	200
Mr. Thomas Buttler	pt. "Hermitage"	352½
Mr. William Moore (Carolina)	pt. "Moores Addition"	35
Mr. John Evans	pt. "Cole Spring Manor"	160
Mr. Charles Feanly	"Nonsuch"	136
Mr. William Hillary	"Williams Lott" pt. "3 Sisters"	87
Mr. Robert Langford	"Shady Grove"	50
Mr. James Beall s/o James	"Longhead"	600
Mr. Alexander Frazer (blacksmith)	pt. "Littleworth"	91
CP:1750:110 ...		
Mr. Jacob Fray	"Frys Habitation"	80
	"Frys Addition"	50
Mr. William Kerly	"Cornwall"	80
	"Leonards Range"	100
	"Addition to Cornwall"	50
Mr. John Macky	"Mount Pleasent"	50
Mr. Henry Avey	"Scott Lott"	202
Mr. John Ryley	pt. "Chesnut Ridge"	219
	"Ryleys Chance"	80
Mr. Daniel Spenghell	"High Spring"	100
Mr. Jacob Duckett	"Friendship"	100
Mr. John Mason	"Masons Folly"	17
Mr. Martin Hildebidle	"Providence"	50
Mr. Nathaniel Maynard	"Maynards Goodwill"	50
Mr. John Nash	"Ivey Reach"	40
Mr. Larkin Pairpoint	"Second Addition"	42
Mr. John Symson	"Symsons Garden"	35
Mr. Thomas Wenmameaden	"Long Choice"	50

Mr. Thomas Hawkins	"Uncles Gift"	160
John Ross, Esq.	"Wolfpit"	100
	"Wingfields Delight"	100
CP:1750:111 ...		
Mr. Joseph Chaplin	"Rush Bottom"	100
	"Josephs Chance"	100
	"Abstons Forrest"	156
	"Content"	100
	"Exchange"	100
Mr. Samuel Kelly	pt. "Hunting the Hare"	50
Mr. Daniel Kelly	pt. "Hunting the Hare"	50
Mr. John Woodfield	pt. "Hunting the Hare"	50
Mr. Thomas Wales	pt. "Hunting the Hare"	50
Mr. Henry Banner	"Batchellors Delight"	100
h/o Rev. Mr. John Lang	"Inverness"	575
Mr. Edmund Martin	"Martins Choice"	35
Mr. George Smith	"Cattail"	100
Mr. Henry Touchstone	"Chance"	50
Mr. John Greenup	"Red Oak Slipe"	32
Mr. William Brashears, Jr.	"William & John"	200
Mr. Caleb Dorsey	"Sparks Chance"	50
	"Harveys Brough"	50
	"State Hill"	50
	"Sparks Round"	50
	"Benjamins Folly"	50
Mr. George French	"Georges Venture"	50
	"Barrens"	100
CP:1750:112 ...		
Mr. Josias Darby	"Darbys Delight"	125
Mr. Jacob Rozer	"Rozers Lott"	50
	"Addition to Rozers Lott"	100
	"Hagars Fancy"	507
	"Welter"	10
Mr. Cornelius Poulson	"Poulsons Chance"	50
Mr. George Winters	"Batchellors Hall"	125
	"Winters Addition to Batchellors Hall"	75

Mr. John Cooe	"Locust Neck"	100
Mr. Joshua Hickman	"Elizabeth"	121
Mr. Kennedy Ferrell	"Fortune"	100
Mr. Jacob Kemnemar	"Long Meadow"	25
Mr. William Ingleman	"Carpouch"	50
Mr. Daniel Steward	"Indian Field"	50
Mr. Robert Leith	"Samuels Lott"	50
Mr. John Toms	"Toms Chance"	150
Mr. Thomas Prather	"Choice"	185
	"Richards Choice"	100
Mr. William Rayman	"Wards Spring"	200
Mr. William Wheat	"Wheats Purchase" a/s pt. "Smiths Pasture"	100
	"Wheats Purchase"	100
Mr. Mareen Duvall, Jr.	pt. "Vale Benjamin"	50
CP:1750:113 ...		
Mr. Thomas Baker	pt. "Taskers Chance"	260
Mr. James Edelen	"James"	166
	pt. "Partnership"	25
	pt. "Hazard"	5
	"Friendship"	200
Mr. Henry Brooke	pt. "Poplar Neck"	310
Mr. John Alexander	pt. "Three Cousins"	50
Mr. Gorah Davis	pt. "Gunders Delight"	64½
	"Addition to Gunders Delight"	70
	pt. "Bealls Manor"	108
	"Whiskey"	282
Mr. Barnard Weymer	"Addition"	200
	"Sandis Run"	200
Mr. John Casteel	"Littleworth"	50
Mr. Christian Steegle	"Empty Cupboard"	112
Mr. Thomas Walker	pt. "Dormans Folly"	73
Mr. Matthew Sparks	pt. "Bedfordshire Carrier"	168
Mr. William May	pt. "Maidens Choice"	53
Mr. John Baynes	pt. "Littleworth"	1
Mr. Martin Carsner	"Youngs Folly"	50
CP:1750:114 ...		

Mr. John Baley	"Mountain"	50
Mr. Thomas Baden	pt. "Sarum"	122
Mr. Daniel Moore	"Moores Delight"	100
Mr. James Crow	"Locust Levells"	119
	"Addition to Samuel Forrest"	150
	"Farmers Chance"	71
Mr. Theobald Foutz	"Cool Spring"	180
Mrs. Catherine Jennings	"Good Luck"	87
Mr. Joseph Welgamout	pt. "Dutch Folly"	34
	pt. "Dutch Folly"	78
	"Free Stone"	100
Mr. Gideon Howard	"Whiskey Ridge"	500
	pt. "Whiskey Ridge"	563
Mr. John Ridgeley	"Disappointment"	46
Mr. William Gibson	"Gibsons Chance"	100
Mr. Thomas Boylstone	"Boylestones Discovery"	39
Mr. Andrew Heaver	"Addition to the Miry Spring"	50
	"Miry Spring"	50
Mr. Erhart Appler	"Deeps"	220
Mr. Joseph Dolbridge	"Anteatum Levell"	50
Mr. Joseph Beal s/o Ninian	"Choice"	167
	"Lost & Found"	85
Mr. John Everett	"Goose Quarter"	125
CP:1750:115 ...		
Mr. Adam Myers	"Black Oak Hill"	50
Mr. Ninian Ryley	"Haly"	100
Mr. Caleb Touchstone	"Rich Thickett"	10
	"Bachellors Hall"	40
	"Whiskey Ally"	76
Mr. Joseph Smith	"Elswick Dwelling"	180
	pt. "Elswick Dwelling"	99
	"Smiths Purchase"	63
Mr. Edward Busy	"Blackwalnutplains"	100
Mr. Charles Wood	"Charles's Choice"	350
Mr. Telar Meisner	"Stoney Hill"	50
Mr. Nicholas Vitzell	"Jerusalem"	75

Mr Henry Bytesall	"Smiths Happ"	100
Mr. John Howard s/o Gideon	"Pretty Sally"	20
	"Second Adventure"	54
Dr. Charles Carroll	"Sluf Galluon"	50
	"Iron Hill"	31
	"Iron Mountain"	50
	pt. "Barbadoes"	250
	pt. "Scotland"	200
	"Meadows"	275
Mr. Basil Williams	"Williams Lott"	40
CP:1750:116 ...		
Edward Dorsey, Esq.	"Middle Way"	295
	"Brandy Wine Spring Enlarged"	377
	"Darbys Delight"	100
	"Brandy Wine Spring"	50
Mr. Michael Havanear	"Vulserhum"	50
Capt. Darby Lux	"Kenton"	100
	"Hunting Lott"	159
Mr. Thomas Maynard	"Maynards Chance"	50
Mr. Solomon Turner	pt. "Ralpho"	202
	"Solomons Flower"	50
Mr. Matthew Syler	"Misery"	50
Mr. Edward Ward	"Wards Delight"	100
	"Wards Delight"	100
Mr. Philip Turner	"Turners Delight"	30
Mr. Samuel Offutt	"Offuts Pasture"	613
	pt. "Younger Brother"	200
	"Offutts Adventure"	93
	"Addition to the Pasture"	19
Mr. Thomas Clagett Prather	"Maids Fancy"	100
Benjamin Penn	"Moores Delight"	100
Mr. Nathan Magruder	"Point"	30
Mr. Francis Hartley	"Hartleys Lott"	10
Mr. William Curron	"Peach Blossom"	50
Mr. John Whiteside	"Leonards Good Luck"	100
CP:1750:117 ...		

Alexander <t>	<t>	<t>
Mr. Bigger Head	"Marthas Delight"	85
Mr. Samuel Read	"Creve"	100
Capt. John Dorsey	"Mount Pleasent"	400
	"Johns Good Luck"	50
Mr. Hans Warbuck Waggoner	pt. "Maidens Choice"	549
	"Flagg of Meadow"	121
Mr. James McDonald	"Galloway"	175
Mr. John Barnwell	"Barnwells Choice"	50
Mr. John Bragilton	"Levell Spring"	100
Mr. Michael Miller	"Ash Swamp"	150
	"Skipton in Craven"	100
	pt. "Skipton in Craven"	180
Mr. Daniel Arnoll	"Goats Horn"	50
Mr. Alexander Perry	"Bachellors Purchase"	100
Mrs. Elizabeth Wilson	"Wilsons Fancy"	100
Mr. Richard Clagett, Jr.	pt. "Dann"	150
	pt. "Dann"	150
Mr. Leonard Allbrach	"Allbrachs Folly"	50
Mr. Edward Tyler, Jr. s/o Samuel	"Hopewell"	80½
CP:1750:118 ...		
<t>	<t>	350
Mrs. Isabella Hussey	"Mackeys Delight"	47
Mr. Walter Moore	"Wolf Harbour"	100
Mr. Stephen Richards	"Spring Garden"	50
Mr. William Dent	pt. "Dann"	150
Mr. Thomas Davis, Jr.	"Golds Branch"	257
	"Hyam"	100
	"Saplin Ridge"	72
	pt. "Benjamins Lott"	166
Mr. John Hammon	pt. "Gathers Chance"	177½
Mr. Henry Gather	pt. "Benjamins Lott"	200
h/o Mr. Benjamin Gather	pt. "Gathers Chance"	684½
	pt. "Benjamin"	150
	"Gathers Chance"	200

Mr. Clement Davis	"Hunting Hill"	300
	pt. "Pines"	78
Mrs. Lemar widow of Thomas	pt. "Two Brothers"	300
Mr. John Lemar s/o Thomas	"Pigpen"	50
	pt. "Joseph & James"	135
	pt. "Conclusion"	85
	pt. "Pines"	52½
Mr. Samuel Lemar	"Anns Garden"	50
	pt. "Conclusion"	213
Mr. James Weemes	"Billingsley"	1169
CP:1750:119 ...		
<t>	<t>	<t>
	"<t> Hatchett"	<t>
	"<t> Begenning"	100
	<t>	50
<t> Russell	pt. <t> a/s "Read Farm"	337
	pt. <t>	132
	"Pine Yard"	47
	"Widows Mite"	339
	"<t>kill"	236½
	"<t> Discovery"	33½
	"Cross Cloth" & "Brook <t>"	484
	pt. "Cucolds Point"	217
Mr. James Wardrop	"<t> Pasture" & pt. "Horse <t>"	254
	pt. "Addition to Darnalls Chance"	4¾
	pt. "Partnership"	285
	pt. "Friendship"	250
	"Wooden Platter"	100
	"Dear Bought"	100
Mr. George Frazer	pt. "Blue Plains"	300
Mr. Thomas Cross	pt. "St. Andrews"	56
	pt. "Orphans Gift"	150
Mr. John Needham	"Widows Mite"	76
	"Vine Yard"	76
	"Addition to Vine Yard"	33
Mr. James Lee	pt. "Labyrnth"	100

Mr. Abiezen Plummer	pt. "Dundee" & "Simonds Delight"	25
	"Swansons Lot"	75
	"Lyford"	48
Mr. Teder Laney	"Sasafras Bottom"	<t>
CP:1750:120 ...		
<t> Wickham	<t>	200
Mr. Lewis Duvall	"Tylors Range"	200
Mr. William Biggs	pt. "Benjamin Good Luck"	168

22:1753:1 ...		**Acres**
Mr. Henry Broone	pt. "Easycomeby"	200
h/o Col. Thomas Addison	"Addisons Choice"	2300
	½ "Whitehaven"	409
	"Philip & Jacob"	400
	pt. "Friendship"	1600
Mr. Thomas Harris	pt. "Charles & William"	251
Mr. Robert Pottenger	pt. "Charles Purchase" a/s pt. "Charles & William"	297
	pt. "Fenwick"	35
	"Brothers Request"	500
Mr. Charles Clagett	pt. "Clagets Purchase"	286
Mr. Jeremiah Berry	pt. "Charles & Benjamin"	1090
	"Addition to Charles & Benjamin"	31
Hon. George Plater, Esq.	"Brightwells Hunting Quarter"	1086
	pt. "Bradfords Rest"	4795
h/o Mr. Meredith Davis	"West Tract"	100
	"Good Luck"	245
	"Josiah"	200
	"Best Breeches"	100
	"Meredith"	118
	"Friends Good Will"	57
	"Resurvey on Meredith's Hunting Quarter"	498
Rev. Mr. John Eversfield	pt. "Deer Park" & "Bear Garden Enlarged"	200
	pt. "Friendship Enlarged" now called "Upper Tract"	204
	pt. "Eversfields Addition to Necessity"	50
	pt. "Grove"	43
	pt. "Enlargement"	90
Mr. Nathaniel Offutt	<t>	230
	<t>	200
	<t>	100
	<t>	<t>
<page is torn from here to bottom>		
James Swann	<t>	<t>
Edward Willet	<t>	<t>
22:1753:2 ...		

Mr. John Riddle	pt. "Poplar Thicket"	50
	"Addition to Poplar Thicket"	63
Mr. Clement Hill	pt. "Partnership"	1000
	pt. "Addition to Partnership"	200
Mr. John Needham	"Forrest"	612
	pt. "Huntington"	308
	pt. "Prichards Purchase"	45
	pt. "Forrest"	100
widow Culver	"Batchelors Forrest"	200
	"Chance"	100
	"Addition to Chance"	200
	"Second Addition to Chance"	400
Mr. Thomas Clagett	pt. "Dann"	250
Mr. John Carmack	pt. "Duckers Wood"	56
h/o Mr. Arnold Livers	pt. "Duckers Wood"	521
	pt. "Ogles Good Will"	105
	"Arnolds Chance"	600
	pt. "Backland" a/s "Arnold's Delight"	1074
Mr. William Carmack	pt. "Duckers Wood"	56
	"Lubberland"	99
Mr. John Cash	pt. "Millland"	50
Mr. Benjamin Becraft	"Becrafts Delight"	50
Hon. Benedict Calvert, Esq.	pt. "Hermitage"	873¼
Mr. Benjamin Boyd	pt. "Castle Plains"	350
	"Richland"	<t>
	"Shelbys Addition"	<t>
Mr. William Boyd	<t>	<t>
<page is torn from here to bottom>		
John Boyd, Jr.	<t>	<t>
Abraham Boyd, Jr.	<t>	<t>
Thomas Lancaster	<t>	<t>
22:1753:3 ...		
Mr. Rignall Odell	pt. "Three Bealls Manor"	216
Mr. John Beall, Jr. (cnp)	pt. "Allisons Park"	305
	pt. "Lay Hills"	649
	pt. "Drummonderry"	152

	pt. “Bealls Reserve”	253
	“Cowpen”	70
Mr. Joseph Ray	“Lashmeats Folly”	50
Mr. Joshua Busey	pt. “Charles & Thomas”	60
	“Jones Slipe”	50
	pt. “Charles & Thomas” called “Gift”	70
Mr. Nathaniel Wickham, Sr.	pt. “Berrystone”	100
Mr. Joseph Evans	pt. “Batts Hunting Quarter”	200
Col. Joseph Belt	“Seneca Hills”	200
	“Chevy Chase”	520
	“Friendship”	200
Mr. James Dooly	pt. “Chevy Chase”	40
	“Roberts Lott”	50
	“Robinsons Low Grounds”	10
h/o Mr. John Bowie, Jr.	“Piney Thickett”	200
	“Piney Thickett Enlarged”	200
	pt. “Hermitage”	602¾
	“Allen & James”	34
John Brice, Esq.	“Wintersels Range”	400
Mr. Thomas Clayland	pt. “Hermitage”	100
	“Bersheba”	5½
	“Dann”	250
Mr. Richard Richardson	pt. “Henry”	280
	pt. “Mill Lot”	92
	“Battengers Endeavour”	50
widow Mason (VA)	“Barbadoes”	75
Mr. Peter Dent	“<t> Spring”	50
22:1753:4 ...		
Mr. Alexander Harbert	pt. “Exchange Enlarged”	250
Mr. William Harbert	pt. “Dunghill”	197
Mr. George Frasier	pt. “Four Gallons & a Half of Rum”	350
	“Cut Knee”	315
Mr. Thomas Digges	“Mountain Prospect”	600
h/o Mr. John Thompson (cnp)	“Thompsons Purchase”	227
	“Cool Spring”	190
	“Small Island”	12

	"Thompson Hopyard"	110
	"Dutch Folly"	105
	"Long Island"	20
	"Darby Island"	70
	"John Jackymanly"	445
Mr. Henry Clagett	"Adderton"	200
Mr. George Scott	pt. "Hermitage"	200
	"Friendship"	600
Mr. Charles Walker	pt. "Virgins Delight"	75
Mr. Nathaniel Walker	pt. "Virgins Delight"	75
Mr. Henry Allison	pt. "Allisons Adventure"	150
Mr. John Baker	pt. "Snowden's Mill"	273
Mr. John Jackson	"Jackson's Improvement" & pt. "Friendship Enlarged"	194
Mr. William Thomas	pt. "Second Addition to Snowden's Manor"	415
	pt. "Fourth Addition to Snowden's Manor"	84
h/o Mr. John Thomas	pt. "Snowdens Manor"	549
	"Thomas's Discovery"	1480
Mr. John Adamson	"Clean Shaving"	277
	"Lucas Friend"	10
	"Largo"	30
Mr. George Moore	"Gideon"	20
22:1753:5 ...		
Mr. Richard Snowden	pt. "Snowdens Manor"	451
	pt. "Addition to Snowdens Manor"	573
	pt. "Third Addition to Snowdens Manor"	109
	pt. "Fourth Addition to Snowdens Manor"	4111
	pt. "Bealls Manor" tbc (N) Davis (41 a.)	523
	"John & Sarah"	200
	pt. "Snwodens Mill Land"	153
	"Moors Rest"	185
	"Walnut Levels" tbc D. Carrol	50
	pt. "Gunders Delight"	73
	pt. "Snowdens Second Addition to His Manor"	70
	"John & Catherine"	76
	pt. "Fourth Addition to the Manor"	1025

Mr. James Holmeard, Jr.	"Addition to James"	630
	"Discovery"	100
Mr. Thomas Lucas, Jr.	pt. "Plumyard"	100
	"Thomas & Nancy"	50
Mr. William Lucas	pt. "Plum Yard"	100
Mrs. Sarah Lucas	pt. "Plumyard"	100
Mr. James Holmeard	"James"	600
	"James Park"	52
	pt. "Token Love"	100
	pt. "Widows Mite"	206
	"No Name"	38
	"Bealls Plains"	508
	"Outlet" a/s "Lamar's Hills"	450
	"Mill Seat"	30
	pt. "Elizabeth"	25
Mr. Hancock Lee	"Addition"	576
Mr. William Masters	pt. "Progress"	49
John Darnall, Esq.	pt. "Hope"	2757
	pt. "Good Luck"	155
Mr. Thomas Waring	<t>	<t>
Mr. Jeremiah Belt	"Belts Tomahauk"	150
Mr. David Cox	"<t>"	50
John Wilcoxon	<t>	200
	<t>	36
	pt. "Gleanings"	64
22:1753:6 ...		
Mr. Caleb Litton	"Oatory"	405
	"St. Mary"	67
Mr. Thomas Catterall	pt. "James & Mary"	636
	pt. "Brothers Content"	360
	pt. "Bear Garden"	206
	pt. "Prevention"	218
MM Alexander & Robert Beall	pt. "Batchelors Forrest"	405
Mr. John Flemming	pt. "Hemsley"	100
Mr. Jeremiah Stimpson	pt. "Hermitage"	100

h/o Mr. Bryan Kelly	pt. "Brothers"	100
	"Advantage"	135
	pt. "Discontent"	100
h/o Mr. Osborn Sprigg	pt. "Stock Quarter"	160
	"Forrest"	85
John Hepburn, Esq.	pt. "Hermitage"	400
	"Hannover"	1500
	"Piles Grove"	566
Mr. William Wallace	pt. "Brothers Industry"	500
Mr. James Wallace	pt. "Brothers Industry"	929
	"Hopson's Choice"	134½
	"Discovery"	83
	"Weavers Denn"	200
	"Piney Level"	130
h/o Mr. James Offutt	"William & James"	530
	"James's Park"	200
	"Youngman's Folly"	100
Mr. James Offutt, Jr.	pt. "Clever Will Enlarged"	1000
Mr. William Offutt	pt. "Clever Will Enlarged"	<t>
	<t>	200
Mr. Alexander Offutt	pt. "Clever Will Enlarged"	600
h/o Mr. John Rogers	pt. "Bealls Manor"	281
	pt. "Snowden's Gift"	40
22:1753:7 ...		
Mr. John Gaither	pt. "Bealls Manor"	200
Mrs. Crabb	"Deer Park"	470
	"Bowling Green"	128
	pt. "Two Brothers"	28
	"Valentine Garden"	950
	pt. "Crab's Purchase"	100
Mr. John Phillips	"Walnut Bottom"	50
Mr. Milburn Simms	pt. "Easy Comeby"	100
Mr. John Smoot	"Cranford"	100
	"Beall's Design"	100
Mr. John Flint (cnp)	pt. "Newton"	100
	pt. "Elizabeth"	25

	pt. "Partnership"	12½
Mr. Thomas Flint	pt. "Newton"	100
Mr. John Flint, Jr.	pt. "Newton"	100
Mr. William John Jackson	pt. "James & Mary"	54
	pt. "Bealls Lott"	100
Miss Elizabeth Bordley	pt. "Backland"	542
	pt. "Backland"	90
Mr. John Riggs	"Bordleys Choice"	1000
Mr. Beale Bordley	"New Years Gift"	1143
Mr. Mathias Bordley	pt. "Backland"	2030
Mr. Richard Keene	"New Exchange Enlarged"	100
	<t>	<t>
John Davis s/o Charles	<t>	<t>
William Hughs	<t>	<t>
22:1753:8 ...		
Mr. John Beall (taylor)	"Resurvey on James & Mary"	270
	pt. "Grove"	219
	"Bealls Seat"	100
	pt. "Grove"	89
h/o Mr. John Radford	pt. "Seneca Landing"	52
	pt. "Long Acre"	52
	pt. "Elizabeth"	50
	pt. "Henry"	105
John Maddings	"Stoney Point" a/s "Labyrinth Point"	100
	"Addition to Stoney Point"	50
Mr. James Plummer	"Wickhams Good Will"	270
Mr. John Vanmetre	"Pipe Meadows"	200
Mr. David Shephard	"Pell Mell"	162
Mr. Thomas Palmer	pt. "Metre"	158
	"Palmers Choice"	58
	pt. "Metre"	142
Mr. Basil Adamson	"Adamsons Choice"	100
h/o Mr. Edward Crabb	"Crabbs Purchase"	356
Mr. Peter Butler (cnp)	"Paradise"	210
	"Magruders Hazard"	100
	"Locust Thickett"	100

	"Paradise Enlarged"	100
	"Butlers Lot"	120
Mr. James Lamar	pt. "Pines"	103½
Mr. Robert Lamar	pt. "Joseph & James"	200
	pt. "Two Brothers"	200
	pt. "Pines"	<t>
Capt. Samuel Magruder	<t>	<t>
James Perry, Jr.	<t>	<t>
Thomas Lamar	<t>	<t>
22:1753:9 ...		
Mr. Thomas Beall 2nd	"Frazers Levell"	200
Mr. Richard Duckett	"Ducketts Misfortune"	200
Mr. Joseph Wheat	"Wheats Choice"	53
Mr. David Trayle, Jr.	"Good Will"	100
Mr. Thomas Owen	"Haymonds Addition"	75
	pt. "New Exchange Enlarged"	73¾
Mr. James Beall s/o Robert	"Enster"	225
	"Farm"	128
Mr. Pharoah Riley	pt. "Dann"	100
Mr. Hugh Ryley	pt. "Dann"	250
Mr. Ninian Tanyhill	pt. "Fenwick"	263
h/o Mr. John Watkins	pt. "Paschaham"	100
	"Watkins's Range"	100
	"Addition to Watkins's Range"	320
h/o Mr. John Aldridge	pt. "Paschaham"	100
Mr. Mathew Robinson	"Joseph's Good Will"	150
Mr. John Leach	"Rocky Spring"	100
Mr. William Pritchett	pt. "Dunghill"	100
	"Harberts Chance"	100
	"Eleanors Green"	150
h/o Samuel Magruder	<t>	300
Mr. William Williams or Sarah Williams	pt. "Smiths Pasture"	100
Mr. Thomas Fletchall	pt. "Flints Grove"	150
Mr. Daniel Clary	pt. "Bradfords Rest"	115
	"Buck Bottom"	100

22:1753:10 ...		
Dr. Andrew Scott	"Fancy"	144
	"Satton"	200
	"Venus"	200
	"Badger Hole"	22
Mr. Benjamin Brown	pt. "Bradford's Rest"	115
h/o Mr. Samuel Magruder	pt. "Magruder & Bealls Honesty"	322
	pt. "Prevention"	140
h/o Mr. James Edmonston	pt. "Brother's Content"	360
	"Amsterdam"	30
	"Accord"	100
	pt. "Prestons March"	334
	pt. "Lubberland"	27
	"Batchelors Forrest"	405
	"Prevention"	281½
	"Western Fields"	32
	pt. "Hermitage"	131
	pt. "Discovery"	41¼
	"Land of Ease"	40
	"Georges Delight"	20
	"Piles Delight"	500
	pt. "Piles Hall"	360
Mr. Samuel Selby	pt. "Bailey Crist"	200
Mr. Alexander Magruder 3rd	pt. "Magruder & Bealls Honesty"	121
Mr. William Condon	pt. "Hermitage"	100
Mr. John Tolson	"I Never See It"	400
Mr. Thomas Thompson (Rock Creek)	pt. "Rattle Snake Den"	150
	"Thompson's Hop Thicket"	34
Mr. Patrick Readen	pt. "<t>"	50
Mr. John West	pt. "Two Brothers"	200
	pt. "Joseph"	200
Mr. Clement Mosely	pt. "Clagetts Purchase"	50
Mr. Stephen Hampton	pt. "Bear Den"	100
22:1753:11 ...		
h/o Dr. John Haswell	"Allison's Park"	153

Mr. Joseph Richardson	pt. "Charles & Benjamin"	100
	pt. "Brookes Reserve"	200
	"Rogues Harbour"	50
Mr. Grove Tomlinson	"Fletchall's Good Will"	100
	pt. "Goodluck"	200
	"Addition to Fellowship"	20
	"Groves Hunting Lot"	136
Mr. Benjamin West	"Younger Brother"	370
Mr. George Beckwith	"Beckwith's Range"	250
Mr. John Halsel	pt. "Cuckolds Delight"	100
h/o Mr. William Cumming	pt. "Accord"	100
	pt. "Amsterdam"	80
	pt. "Norway"	630
	pt. "Prestons March"	334
	"Drummine"	668
	"Barbers Beginning"	100
	"Sluce"	100
Mr. John Waters (PG)	pt. "Maiden Fancy"	430
	"Bear Neck"	151
	"Mothers Gift"	400
Mr. Brock Mockbee	pt. "Fellowship"	200
Mr. John Nelson	pt. "Chance"	25
	"Hopson's Choice"	555
Mr. John Delashmet	pt. "Swedes Folly"	100
Mr. Elias Delashmet	pt. "Swedes Folly"	100
	"Ramble"	100
	"Addition to Swedes Folly"	25
Mr. Weaver Barnes	pt. "Snowdens 2nd Addition to His Manor"	200
	pt. "Snowdens 2nd Addition to His Manor"	200
	"Inspection"	150
22:1753:12 ...		
Mr. George Moore (PG)	"Chance"	50
Mr. George Moore	"Moores Industry"	100
h/o Mr. John Cramphin	"Grand Mothers Good Will"	150
	"Henry & Mary"	110
Mr. Philip Murphy	"Bucklodge"	100

Mr. William Luckett	"Kittocton Bottom"	100
Mr. Stephen Julian	"Hedgehogg"	258
Rev. Mr. George Murdock	"Friends Good Will"	150
	"Glebe of Rock" a/s "Generosity"	100
	pt. "Mill Land"	2
	pt. "Charles & William"	248
Mr. Abraham Eltinge	"Abrahams Lott"	312
	pt. "Concord"	100
	"New Esopus"	100
Mr. Isaac Hite (VA)	pt. "Black Walnut Tree Island"	142
	pt. "Forrest"	140
Mr. Abraham Fore	"Eltings Right"	325
Mr. John Hite (VA)	pt. "Black Walnut Tree Island"	142
	"Discord"	215
	"Discovery"	37
	pt. "Forrest"	140
h/o Dr. Samuel Stringer	"Joy Church"	1045
	pt. "Stringers Chance"	300
Col. John Colvel	"Maryland"	6300
Mr. John Dickerson, Jr.	pt. "Charley Forrest"	100
Mr. Thomas Hilleary	"Pick Axe"	58
	"Sugar Loaf"	80
	pt. "Stock Quarter"	100
22:1753:13 ...		
Mr. Cornelius Eltinge (cnp)	pt. "Partnership"	100
	"Overplus"	170
	"Troy Island"	30
	"Millburn"	270
	pt. "Darby Island"	76
	"Fork Gruffy Hill"	305
	"Seneca Ford"	160
	"Fountain"	100
	pt. "Concord"	201
	pt. "Long Acre"	52
	"Fortune"	118
	"Eltings Rest"	60

	"Addition"	50
	"Mill Road"	240
	"Isaac Elting"	112
	"Fair Island"	172
	"Hills"	105
Mr. John Hilleary	"Walnut Point"	100
Mr. Joseph Waters	pt. "Moores Industry"	30
Mr. Thomas Odell	pt. "Grubby Thickett"	200
h/o Mr. James Magruder, Jr.	"Lost Jacket"	200
Mr. Nathaniel Magruder	pt. "Grubby Thickett"	166½
	pt. "Friendship"	101
Mr. Nathan Magruder	"Point"	30
	"Knaves Dispute" & "Ridge"	180
	pt. "Charles & Benjamin"	50
	"Knaves Dispute"	40
	"Addition to Turkey Thicket"	40
Mr. Zadock Magruder	"Turkey Thickett"	350
	"Robert & Sarah"	100
	"Ridge"	78¼
Mr. John Magruder, Jr.	pt. "Friendship" & "Magruders Purchase"	316
	pt. "Grubby Thickett"	166
Mr. James Magruder s/o Ninian	pt. "Magruder & Bealls Honesty"	300
Mr. Zachariah Magruder	pt. "Friendship"	220
	"Zachariah"	100
22:1753:14 ...		
Mr. Basil Beall	"Industry"	163
	"Archibalds Lott"	100
Mr. Samuel Magruder 3rd	pt. "Friendship" & "Addition to Magruder & Bealls Purchase"	320
	"Will Use"	25
	"As Good As We Could Get"	200
	"Samuel's Delight"	200
	"Hemsley"	100
	"Addition to Hemsley"	50
	pt. "Magruder & Beall's Honesty"	83

Mr. Archibald Edmonston	pt. "Deer Park" & "Bear Garden Inlarged"	458
	"Bealls Good Will"	50
Mr. William Davis	pt. "Hermitage"	197
Mr. Thomas Dowden	pt. "Hermitage"	70
Mr. William Davis s/o Griffith	"Hazard"	60
Mr. Charles Williams	"White Oak Valley"	100
Mr. Benjamin Perry	pt. "Hermitage"	250
Mr. John James (Pipe Creek)	"Dispute"	50
Mr. Edward Offutt	pt. "Coolspring Levels"	296
	pt. "Outlet"	520
Mr. John Dalyzell	pt. "Outlet"	80
Mr. Flayl Payne	"Paynes Delight"	100
	"Paynes Industry"	50
h/o Mr. George Noble	pt. "Wetwork"	350
	pt. "Spring Garden"	170
	pt. "Dry Work"	42½
Mr. Thomas Noble	pt. "Spring Garden"	170
	pt. "Wetwork"	350
	pt. "Dry Work"	42½
22:1753:15 ...		
Mr. Edward Owen	"Shephards Fortune Resurveyed"	292
	"What You Please"	120
Mr. Ninian Beall, Sr.	"Friendship Inlarged" now "Upper Tract"	322
Mr. Thomas Lucas	"Lucas Adventure"	100
Mr. John Smith Prather	pt. "Beer Garden Inlarged" & "Deer Park"	620
Mrs. Ann Magruder	"Friendship"	310
	pt. "Elizabeth" & "Partnership"	<n/g>
Mr. Hezekiah Magruder	pt. "Friendship"	100
Mr. Nathaniel Magruder	pt. "Grubby Thickett"	333
Mr. Charles Williams 3rd	pt. "Bealls Manor"	73
Mr. Thomas Case	pt. "Bealls Manor"	100
Mr. John Cartwright	pt. "Charles & Thomas"	150
Mr. James Moore	pt. "Allisons Park"	100
Mr. Charles Allison	pt. "Allisons Park"	52
Mr. William Black (London) (cnp)	pt. "New Exchange"	700
	"Gordon's Purchase"	150

	pt. "Friendship"	400
	"Black Acre"	435
Mr. George Gordon	pt. "Knaves Disapointment"	236
Mr. Henry Chappel	pt. "Allison's Park"	50
Mr. John Dowden	pt. "Addition to Fellowship"	49
	"John & Molly"	106
	"Johny's Poplar Spring"	42
	pt. "John & Molly"	137
22:1753:16 ...		
Mr. Robert Wells	"Cannoe Bottom"	50
Mr. John Beall s/o Robert	"Snowdens Mill Land"	120
	pt. "Three Beall's Manor" a/s "Elizabeth & John"	108
Mr. Edward Beatty	"Poplar Bottom"	52
	pt. "Dulany's Lott"	166
	"Patricks Colt"	60
Mr. William Oneale	pt. "Token of Love"	197
	"Wheel of Fortune"	100
Mr. John Buckston	"Buckson's Delight"	100
MM Arthur Lee & Charles Jones	pt. "Croucher's Gift"	250
	"Clean Drinking"	700
Mr. Peter Murphy	"Bear Garden"	100
h/o Mr. Joseph White or James Wallace, Jr.	"Fletchall Garden"	65
	pt. "Reads Delight"	100
	"Robinson's Low Grounds"	10
Mr. Richard Deane	pt. "Hunting the Hare"	50
Mr. Moses Chapline	"Mount Pleasant"	100
	"Resurvey on the Three Springs"	739
	"Joyners Fancy"	50
Mr. Thomas Willett	"Lick Hill"	100
	pt. "Little Den"	26
Mr. William Farquar (cnp)	pt. "Rockland"	74
	"Kilfadogh"	200
	pt. "Mount Pleasant"	40
	"Swamp Miserable"	60
	"Forrest in Need"	120
	"Unity"	25

	"Williams Defence"	270
widow Franceway	pt. "Nancys Delight" a/s pt. "Labyrinth"	100
Mr. Samuel Blackmore	pt. "Discovery"	100
22:1753:17 ...		
Mr. Cornelius Vernoy	pt. "Concord"	226
	pt. "Forrest"	142
	½ of "New Esopus"	100
Mr. William Williams	"Fork"	400
	"Mill Lands"	162
	"Addition to the Fork"	80
	"Haymans Addition"	75
	pt. "New Exchange Inlarged"	73¾
Mr. James Holland	pt. "Gittings's Hall Hat"	117
	"Panthers Range"	50
Mr. Thomas Stump	pt. "Stump's Valley"	133½
Mr. James Lee, Jr.	pt. "Discovery" & "Labyrinth"	100
Mr. William Beall	"William & Elizabeth"	135
	pt. "Friendship Inlarged"	290
	pt. "Discontent"	100
	"Hill & Dale"	66
	"Prevention"	141
	"Resurvey on Fatt Oxon"	878
Mr. John Tanyhill	pt. "Hills & Dales"	70
Mr. Samuel Beall	pt. "Laybrinth"	240
Mr. Humphry Batts	pt. "Magruder & Bealls Honesty"	233
	pt. "St. Elizabeths Manor"	100
	pt. "Partnership"	200
h/o Col. Thomas Lee (VA)	"Morton"	165
	"Eden"	320
	"Hill in the Middle"	315
Mr. Thomas Plummer	pt. "Plummers Island"	100
	"Greenland"	37
Mr. Thomas Plummer, Jr.	"Saplin Hill Resurveyed"	177
Mr. Thomas Kinderick	pt. "Addition to Remains"	100
	pt. "Division of the Tythe"	29
22:1753:18 ...		

h/o Mr. Isaac Down or Edward Doran	pt. "Bear Bacon"	223½
Mr. Joseph Peach	pt. "Bear Bacon"	200
Mr. Peter Apple	pt. "Rocky Creek"	150
	pt. "Arnolds Delight" a/s "Backland"	100
	pt. "Small Hope"	20
Mr. Ninian Magruder, Jr.	pt. "Friendship" & "Addition to Magruders Purchase"	300
	pt. "Pritchets Purchase"	50
	"Magruders Lott"	100
	"Addition to Magruders Lott"	50
	"Black Oak Thickett"	150
	"Addition to Magruders Purchase"	18
	pt. "Magruder & Bealls Honesty"	83
h/o Mr. Jacob Fout	pt. "Rocky Creek"	539
	pt. "Mill Lott"	50
	pt. "Small Hope"	10
	"Goose Nest"	30
Hon. Richard Lee, Esq.	"Angle"	300
	"Cuckolds Delight"	100
	"Scotts Ordinary"	100
	"Terrels Green"	170
	"Boling Green"	86
	"Thomas's Last Shift"	200
	pt. "Dan"	500
MM Francis & Charles Pierpoint	pt. "Rocky Creek"	250
	"Small Hopes"	80
Mr. Edward Tulley	"Hard Lodging"	322
Mr. Daniel Sing	"Breeches"	100
Mr. Benjamin Norris s/o John	pt. "Hopewell"	125
Mr. Zachariah Lyles	pt. "Hopewell"	50
Mr. William Holland	pt. "Charles & Benjamin"	187
	"Holland's Addition"	80
Mr. Francis Hall	pt. "Hope"	216
22:1753:19 ...		

Mr. Ignatius Digges	"Chittam Castle"	218
	"Clear Spring"	50
Mr. Stephen Lewis (VA)	"Strife"	500
	"Lewis's Discovery"	65
h/o Mr. Thomas Charter	pt. "Henry"	193
Mr. Holland Middleton	"Maiden's Bower"	100
Mr. Thomas Conn	pt. "Labyrinth"	184
	"Macgiligan" pt. "Labyrinth"	183¾
	"Lost Knive"	150
Charles Carroll, Esq.	"Carrolls Forrest"	500
	"Clown Core"	925
	"Carrollton"	10000
	"Stage"	228
	"Addition to Carrolton" originally "Joseph's Rest"	2700
	"Martins Fields"	100
	"Melkin Fields"	153
	"Carroll's Delight"	5000
	"Carrollsburgh"	5000
	"Girls Portion"	1700
Mr. George Gump	"Chesnut Hill"	142
	"Four Springs"	50
h/o Mr. Daniel Carroll	"Batchelor's Chance"	100
	"Batchelor's Content"	176
	"Killman"	1300
	pt. "Aixlachapell"	942
	pt. "Refuse"	150
	pt. "Elizabeths Delight"	100
	pt. "Joseph's Park"	1435¼
Mr. Daniel Carroll	pt. "Joseph's Park"	2058½
	pt. "Aixlachapelle"	850
	"Henry"	100
	pt. "Joseph's Park"	100
Mr. William Moore	"Sprigg's Delight"	75
22:1753:20 ...		
Mr. Higginson Belt	"Spring Garden"	250
	"Rogers Chance"	200

h/o Mr. William Parks (VA)	"Park Hall"	1550
Mr. Robert Lazensby	pt. "Woolf Den"	217
Mr. Richard Petty, et. al.	"Wickhams Chance"	300
Mr. Thomas Sprigg	pt. "Woodstock"	1000
Mr. Charles Beall s/o Capt. Charles	"Pickleton's Rest"	100
Miss Rachel Beall	pt. "Grubby Thickett"	133¾
	pt. "Magruder & Bealls Honesty"	287
Mr. Samuel White, Sr.	pt. "Charles & Benjamin"	170
Mr. Samuel White, Jr.	pt. "Charles & Benjamin"	250
Mr. Samuel Richardson	pt. "Addition to Charles Forrest"	1470
h/o Col. Edward Sprigg	"Three Partners"	75
	pt. "Happy Choice"	593
	"Little Cave"	83
	pt. "Resurvey of the Addition to Piles Delight"	1800
h/o Mr. Hugh Parker	"Astill's Delight"	150
	"Salisbury" composed of: • "Salisbury Plain" • "Addition to Salisbury's Plain" • "Vennemons Struggle" • "Salisbury Plains" • pt. "Nazareth Resurveyed"	4119
Mr. Samuel Ryley	pt. "Chesnut Ridge"	182
h/o Mr. William Tanyhill	"Buckingham House"	289
Mr. John Coffee	pt. "Labyrinth" & "Discovery"	155
Mr. William Norris s/o John	pt. "Hopewell"	125
22:1753:21 ...		
Mr. Robert Turner	"Nelsons Folly"	500
Mr. Thomas Pritchet	pt. "Cuckolds Delight"	140
Mr. Alexander Barrett	pt. "New Exchange"	200
Mr. Charles Bussey	"Red Oak Bottom"	60
	"Self Defence"	113
	"Cool Spring Manor"	50
Mr. James Hook	"Kittocton Bottom"	100
	"Hooks Hills"	55
Mr. Samuel Thomas	pt. "Winexburgh"	493
	pt. "4th Addition to Snowdens Manor"	1029

Mr. Samuel Beall, Jr.	pt. “Benjamin”	139
	“Charles & William”	330
	“Addition to Mill Seat”	325
Mr. Joseph Glass	pt. “Dan”	93
Mr. William Callioner	pt. “Dann”	67
h/o Mr. John Beall	“Friends Delight”	100
	“Dispute or Discontent”	200
Dr. David Ross	“Poplar Thickett”	370
Mr. Josiah Beall s/o John	“Easy Purchase”	300
	pt. “Easy Purchase”	75
Mr. Charles Jones	pt. “Clagets Purchase”	50
Mr. Micajah Plummer	“Plummers Hunting Lott”	50
	“Plummers Delight”	50
Mr. Jacob Sinn	“No Name”	242
22:1753:22 ...		
Mr. James Perry, Jr.	pt. “Wickhams Park”	200
	“Wickhams & Pottengers Discovery”	200
	“Addition to Wickhams & Pottengers Discovery”	50
Mr. James Winders	“Medcalfes Meadows”	100
Mr. Lancelot Wilson	“Wilsons Discovery”	53¾
Mrs. Mary Cramphin	“Cramphins Delight”	100
	pt. “Grandmothers Delight”	150
h/o Mr. Edmund Cartledge	“Hickory Tavern”	200
Mr. Mathew Lodge	“Dear Stone”	150
John Cooke, Esq.	“Mount Pleasant”	150
	“Mothers Delight”	200
	“Mothers Delight” & “Addition to Mothers Delight”	200
Mr. Richard Purnell (AA)	pt. “Wickham & Pottenger’s Discovery”	100
	“Newberry”	98
Mr. George Wilson	pt. “Clagets Purchase”	50
Mr. Zachariah Lanham	“Addition to Remains”	100
Mr. William Hardy	pt. “Addition to Remains”	100
Mr. William Waters	pt. “Charles & Benjamin”	152
Mr. Michael Dowden	pt. “Hermitage”	76
	“Hammer <t>”	50

Mr. Tobias Belt	"Lost Hatchet"	192
	"Oronoco"	290
	"Belts Delight"	120
Mr. Ignatius Mitchell	pt. "Remains & Addition"	100
	"Mitchells Fancy"	100
22:1753:23 ...		
Mr. William Allyburton	pt. "Fox'es Denn" a/s pt. "Snowdens Second Addition to His Manor"	150
Mr. Joseph Lazear	pt. "Fox'es Denn" a/s pt. "Snowden's Second Addition to His Manor"	126
Mr. John Vertrees	"John Mounting"	128
Mr. John Bayne	"Hermitage"	100
	"Saturdays Work"	50
Mr. John Bayne (Andictum)	"Anything"	50
Mr. John Martin, Sr.	pt. "Dulany's Lott"	100
Mr. Joseph Bonnett	pt. "Dulany's Lott"	52½
Rev. Mr. Hugh Conn	"Joseph's Park"	300
h/o Mr. Samuel Chew	"No Name"	5000
Mr. Luke Barnard	"Barnards Desire"	236
Mr. Walter Evans	pt. "Dunghill"	100
	pt. "Island"	32½
	"Beggars Benison"	50
Mr. Ninian Hamilton	"Aberdeen"	100
	"Hamilton's Lott"	50
Mr. William Plummer	pt. "Bealls Pleasure"	64
Mrs. Jane Wyvell	"Sugar Bottom"	37
Mr. Charles Friend	"Swedes Delight"	260
	"Dear Bargain"	25
Mr. John Jack	"Jacks Bottom"	175
22:1753:24 ...		
Mr. Charles Chaney	pt. "Strife"	50
Mr. John Rutter	"Rutters Delight"	100
	"Gaming Alley"	100
Mr. William Kelly	"Cheneys Delight"	47
	"Tower Hill"	50
	"Rutters Delight"	50

Mr. Thomas Gatterd	"Farewell"	50
Mr. James Shaw	"Brothers Chance"	223
Capt. George Beall	"Long Life to the Lord Baltimore"	150
	"Rock Dunbarton"	795
	"Addition to Rock Dunbarton"	1380
	"Pens Disapointment"	80
	"Conjurers Disapointment"	46
	pt. "Lubberland"	27
	"Bealls Chance"	100
Mr. Miles Foy	"Hunting Bottom"	80
Mr. Enock Enockson	"Enocksons Lot"	100
Mr. Edward Charlton	"Charlton's Forrest"	275
h/o Mr. Evan Shelby	pt. "Maidens Choice"	268
	pt. "Hazard"	100
Mr. James Gilliland	"Bigg Spring"	150
	"Bealls Fort"	50
Mr. Charles Dorrecho	"Mouldy Pone"	100
Mr. James Jack	pt. "Mouldy Pone"	50
Mr. John Williams, Jr.	pt. "Maidens Choice"	100
Mr. John Darling	"Darlings Choice"	150
	"Deceit"	108
22:1753:25 ...		
Mr. Isaac Baker	"Alloway"	150
	"Pleasant Bottom"	226
Mr. Michael Risener	"Spring"	200
Mr. Peter Rench	"Hickmans Meadows"	150
	pt. "Spriggs Delight"	75
	"Strife"	150
	"4 Springs"	200
Mr. John George Arnold	"Rams Horn"	392
	"Hoggyard"	100
Mr. Jacob Fore	"Batchelor's Hall"	100
Mr. Thomas Cherry	pt. "Sky Thorn"	120
	"Chance"	138
Col. Thomas Cresap (cnp)	"Forrest of Needwood"	146
	pt. "Sky Thorn"	10

	"Indian Field"	250
	"Indian Purchase"	330
	"Tinton"	155
	"Conquest"	275
	"3 Fields"	165
	"Good Hope" originally "Indian Field"	420
	"Enocksons Delight"	80
	pt. "Sky Thorn"	95
	"Boyles Cabbin"	60
Mr. Casper Smith	"Mount Olivet"	364
Mr. William Anderson	"Andersons Delight"	212
Mr. William Gilliland	pt. "Darlings Delight"	100
Mr. Joseph Perry	"Ash Swamp"	200
Mr. Joseph Tomlinson	"Water Sink"	150
	pt. "Water Sink"	50
22:1753:26 ...		
Mr. John Fellingragh	"Fellingrah"	150
	"Felts Addition"	120
	"Batchelors Delight"	818½
Mr. John Lemon	"Lamond Choice"	200
	"Addition to Lamond Choice"	40
Maj. Joseph Ogle	"Peace"	250
	"Peace & Plenty"	750
	"Fountain Low"	1050
	"Content"	210
	pt. "Creve"	50
	"Werleys Delight"	104
	"Grasing Ground"	100
	"Resurvey on Black Walnut Bottom"	310
Mr. Samuel Waters	pt. "Charles & Benjamin"	4
Mr. Jeremiah Mullican	pt. "Charles & Benjamin"	96
Mr. Isaac Simmons	"Charlton Rack"	100
	"Simmons Rack"	200
	pt. "Simmons Rack"	245
Mrs. Susannah Beatty	pt. "Dulany's Lott" & pt. "Rocky Creek"	298
	pt. "Providence"	72

Mr. James Brooke	"Brook Grove"	3154
	pt. "Brothers Content"	222
	pt. "Charly Forrest"	1080
	"Fork"	100
	"Brook Chance"	20
	"Crows Content"	150
	"Brooke Park Resurveyed"	1040
	pt. "Snowdens Manor Inlarged"	392
	pt. "2nd Addition to Snowdens Manor Inlarged"	218
	"Long Chohice"	50
	"Brookes's Black Meadow"	262
	"Brookes's Bottom"	584
	"Brooke's Discovery on the Rich Land"	440
Mr. Thomas Beatty	pt. "Dulany's Lot"	158
	"Well Waterd Bottom"	76
	"Mackeys Choice"	50
Mr. Peter Crepple	"Beatty's Venture"	100
22:1753:27 ...		
Mr. William Beatty	pt. "Dulanys Lott"	268
Mr. John Beatty	pt. "Dulanys Lot"	166
	pt. "Rocky Creek"	85
Mr. James Beatty	pt. "Dulanys Lot" & pt. "Rocky Creek"	245
Mr. Johannes Middagh	pt. "Dulanys" & pt. "Rocky Creek"	251
Mrs. Agnes Beatty	pt. "Dulany's Lott" & pt. "Rocky Creek"	300
Mr. Benjamin Stoddert	pt. "Friendship"	230
Mr. Zachariah Maccubbin	pt. "Friendship"	380
	pt. "Pritchets Purchase"	81½
Mr. William Ray	pt. "Charles & Thomas"	70
Mr. Robert Masters	"Thorough Fare"	100
Mr. Richard Simmonds	pt. "Gittings's Hah Hah"	200
	pt. "Wickham's & Pottengers Discovery"	100
Capt. Charles Higginbothom	"Charly Mount"	300
	pt. "Piles Delight"	117
	"Bedlam Green"	8
Mr. William Flintham	"Neglect"	150
Mr. Samuel Plummer, Jr.	"Plummers Delight"	50

Mr. Conrod Crosh	"Foutz Delight"	150
Mr. George Kersner	"Dutch Folly"	100
	"Addition to Dutch Folly"	100
Mr. Michael Kirkpatrick	"Narrow Point"	50
22:1753:28 ...		
Mr. John William Smith	"Smiths Field"	150
h/o Mr. Edward Fotterell	"Cotters Hall"	100
Mr. Isaac Plummer	"Trade Land"	40
Mr. William Spurgin	pt. "Andietum Bottom"	50
Mr. John Shephard	pt. "Andietum Bottom"	50
Mr. John Vandever	pt. "Andietum Bottom"	50
Mr. James Spurgin	pt. "Andietum"	50
	"Trenton"	120
	pt. "Stony Hill"	50
Mr. John Moore	pt. "Andietum Bottom"	50
Mr. Michael Crager	"Anchor & Hope"	150
	"Batchelor's Hall"	40
Mr. Amos Thatcher	"Johns Bottom"	100
Mr. Butler Evans	"Evans's Lookout"	20
Mr. Thomas Elder	pt. "Dann"	100
Mr. Samuel Ellis	pt. "Chance Resurveyed"	273
Mr. John Kellor	"Head of Ash Spring or Swamp"	150
h/o Mr. Isaac Wells	"Lowland"	100
	"Childrens Chance"	225
Mr. Henry Thomas	"Perry's Lott"	50
Mr. John Hanthorn	"St. John Resurveyed"	218
Mr. Charles Polke	"Hanthorns Rest"	100
22:1753:29 ...		
Mr. William Haynes	"Polke Meadows"	100
Mr. John Harding	pt. "Hardins Choice"	126
	pt. "Hermitage"	58½
Mr. John Harding, Jr.	pt. "Gunders Delight"	62½
Mr. James Walling	"Dumb Hall"	50
	"Wives Chance"	50
	"Adventure"	50

Mr. George Moore (Andietum)	"Moor's Delight"	50
Mr. William Elder	"Beaver Dam Level"	100
	"Black Walnut Bottom"	100
	pt. "Ogles Good Will"	107
	pt. "Arnolds Delight"	300
	"Addition to Beaver Dam Level"	43
	"Elders Choice"	240
Mr. Jacob Mathias	"Slate Ridge"	123
Mr. John Ramsay	"Labyrinth"	100
MM John & Thomas Fletchall	"Two Brothers"	200
Mr. John Digges	pt. "Chance"	25
	"Charles's Discovery"	100
	"Richards Hunting Ground"	366
	pt. "Justices Delight"	150
	"Rich Levels"	252
	"Williams Intention"	246
	"Bear Garden"	568
	"Spring Plains"	848
	"Hazel Valley"	118
	"Digges's Lot"	547
	"Meadows"	172
	"Disapointment"	182
	"Cedar Clift"	290
MM Edward Digges, Ralph Taney, & Ralph Neale	"Brothers Agreement"	60
	"Brothers Tryal"	30
Mr. John Justice	pt. "Justices Delight"	100
22:1753:30 ...		
Mr. Charles Coots	"Flints Grove"	100
Mr. Richard Davis (AA)	pt. "Dear Bought"	58
Mr. Edward Gillimore	"Owens Rest"	107
Mr. William Davis (Monococy)	"Stone Hill"	50
h/o Mr. John Settem	"Desire"	47
Mr. Thomas Mennard	"Forrest"	60

Mr. William Turner	"Turners Promise"	50
	"Turners Lott"	40
Mr. John Cook (Back Woods)	"Turley's Chance"	50
	"Cookes Choice"	87½
Mr. James Turley	pt. "Rattle Snake Den"	100
Rev. William Williams	"Green Bottom"	250
	"Williams Project"	250
Mr. Evan Jones	"Jones's Lott"	100
	"Evans's Chance"	50
h/o Capt. Henry Munday	"Truse"	844
Mr. George Read	"New Seat"	300
	"Earl Douglas & Earl Pearcey"	73
Mr. Mark Bigler	"Stulls Choice"	100
	"Hickory Bottom"	26
	"Marks Delight"	26
	"Biglers Addition to Stulls Choice"	50
Mr. George Swineheart	pt. "Lost Spring" a/s "George & Margaret"	150
Mr. George Hutsel	pt. "Lost Spring" a/s "George & Margaret"	55
Mr. Edward Shippen	"Addition to Lafferdy's Lott"	186
	"Addition"	52
22:1753:31 ...		
MM Stephen Geo. Woolbrey & James Gripe	"Lafferdays Lott"	100
	"Marsh Head"	100
	"Walnut Grove"	175
Mr. William Collier	"Stubb Hill"	100
	"Elders Delight"	50
	pt. "Dan"	67
Mr. Joseph Skidmore	"Monocan"	50
Mr. John Friend	"Hogg Hall"	66
Mr. James Maccollum	"Chesnut Levels"	50
Mr. Godfred Mong	"Delight"	100
Mr. Edmund Rutter	pt. "Strife"	50
Mr. Abraham Neighbours	"Abrahams Choice"	50
Mr. David Jones	pt. "Bakers Purchase"	100
	"Addition to Bakers Purchase"	100
Mr. Baltis Miller	pt. "Bakers Purchase"	100

Mr. Joseph Beall	pt. "Layhill"	649½
Mr. John Clagett, Jr.	pt. "Clagetts Purchase"	286
	pt. "Pritchets Purchase"	32½
Mr. Charles Brooke	pt. "Dann"	150
Mr. Peter Youngblood	"Catail Marsh"	200
Mr. John Pigman	pt. "Charly Forrest"	50
Mr. Henry Holland Hawkins, Jr.	"Grand Fathers Gift"	305
h/o Col. Thomas Lee (MD)	"Buckland"	350
h/o MM Col. Edward Sprigg & Osborn Sprigg	"Swedeland"	150
22:1753:32 ...		
Mr. Thomas Brooke	pt. "4 Gallons & ½ Rum"	350
Mr. James Docker	"Dockermite"	40
Mr. William Roberts (Pipe Creek)	"Broowood"	200
Madam Lucy Brooke	pt. "Dann"	947
Mr. Charles Clagett s/o Thomas & Philip Berry	pt. "Dan"	200
Mr. Edward Burch	pt. "Dan"	100
	pt. "Division Syth"	29
Mr. Francis Burrell, Sr.	"Burrels Bower"	50
Mr. Francis Burrell, Jr.	"Burrels Choice"	50
Mr. Daniel Vear	"Rum Punch"	60
Mr. Samuel Farmer	"Jack of the Green"	100
Mr. Charles Trayle	"Trayles Choice"	50
Mr. James Dickson	"Mathews Lott"	100
	"Content"	112
	"Kingsteadestead"	100
	"Connoloways Luck"	100
	"Chance on Beaver Creek"	100
	"Dicksons Struggle"	229
	"Whiskey Alley"	115
	"Secret Bottom"	104
Mr. William Field	"Bedforshear Carrier"	108
Mr. William Inman	"Inmans Plains"	50

Mr. Christian Getsetner	"Christian's Choice"	100
	"Alamingle"	50
	"Frankfort Resurveyed"	200
Mr. Robert Burchfield	"Roberts Purchase"	50
	"Crooked Piece"	50
22:1753:33 ...		
Mr. Handel Barrick	"Mill Place"	100
Mr. Thomas Macferson	"Dan"	100
Mr. Arthur Charlton	"Charlton's Purchase"	100
	"Friendship"	106
Mr. William Downey	"Walnut Point"	164
	"Downeys Contrivance"	61
Mr. James Crouch	"Pleasant Valley"	84
Mr. Benjamin Warfield	"Walnut Ridge"	278
Mr. John Jones	"Linthrins Discovery"	84
	"Mill Race"	10
Mr. John Pool	"Pools Delight"	100
Mr. David Watson	"Sarah's Delight"	90
	"Harry's Grave Resurveyed"	140
	"Nicholas Mistake"	10
Dr. James Dowell	"James's Field"	100
	"Finis Coronat Opus"	290
	"Dowells Chance"	143
	"Dowells Folly"	166
	"Twenty Acres"	20
	"Hay Park"	40
	"Hunting Park"	50
	"Dowell's Discovery"	123
	"Controversy"	15
Mr. James Downey	"Nicholas's Contrivance"	75
Mr. Charles Hedges	"Hedges Delight"	192
	pt. "Charles & Mary"	100
	"Whiskey"	100
Mr. John Wofford	"William & John"	100
Mr. Thomas Wilson (Pipe Creek)	pt. "Rockland"	100
	"Addition to Rockland"	50

22:1753:34 ...		
Mr. Thomas Wilson (Toms Creek)	"Disapointment"	46
	"Mary's Fancy"	104
Mr. John Lewis	pt. "Do Little"	50
Mr. James Beall s/o Ninian	"Poplar Spring"	150
h/o Mr. Charles Cagg	"Caggs Delight"	30
Mr. James Forde	"Turnip Patch"	60
Mr. George Lambert	"Lambert"	200
Mr. Nathan Ward	"Wards Pleasure"	50
Mr. Martin Whetsal	"Wine Garden"	150
Mr. Thomas Hargis, Sr.	pt. "Darlings Delight"	75
Mr. Thomas Hargus, Jr.	pt. "Darlings Delight"	50
Mr. Allen Farquar	pt. "Dulany's Lott"	100
	"Locus Thickett"	50
	"Chance"	118
Mr. Philip Davis	"Save All"	50
Mr. Notley Thomas	"Hazard"	150
Mr. Andrew Barland	"Woodyard"	60
Mr. John Thompson	"Thompson's Adventure"	50
h/o Mr. Patrick Mathews	"Mulingah"	100
Mr. Nicholas Rightenous	"Nicholas Rightenous Pound"	100
Mr. David Candlar	"Swingabarker"	100
Mr. Mathias Riselin	"Beaver Dam"	100
	"Ogles Good Will"	100
22:1753:35 ...		
Mr. Richard Collier	pt. "Token Love"	96
Mr. John Hamilton	"Upper Indian Bottom"	200
	"Hamiltons Recovery"	100
Mr. John Pritchet	pt. "Pritchets Purchase"	38
Mr. Henry Child (AA)	"Wickham & Pottengers Discovery"	100
Mr. Youst Cope	"Range"	420
Mr. Henry Trout	"Rich Bottom"	75
Mr. Christopher Lowndes	pt. "Hermitage"	300
	"Last Choice"	120
	"Mathews Good Will"	176

Mr. John Chalmers (Annapolis)	"Bear Den"	100
Mr. John Chambers	pt. "Stump's Valley"	66½
Mr. Samuel Plummer, Sr.	"Food Plenty"	167
	"Rich Hills"	198
	"Hunting Lot"	226
	"Rocky Hill"	170
	"Supply"	100
	"Hickory Plains"	454
Mr. Joseph Plummer s/o Samuel	"Pleasant Meadow"	184
Mr. Peter Mire	"Cool Spring"	188
Mr. William Morgan	"Thomas's Forrest"	100
Mr. George Childen	"Longate Pough"	100
Mr. George Honey	"Den of Wolves"	100
Mr. Adam Spaugh	"Addition to the Sandy Elizabeth"	100
Mr. Basil Beckwith	"Garter Lost"	200
22:1753:36 ...		
Mr. Peter Dent, Jr.	"Crabby Street"	100
Mr. Daniel Steagle	"Sinking Spring"	100
h/o Mr. Baltus Fought	"Boiling Spring"	47
Mr. William Tracey	"Tracey's Desire"	60
Mr. Robert Ward	"Grubby Hill"	50
Mr. Edward Brawner	"Elders Kindness"	100
Mr. James Trayle	"Rock Head"	60
Mr. Luke Ray	"Rays Venture"	150
Mr. Conrod Hawkersmith	"Low Mill"	100
	"Long Null"	50
Mr. Thomas Lashear	"Square"	50
Mr. David Delantree	"Davids Choice"	100
Mr. John Reator	"Higginbothom's Exchange"	100
Mr. Peter Stitly	"Saplin Ridge Resurveyed"	195
Mr. Robert Twigg	"Bear Range"	50
	"Jerricho"	44
Mr. Thomas Hitchcraft	"Hannah's Purchase"	55
Mr. William Hickman	"Three Springs"	100

Mr. John Smith	"New Germany"	50
	"Addition to New Germany"	50
Mr. Christian Kemp	"Kemps Delight"	100
	"Dispatch"	230
	"Good Luck"	150
Mr. John Thompson	"Griffith Park"	500
Mr. Francis Gatterall	"Grues Lot"	50
Mr. Thomas Hinton	"Saplin Ridge Resurveyed"	290
22:1753:37 ...		
Mr. Henry Leeks	pt. "Gittings's Hah Hah"	200
	"Leeks Lot"	50
	pt. "Leeks Lot"	107
Mr. John Veatch	pt. "Progress"	83
	"Pleasant Nest"	100
	pt. "Poplar Spring"	200
Mr. Absalon Wilson	pt. "Forrest"	100
Mr. Joseph Belt s/o Benjamin	pt. "Joseph's Park"	326½
MM Wadsworth & Thomas Wilson	"Saint Thomas"	150
Mr. John Young	"Buckland" a/s "Arnold's Delight"	100
	"Switzerland Resurveyed"	103
Mr. William Murdock s/o Parson	pt. "Discovery"	268
h/o Mr. John Masterson	pt. "Bear Bacon"	176
Mr. Benjamin Ricketts	pt. "Snowdens Addition to His Manor"	134
	"Green Marsh"	78
Mr. John Perrin	"Perrins Adventure"	222
Mr. Michael Thomas	"Inlet"	60
Mr. Daniel Pettinger	"Reyonton Plains"	261
h/o Mr. Peter Studenbaker	pt. "Bakers Lookout" & "Bakers Lot"	265
	"Shoemakers Purchase"	63
	"Woolf's Lot"	100
Mr. John Long	pt. "Bakers Lookout"	100
Mr. Robert Brightwell	"Sky Thorn"	60
Mr. Nicholas Fink	"Prevention"	50
	"Arabia"	208

h/o Mr. William Griffith (Conocochegue)	pt. "Nazareth"	100
	pt. "Dutch Folly"	66
22:1753:38 ...		
Mr. James Baldwin	pt. "Wickham & Pottengers Discovery"	100
Mr. John Hawkins, Jr.	pt. "Magruders & Bealls Honesty"	101
	"Coxon's Rest"	300
	"Forrest of Needwood"	300
	"John Priscilla"	125
	"Haw Meadow"	50
	"Hawkins Island"	125
	"Contention"	499
	"Chance" a/s "Hawkins Chance"	100
	"Refuse"	137
Mr. William Beall s/o Ninian	pt. "Jovial Ramble"	109
Mr. Nathaniel Wickham, Jr.	"Salisbury"	50
	pt. "Chance"	25
	"Paw Paw Thicket"	160
	"Turkey Thicket"	100
	"Locus Thicket"	190
Mr. William Cumming, Jr.	"Hope"	50
Mr. Ninian Beall s/o Ninian	pt. "Dispute"	200
	"Basrren Hill"	100
	"Gravely Ridge"	50
Mr. Arthur Nelson, Sr.	pt. "Nelsons Island"	56
	pt. "Broken Island"	45
	"Nelsons Adventure"	97
Mr. Arthur Nelson, Jr.	pt. "Nelsons Island"	24
	pt. "Nelsons Island"	150
	pt. "Chance"	25
Mr. John Trammel, Jr. (VA)	pt. "Nelsons Island"	136
Mr. Urill Virgin	pt. "Dicksons Delight"	133
h/o Mr. John Dickerson	"Dickersons Chance"	30
Mr. Serrat Dickerson	"John & James's Choice"	150
Mr. Abel Brown	"Abells Levels"	400
Mr. Martin Howser	"Howsers Choice"	110
Mr. Thomas Whitten	"Small Hope"	60

22:1753:39 ...		
Mr. Jacob Brunner	"Inlet"	25
	pt. "Taskers Chance"	248
	"Chevy Chase"	100
Mr. William Fee	"Batchelors Purchase"	150
Mr. Jacob Clount	"Hollow Spring"	100
Mr. Steffill Shaugh	"Half Moon"	108
Mr. John Pastall	"Blacksmiths Lot"	50
	"Smiths Lot"	50
Mr. James Maccollum	"Ovel"	100
Mr. Lodowick Davis	"Lodowicks Range"	150
	"Benjamin's Squall"	50
	"Davis's Content"	50
Mr. John House	"Strife"	100
	pt. "Andietum Bottom"	50
	"Two Wives"	33
	"Houses Addition"	70
	"Mill Place"	25
Mr. Stephen Gatherill	"Gatherills Venture"	100
	pt. "Leeks Lot"	78
Mr. Jacob Staley	"Switzerland"	150
	"Crames Quietness"	100
	"Other Some Resurveyed"	423
Mr. Adam Meyner	"White Gravel Spring"	190
Mr. James Smith (Andietum)	"Smith's Hills"	200
Mr. George Bond	"Sawpit"	150
	"Forrest"	100
Mr. Adam Stull	"Chesnut Hill"	150
	pt. "Chesnut Hill"	100
Mr. Robert Owen	"Horse Shoe"	96
Mr. Thomas Harris	"Pleasant Levels"	50
	"Maidens Point"	100
22:1753:40 ...		
Mr. David Scott	"Charlton's Victory"	50
Mr. Mathew Pigman	"Rich Bottom"	15
	"Very Good"	100

Mrs. Martha Lakins widow of Abraham	"James & Marriots Lott" pt. "Two Brothers"	100
Mr. Joseph Lakins	pt. "Two Brothers"	50
Mr. Abraham Lakins	"Lakins Lot" pt. "Two Brothers"	50
	pt. "Two Brothers"	52
Mr. Peter Shaver	"Palantine"	100
Mr. John Kennedy	"Dublin"	200
Mr. James Brown	"Browns Choice"	50
	"Browns Delight"	100
Mr. Nicholas Haile	"Mellchers Garden"	200
Mr. Joseph Wilson (Monococy)	"Boys Lot"	100
	"Mill Tract"	93
	"Roberts Delight"	300
MM John & Benjamin Mekingly	"Benjamins Inspection"	300
Mr. John Campbell (AA)	"Johns Good Luck"	130
	"Partnership"	300
	"Johns Delight"	59
Mr. Jacob Weller	"Taylors Lot"	200
	"Taylors Piglouse"	50
	"Taylors Shears"	50
Mr. John Weller	"Beauty"	50
Mr. Charles Davis s/o Griffith	"Davis's Forrest"	70
Mr. George Mathewes	pt. "Good Luck"	212
	"Davis's Delight"	100
Mr. William Hayes	"Dove Harbour"	90
Mr. William Chambers	"Chambers Desire"	44
Mr. Ignatius Perry	"Perry's Delight" a/s "Woolf Den"	100
22:1753:41 ...		
h/o Mr. John Perry	"Perrys Range"	100
	"Bushy Neck Hill"	100
Mr. Robert Constable	"Constable Range"	100
Mr. Jacob Hove	"Hoves Patcoson"	100
Mr. Lawrance Creager	"Creagers Delight"	100
	"Middle Choice"	100
	"Longapaw Resurveyed"	140

Mr. Joseph Bruner	pt. “Taskers Chance”	303
h/o Mr. Francis Wise	pt. “Taskers Chance”	206
	“Stumbling Block”	10
Mr. Casper Myre	pt. “Taskers Chance”	273
Mr. Jacob Storum	pt. “Taskers Chance”	202
h/o Mr. Peter Hufman	pt. “Taskers Chance”	225
Mr. Christian Thomas	pt. “Taskers Chance”	209½
Mr. George Lay	pt. “Taskers Chance”	213
Mr. Henry Sinn	pt. “Taskers Chance”	145
Mr. Gilbert Kemp	pt. “Taskers Chance”	115
	“Kemp’s Discovery”	30
	“Above House”	150
Mr. Conrod Kemp	pt. “Taskers Chance”	220
	“Peace & Quietness”	50
	“Wilbersign”	30
	“<t> Lot”	10
Mr. Stephen Ransberger	pt. “Taskers Chance”	465
	“Shoemakers Choice”	100
	“Stoney Hill”	100
	“Ransbergers Chance”	190
Mr. Henry Trought	pt. “Taskers Chance”	171
22:1753:42 ...		
Mr. Henry Bruner	pt. “Taskers Chance”	215
Mr. Conrod Kellor	pt. “Taskers Chance”	159
Mr. Abraham Miller	“Millers Chance”	100
	“Coopers Point”	200
Mr. Melock Wherfield	pt. “Taskers Chance”	352¾
h/o Mr. Robert DeButts	pt. “Taskers Chance”	217½
	“DeButts Hunting Lott”	72
	“Sun is Down & The Moon is Up”	500
Mr. John Brunner	pt. “Taskers Chance”	232
	“Good Luck”	100
h/o Mr. Jacob Stonar	pt. “Taskers Chance”	571¾
	“Isaac’s Inheritance”	200
	“Stoners Chance”	75

h/o Mr. Mathew Hopkins	"Salop"	565
	pt. "Knaves Disapointment"	64
Mr. Christopher Ellis	"Beginning"	50
Mr. William Ridgley	"Pocoson"	13
	"Hobsons Choice"	337
	"Round About Hill"	12
	"Jones Addition"	40
	"Ridgleys Ridge"	50
	"Meeks Delight"	50
Mr. Jacob Miller	"Meadows"	33
	"Swamp"	50
Mr. Jacob Miller (Quaker)	"Hazel Thicket"	100
	"Addition to Hazel Thicket"	50
Mr. Thomas Taylor	pt. "Addition to Hazel Thicket"	50
	"Mount Pleasant"	50
Mr. Henry Fortney	"Deer Spring"	200
Mr. Alexander Warfield s/o John	"Warfields Vineyard"	270
Mr. Robert Miller	pt. "Brothers Generosity" a/s "Pork Hall"	587
22:1753:43 ...		
Mr. Alexander Warfield s/o Richard	pt. "Stringers Chance"	195
Mr. Elisha Laurance	"Good Luck Resurveyed"	245
	pt. "Maidens Choice"	24
Mr. George Hartman	"Hartman"	100
Mr. Jacob Henry	pt. "Good Luck"	100
Mr. Leonard Decose	"Leonard's Frolick"	50
Mr. Melchor Staley	"Maswander"	30
	"Onodrandy"	7½
Mr. Oliver Mathews	pt. "Georges Discovery"	100
	"Chesnut Valley"	25
Mr. Daniel Mathews	pt. "Georges Discovery"	75
	"Daniels Addition"	25
Mr. Michael Jesserang	"Piny Neck"	100
Mr. Edward Lamb	"Lambs Choice"	150
	"Good Fellowship"	150

Mr. Henry Coocus	"Shear Spring"	100
	pt. "Shear Spring"	135
Mr. William Kearley	"St. Patricks Lot" originally called "St. Patrick"	127
Mr. Edward Stephenson, Jr.	"Cromwells Resurvey"	213
	"Leonards Range"	100
Mr. Henry Avey	"Scott Lott"	202
Mr. Valentine Myre	"Michaels Fancy Resurveyed"	186
Mr. Benjamin Biggs	"Benjamins Good Luck"	100
	pt. "Benjamins Good Luck"	43
Mr. Casper Venrode	"Addition to Woolf Pit"	50
Mr. George Gue	"St. George That Slew the Woolf"	50
22:1753:44 ...		
Mr. Jacob Peck	"Lambson Resurveyed"	196
	pt. "Addition"	100
Mr. William Kersey	"Gravely Spring"	56
Mr. William Richardson	pt. "Snowdens Fourth Addition to His Manor"	200
	pt. "Second Addition to His Manor"	218
Mr. Mathew Ambroser	pt. "Backland" a/s "Arnolds Delight"	125
	"Swedeland"	50
	"Gap"	100
h/o Mr. Samuel Hyde	pt. "Progress"	173
	pt. "Concord"	553
	pt. "Conclusion"	956½
	pt. "Middle Plantation"	361
	"William & Elizabeth"	150
h/o Mr. John Stull	"Whiskey"	380
	"Stull's Addition to Whiskey"	160
	"Second Addition to Whiskey"	40
Mr. Joseph Wood (Pipe Creek)	pt. "Woods Lot"	862
Mr. Mathew Jones	"Jones Addition"	20
Mrs. Mary Jones	"Fletchal"	253
Mr. Nicholas Baker	"Hazard"	300
	pt. "Knaves & Richard's Dispute"	133
	"Pig Pen"	50

Mr. Mathias Gray	"Grays Delight"	50
	"Grays Choice"	10
	"Grays Neck"	119
Mr. Moses Shelby	"Hunts Cabin"	310
Mr. John Huse	"William & John"	50
	"Retreat"	15
Mr. Joseph Wilson (CV)	"New Exchange"	100
Mr. Thomas Mills	"Batchelors Hall"	100
	"Lanes Fields Resurveyed"	231
Mr. Benjamin Hiskett	"Hiskets Choice"	50
22:1753:45 ...		
Mr. Evan Macdonald	"Watsons Welfare"	100
Mr. Martin Earnelt	"Martins Intention"	31
Mr. William Mathews	"Widows Rest"	100
Mr. William Dyal	"Dyals Delight"	50
Mr. James Burgess	"Burgess Choice"	50
	"Halsel's Folly"	50
Mr. Richard Watts	"Susannah & Elizabeth"	50
	"Peach Tree Hill"	75
Mr. Edward Mobberly	"I Lookt Many Places Now I Like"	100
	"Peace & Quietness"	68
Mr. Michael Ramar	"Meadow"	150
Mr. John Owens	"Rich Plains"	100
	"Owens Choice"	80
Mr. Mark Whiteacre	pt. "Delight"	50
Mr. Thomas Swift	pt. "Delight"	50
Mr. John Sweringen	"Piney Hills"	50
	"Piney Hills Inlarged"	270
Mr. Robert French (CV)	pt. "Ridge" & "Knaves Delight"	100
Mr. Shadrack Hyat	pt. "Hermitage"	101
Mr. John Nicholls (Linton Hundred)	"Butter & Cheese"	80
Mr. Jonathan Hagar	"Dicksons Rest"	100
	"Dickson's Fatiguing Journey"	100
Mr. Jeremiah Virgin	pt. "Dickson's Delight"	100
Mr. Joseph Faress	"Faress's Delight"	100

Mr. James Odell	"Ball Christ"	303
22:1753:46 ...		
Mr. Joseph Robinet	pt. "Piles Delight"	129
	pt. "Piles Delight"	17
Mr. William Williams	"Williams Range"	132
	"Ned Quarter"	21
	pt. "Conclusion"	200
Mr. Charles Fenley	"Nonsuch"	136
Mr. Edward Crow	"Shady Grove"	50
	"Addition to Shady Grove"	54
	"Abell's Levels"	400
Mr. Jacob Fry	"Fry's Habitation"	80
	"Frys Addition"	50
Mr. Joseph Hains	pt. "Cromwell's Resurvey"	250
	"Addition to Cromwell's Resurvey"	50
	"Woolf Harbour"	100
	"Pleasant Grove"	52
Mr. Unckle Unckles	pt. "Cromwells Resurvey"	219
	"Buck Range"	100
Mr. John Ryley	pt. "Chesnut Ridge"	219
	"Ryleys Chance"	80
Mr. Daniel Spengle	"High Spring"	100
Mr. Jacob Ducket	"Friendship"	100
	"Flaggy Pond"	406
Mr. John Mason	"Mason's Folly"	17
Mr. Martin Heildebidle	"Providence"	50
Mr. Nathan Maynard	"Maynards Good Will"	50
Mr. John Nash	"Ivy Reach"	40
Mr. John Sympson	"Simpson's Garden"	35
Mr. Thomas Hawkins	"Unckles Gift"	160
h/o Mr. Samuel Kelly	pt. "Hunting the Hare"	50
22:1753:47 ...		
John Ross, Esq. (cnp)	"Woolfpit"	100
	"Winkfields Delight Resurveyed"	1300
	"Plains"	50
	"Resurvey on Ross's Range"	3400

	"New London"	1360
	"Long Hope"	100
Mr. Joseph Chapline	"Rush Bottom"	100
	"Joseph's Chance"	100
	"Abston's Forrest"	156
	"Content"	100
	"Exchange"	100
	"Hills & Dales"	45
	"Grove"	195
	"Mendall"	66
	"Watsons Welfare"	260
Mr. Daniel Kelly	pt. "Hunting the Hare"	50
Mr. John Woodfield	pt. "Hunting the Hare"	50
Mr. Thomas Wales	pt. "Hunting the Hare"	50
Mr. Henry Banner	"Batchelors Delight"	100
h/o Rev. Mr. John Lang	"Inverness"	575
Mr. Edmund Martin	"Martins Choice"	35
Mr. George Smith	"Catail"	100
Mr. John Greenup	"Red Oak Slipe"	32
Mr. John Prather s/o William	"William & John"	100
	"Prathers Adventure"	75
	"Turkey Flight"	25
Mr. Caleb Dorsey	"Sparks Chance"	50
	"Harveys Borough"	50
	"Slate Hill"	50
	"Spark's Rounds"	50
	"Benjamin's Folly"	50
	"Caleb's Delight"	375
22:1753:48 ...		
Mr. George French	"Georges Venture"	50
	"Barrens"	100
Mr. Josiah Darby	"Darby's Delight"	125
Mr. Jacob Rorar (PA)	"Hagars Fancy"	507
Mr. Jacob Rorar (MD) (cnp)	"Rorar's Lot"	50
	"Addition to Rorar's Lot"	100
	"Weter"	10

	"Defyance"	100
Mr. Cornelius Poulson	"Poulson's Chance"	50
Mr. George Winters	"Batchelors Hall"	125
	"Winters Addition to Batchelors Hall"	75
Mr. Joshua Hickman	"Elizabeth"	121
	"Barsheba"	179
Mr. Kennedy Farrell	"Fortune"	100
Mr. Hans Wilaric Waggoner	"Flaggy Meadow"	121
	"Long Meadow"	25
	"Jemima" originally "Maidens Choice"	435
Mr. William Ingleman	"Karpouch"	50
Mr. Daniel Stewart	"Indian Field"	50
Mr. Robert Leith	"Samuel's Lot"	50
Mr. Lodowick Miller	"Tom's Chance"	150
Mr. Thomas Prather	"Choice"	185
	"Richards Choice"	100
	"Dutchman's Misfortune"	100
Mr. William Rayman	"Wards Spring"	200
Mr. William Wheat	"Wheats Purchase"	100
Mr. James Smith (Bk Ck)	pt. "Tasker's Chance"	260
	"Bakers Ramble"	50
	"Salisbury Plains"	50
22:1753:49 ...		
Mr. Garah Davis	"Gunders Delight"	64¼
	"Addition to Gunders Delight"	70
	"Whiskey"	282
Mr. Barnet Waymour	"Addition"	100
	"Sandy Run"	150
Mr. John Waymour	pt. "Sandy Run"	50
	"Waymours Cheges"	100
Mr. John Casteel	"Little North"	50
Mr. George Clapsaddle	"Empty Cupboard"	112
	"Addition to Empty Cupboard"	42
Mr. Mathew Sparks	pt. "Bedforshier Carrier"	68
Mr. William May	"Dutchman's Request" originally "Maidens Choice"	151

Mr. Martin Kersner	"Young's Folly"	50
Mr. John Baley	"Mountain"	50
Mr. Daniel Moore (Andietum)	"Moors Delight"	100
Mr. James Crow	"Locust Level"	119
Mrs. Catherine Jennings (Annapolis)	"Good Luck"	87
	"3 Springs"	525
Mr. Joseph Volgamot	pt. "Dutch Folly"	34
	pt. "Dutch Folly"	78
	"Free Stone"	100
Mr. John Worthington (AA)	"Whiskey Ridge"	500
	pt. "Whiskey Ridge"	563
Mr. John Ridgley	"Disapointment"	46
Mr. William Gibson	"Gibson's Chance"	100
Mr. Thomas Boildstone	"Boildstone's Discovery"	39
22:1753:50 ...		
Mr. Andrew Hever	"Addition to Miry Spring"	50
	"Miry Spring"	50
Mr. Abrahart Apler	"Deeps"	220
Mr. Joseph Dodderidge	"Andietum Levels"	50
Mr. Joseph Beall s/o Ninian	"Choice Improved"	649
	"Lost & Found"	85
	pt. "Fat Oxen"	44
Mr. John Everett	"Goose Quarter"	125
Mr. Adam Miers	"Black Oak Hill"	50
	"Miers's Pleasure"	175
	"White Gravel Spring"	190
Mr. Ninian Ryley	"Haly"	100
Mr. Caleb Touchstone	"Rich Thicket"	10
	pt. "Whiskey Alley"	10
Mr. Philip Kiefalper	pt. "Whiskey Alley"	67
Mr. Joseph Smith	"Ellswick Dwelling"	180
	pt. "Ellswick Dwelling"	99
	"Smiths Purchase"	63
Mr. Edward Busey	"Black Walnut Plains"	100
Mr. Charles Wood	"Charles's Choice"	350
Mr. Teter Meisner	"Stony Hill"	50

Mr. Frederick Wollyde	"Jerusalem"	75
Mr. Henry Bitzel	"Smiths Hap"	100
Mr. Michael Haines	"Meadows"	275
22:1753:51 ...		
Mr. John Howard s/o Gideon	"Pretty Sally"	20
	"Second Adventure"	54
	pt. "Woods Lot"	94
	"Howards Range"	203¼
	"Pears Forrest"	30
	"Many Glades"	25
	"Chance"	50
	"Locust Woods"	25
	"Howards Rest"	172
	"Resurvey on Part Spriggs Delight"	387
Dr. Charles Carroll (cnp)	"Sluce Galleon"	50
	"Iron Hill"	31
	"Iron Mountain"	250
	"Shelby's Misfortune"	250
	"Carrolls Range"	390
	"Hoyts Home"	100
	"Halfer Stodd"	184
	"Carolina"	208
	"Chesnut Ridge"	390
	"Addition"	150
	"Addition to Chesnut Ridge"	70
	"Notch"	18
	"Bear Meadow"	325
	"Forrest"	144
	"Pines"	160
	"Biglars Addition to Hills Choice"	50
	"Black Oak"	225
	"Addition to Backland"	22
	"Barren Hills"	55
	"Addition to Strawberry Plains"	40
	"Hoyls Luck"	116
	"Castle Fur"	112

	"Spring Head"	96
	"Killmore"	190
	"Bearden"	355
	"McCoys Delight"	100
	"Turkey Hill"	110
	"Bottom"	56
	"Earnest Choice"	50
	"Long Acre"	144
	"Peters Park"	216
	"Shiers Bottom"	110
	"Hollygan's Forrest"	50
	"Addition to Base Meadow"	70
	"Stoney Meadow"	96
	"Waddels Delight"	60
	"Adventure"	180
	"Lemons Range"	208
	<t>	200
	"Fryers Delight"	268
	"Chance Medley"	92
	"Addition to the Pines"	264
	"High Germany" originally "Catail Marsh"	1254
Mr. Basil Williams	"William's Lott"	40
22:1753:52 ...		
Edward Dorsey, Esq.	"Brandy Wine Spring Inlarged"	377
	"Brandy Wine Spring"	50
	pt. "Woods Lott"	584
	"Mount Pleasant"	50
	"Addition"	230
	"Resurvey on Pretty Sally"	1244
	"Pleasant Fields" originally "Second Adventure"	1394
	"Resurvey on Darby's Delight"	696
	"Rich Forrest"	125
Mr. Basil Dorsey (AA)	"Middle Way"	295
Mr. Michael Havenor	"Vulsursham"	50
	"Bullfrog"	50

h/o Mr. Darby Lux (BA)	"Canton"	100
	"Hunting Lott"	159
Mr. Thomas Maynard	"Maynards Chance"	50
Mr. Solomon Turner	"Solomons Flower"	50
Mr. Mathew Tyler	"Misery"	50
Mr. John Waters, Jr.	"Wards Delight"	100
	"Wards Delight" [!]	100
Mr. Philip Turner	"Turners Delight"	30
Mr. Samuel Offutt	"Offutts Pasture"	613
	"Offutts Adventure"	93
	pt. "Younger Brother"	200
	"Addition to the Pasture"	19
Mr. Thomas Claget Prather	"Maidens Fancy"	100
Mr. Benjamin Penn	"Moors Delight"	100
Mr. Francis Hartley	"Hartleys Lot"	10
Mr. William Currans	"Peach Blossom"	50
Rev. Mr. Samuel Hunter	"Leonards Goodluck"	100
22:1753:53 ...		
Mr. Alexander Grant	"Alexander & John"	30
Mr. Edward Northcraft	"Molls Rattle"	25
Mr. Biggar Head	"Martha's Delight"	85
	"Heads Goodluck"	19
	"Heads Industry"	19
Mr. Samuel Read	"Newry"	50
	"Bailey's Purchase"	26
	"York"	168
Mr. Benjamin Riddle	pt. "Creve"	50
Capt. John Dorsey (AA)	"Mount Pleasant"	400
	"John's Goodluck"	50
	"Dorseys Search"	856
Mr. James McDonald	"Galloway"	175
	"Macdonalds Chance"	100
	"Isle of Raven"	50
	"Bite the Biter"	144
Mr. John Barnwell	"Level Spring"	100
Mr. Michael Miller	"Ash Swamp"	150

Mr. Michael Miller	"Skipton in Craven"	100
	pt. "Skipton in Craven"	180
Mr. Daniel Arnold	"Goats Horn"	50
	"Luck"	175
Mr. Alexander Perry	"Batchelors Purchase"	100
Mr. William Porter	"Wilson's Fancy"	100
Mr. Richard Clagett, Jr.	pt. "Dann"	150
	pt. "Friendship"	250
Mr. Leonard Albrach	"Albrach's Folly"	50
22:1753:54 ...		
Mr. Darby Ryan	"Mackey's Delight"	47
Mr. Stephen Richards	"Spring Garden"	50
Mr. William Dent	pt. "Dan"	150
Mr. Thomas Davis, Jr. (AA)	"Gold's Branch"	257
	"Hyam"	100
	"Saplin Ridge"	72
	pt. "Benjamin's Lot"	166
Mr. John Hammond	pt. "Gaithers Chance"	177½
	"Discovery"	15
Mr. Henry Gaither	"Benjamins Lott Resurveyed"	238
h/o Mr. Benjamin Gaither	pt. "Gaithers Chance"	684½
Mr. Edward Gaither	pt. "Gaithers Purchase"	100
	pt. "Benjamin"	150
	"Gaithers Chance"	200
Mr. Clement Davis	"Hunting Hills"	300
	pt. "Pines"	78
Mrs. Lamar widow of Thomas	pt. "Two Brothers"	300
Mr. John Lamar s/o Thomas	pt. "Joseph & James"	135
	pt. "Conclusion"	85
	pt. "Pines"	52¼
	"Woolfpit Tract"	50
Mr. Samuel Lamar	"Amts Garden"	50
	pt. "Conclusion"	213
Mr. John Rawlins	"Lost Hatchet"	50
	"Beginning"	100
	"Hobson's Choice"	50

Mr. James Wardrop	"Partnership"	285
	"Dearbought Resurveyed"	500
	"Red Oak Level"	100
	"Wooden Platter Resurveyed"	327
	"Oxford"	54
	"John's Delight"	104
	"Brandford"	35
	"Bloosberry"	104
	"Cool Spring"	75
22:1753:55 ...		
Mr. James Lee	pt. "Labyrinth"	100
Mr. William Biggs	pt. "Benjamin's Good Luck"	168
Mr. Richard Waters	pt. "Charles & Benjamin"	152
h/o Mr. Peter Johnson	pt. "Sky Thorn"	85
	"Johnson's Lot"	139
Mr. Peter Johnson (PA)	"Johnson's Desire"	67
widow Wilson	pt. "Forrest"	100
	"London"	100
	"Suburbs"	90
Mr. John Cow	"Locust Neck"	100
Mr. Jacob Mills	"Beaver Dambottom"	138
Mr. Joseph Belt, Jr.	"Albany"	200
	"Joseph's Chance"	40
Mr. Henry Rhodes	"Round Meadow"	50
Mr. James Green Martin	"Martin's Fancy"	50
Mr. Joseph Harris	"White Oak Swamp"	50
Mr. John Grossnickle	"Grossnickles Delight Resurveyed"	201
Mr. Martin Shope	"Mankin"	231
Mr. Alexander Maccain	"Addition"	80
	"Douthits Chance Resurveyed"	280
Mr. Henry Story	"Storys Grove"	50
Mr. John Martin, Jr.	"Johnson's Chance"	100
Mr. George William Lawrance	"Hogg's Delight"	55
Mr. William Johnson	"Exchange"	50
22:1753:56 ...		

Mr. William Hallum	"Great Hall"	100
	"Hallums Lookout"	215
h/o Mr. John Dunn	"James & Elizabeth"	170
Mr. Joseph Williams	"Collins Folley"	11
Mr. William Wilson	"Long Meadow"	50
	"Wilson's Delight"	50
	"Wilson's Chance"	50
Mr. Mounts Justice	"Hard Quarter"	45
Mr. John Hobbs	"Hobb's Purchase" originally "Bush Creek Hill"	319
Mr. Owen David	"Neighbours Neglect"	52
Mr. John Arnold	"Buck's Horn"	40
Mr. Daniel Richards	"Richards Delight"	50
Mr. Peter Stull	"Stulls Delight"	100
Mr. John Howard s/o B.	"Mary's Delight"	100
Mr. William Sparks	"Sparks Delight"	50
Mr. William Murdock & Rev. Mr. Henry Addison	"Friendship"	1000
Mr. Gabriel Thomas	"Stoney Lick"	100
Mr. John Mellor	"Rocky Ridge"	50
Mr. Philip Knavel	"Shoemakers Knife"	50
Mr. Henry Funk	<t>	54
Mr. Stephen Newton Chizwell	"What You Will"	50
Mr. Frederick Kemp	"Low Kemper"	150
Mr. George Jacob Powe	"Well Taught"	100
Mr. Harmon Greathouse	"Chesnut Spring"	50
22:1753:57 ...		
Mr. Charles Harding	"Pretty Spring"	91
	pt. "Hermitage"	58½
Mr. Jacob Gans	"Egypt"	104
Mr. David Foutz	"Good Spring"	100
Mr. William Griffith (Monocacy)	"Nipple"	53
	"Fairly Got"	200
	"Bubby"	100
Mr. William Cullom	"Hogpen"	64
Mr. John England	"Englands Choice"	100
Mr. John Johnson	"Stoney Hill"	50

Mr. John Purdom	"Bear Garden"	10
Mrs. Ann Kersner	"Widow's Last Shift"	100
Mr. Seth Hyat	"Seths Folly"	50
Mr. Martin Coons	"Parriot Hall"	50
Mr. William Fuller	"Fuller's Folly"	50
Mr. Thomas Sparrow	"Sparrows Request"	100
Mr. Robert Lamar, Jr.	"Wilson's Delay"	500
Mr. John Nicholls (Senecar)	"Hickory Levels"	45
Mr. James Gore	pt. "Allison's Adventure"	150
Mr. William Summers	"Strawberry Patch"	50
Mr. John Hook	pt. "Kittocton Bottom"	50
	"John Sarah"	100
Mr. Robert Kinderick or Isaac McDaniel	"Kindericks Hap"	50
22:1753:58 ...		
Mr. George Fee	pt. "Andrews Folly & Discontent"	25
Mr. Richard Ankrum	pt. "Andrews Folly & Discontent"	25
h/o Mr. Samuel Pottenger	pt. "Wickham & Pottengers Discovery"	200
	"Addition to First Purchase" pt. "Wickham & Potttengers Discovery"	200
Capt. John Stoddert (CH)	pt. "Friendship"	300
Mr. Thomas Cramphin	"Johns Delight"	100
	"Thomas & Mary"	450
	"Hermitage"	200
Mr. Solomon Whitnal	pt. "Charles & Thomas"	69
Mr. William Norris (Sugar Loaf)	"Norris's Seal"	65
h/o Mr. John Hayman	"Constant Friendship"	150
	"Haymans Delight"	225
h/o Mr. William Norris (schoolmaster)	"Ralpho"	65
	"Sarris Love"	100
Mr. Edward Wilson	"Willsons Lott"	40
Mr. Thomas Johnson	"No Name" a/s "Sarah's Delight"	100
	pt. "Boar Den"	100
	"Addition to Sarah's Delight" pt. "New Exchange Inlarged"	24

Mr. Thomas Johnson (shoemaker)	"Fork"	50
	"Thomas Johnson's Chance"	50
Mr. Alexander Beall s/o William	"Jovial Ramble"	91
	pt. "Discovery"	268
	"Jacobs Cowpen"	50
	"Rubbish"	84
	"Refuse"	84
Mr. William Starr	"Star's Fancy"	50
Mr. John Stinchicom	"Stinchicombs Friendship"	150
Mr. William Wilburn	"Leeds"	50
Mr. William Campbel	"Monross"	154
Mr. William Albaugh	"Albaughs Choice"	50
22:1753:59 ...		
Mr. Charles Hammond	"Charles's Lot"	42
Mr. Michael Foutz	"Clear Meadow"	91
Mr. Robert Downey	"Ester" a/s "Chester"	100
	"Downeys Lot Resurveyed"	319
	"Addition to Blares Forrest"	100
Mr. Joshua Owens	"Joshua's Lot"	430
Mr. John Jones	"Resurvey on William & John"	224
Mr. Charles Kelley	"Kelly's Range"	100
Mr. John Stouchyer	"Cumberland"	100
Mr. Henry Ford	"White Oak Spring"	50
Mr. Joseph Benton	"Benton's Lott"	50
Mr. Solomon Braurd	"Rattle Snake Den"	50
Mr. Christian Koone	"Koone's Delight"	54
Mr. Westall Ridgley	"Ridgleys Rest"	100
Mr. John Harmangart	"Dispatch"	50
Mr. George Volantine	"Swifing Swamp"	50
Mr. Handel Han	"Henns Choice"	55
Mr. George Whiddle	"Huckleberry Levels"	80
Mr. John Hutchinson	"Roses Delight"	50
Mr. Theobald Boon	"Boons Content"	50
Mr. Samuel Arnold	"One Horn"	26
	"Pigg Stye"	54
Mr. George Brown	"Resurvey on Brown's Delight"	500

Mr. John Gryder	pt. "Brown's Delight"	100
22:1753:60 ...		
Mr. John Logsdon	"Bedford"	50
Mr. Andrew Young	"Saplin Hill"	100
Philip Key, Esq.	"Paradise Regained"	530
	"Epping Forrest"	1070
	"Friendship"	206
Mr. Richard Smith	"Smithfield"	44
Mr. Joseph Hill	"Mountain Branch"	87
Mr. Charles Hammond s/o John	"Bite Me Softly"	152
Mr. Joseph Grabble	"Strippies Neglect"	74
Mr. Ezekiel Gosling	"Cool Spring"	50
Mr. George Valentine Matzgar	"Quaker's Bite"	38
Dr. Henry Snavely	"Plunks Delight"	100
MM Richard Coombes & Dennis Ensey	"Coom's Inheritance"	203
Mr. Peter Balsell	"Turnoh"	150
Mr. Thomas Jones	"Jones's Chance"	36
Mr. George Smith (Monococy)	"Make Shift"	150
Mr. James Davis	"Nonsuch Resurveyed"	300
Mr. Richard Croxall	"<t> Part Pork Hall"	490
<t> Davis	<t>	50
Mr. John Banks	"Saffy's Lott"	45
Mr. John Huffman	"Bethlem"	100
Mr. Casper Divelbess	"Hunting Lott"	150
Mr. Daniel Hurley	"Friends Good Advice"	30
22:1753:61 ...		
Mr. Jacob Mathews in trust for Matth. Kitts	"Gift"	10
Mr. William Steuart	"Vineyard"	154
Dr. George Steuart	"Marshal Plains"	200
Mr. James Rimmer	pt. "Chance Resurveyed"	145
Mr. James Ellis	pt. "Chance Resurveyed"	65
h/o Mr. William West	"Two Brothers"	400

Mr. Nathaniel Magruder s/o Nin	pt. "Grubby Thicket"	166½
	pt. "Friendship"	101
	pt. "Magruder & Bealls Honesty"	200
Mr. James Smith (blk smith)	pt. "Grove"	37
Mr. Nicholas Haymond	"Constant Friendship Part"	150
Mr. John Youngblood	"Youngbloods Choice"	100
Mr. William Breshears	"William & John"	100
Mr. Thomas Radford	pt. "John & Molly"	100
	"Squabble"	50
h/o Mr. John Abington	"Wetwork"	700
	"Whitehaven"	350
Mr. Larkin Pierpoint	"Second Addition"	42
	"Pierpoints Range"	139
Mr. John Charlton	"Darling's Sale Resurveyed"	420
Mr. Robert Mark	"Shettle"	50
MM William & Alexander McGaughy	"Rich Level"	214
Mrs. Sarah Offutt widow of Samuel	"William & James"	82
Mr. Thomas Gilliland	"Indian Bottom"	100
Mr. Mathew Clark	"Discontent"	100
22:1753:62 ...		
Mr. Nicholas Martin	"Swamp of Experience"	100
Mr. Jeremiah Hays	"Resurvey on Jeremiah's Park"	475
Mr. Abner Lewis	"Abner's Choice"	100
Mr. Jacob Hoof	"Stone Acre"	50
Mr. William Hall	"Hall's Addition"	80
Mr. William Wilkey	"William & Ann"	30
MM Lewis Duvall, Edward Crow, & Samuel Farmer	"Beginning"	29
Mr. Jonas Brown	"Williams Neglect"	50
Mr. James Dawson	"Point Lookout"	85
Mr. Joshua Harbin	"Harbin's Lot"	50
Mr. George Shidelor	"Reeking"	50
Mr. Thomas Thrasher	"Thrashers Lott"	100
Mr. John Beall	"Addition to Anstuther"	70
Mr. Edward Burrage	"Burrages Lott"	50

Mr. Jacob Knave	"Addition to Turkey Plains"	50
Mr. Joseph Hughes	"Tradesman's Value"	35
Mr. Frederick Havener	"Havener's Discovery"	45
Mr. Joseph Sparke	"Spark's Delight"	50
Mr. Isaac Garrison	"Garrison's Choice"	50
Mr. Christopher Robinger	"Isles Mountain"	94
Mr. William Wheat, Jr.	"Lucks All"	50
Mr. Thomas Lintchicum	"Lintchicum's Chance"	50
22:1753:63 ...		
Mr. George Williams	"Williams's Chance"	150
Mr. William Cooper	"Coopers Choice"	80½
Mr. Peter Wedstone	"Hartmans Place"	50
Mr. Edward Ward	"Wards Pleasure"	50
Mr. James Brooke, Jr.	"Younger Brother"	146
	"Knee Drop"	150
Mr. William Warford	"William & Mary"	56
Mr. James Young	"Bite Him Softly"	50
Mr. George Burkett	"Debate Spring"	19
	"Georges Fancy"	31
Mr. Thomas Estop	"Rock Spring"	62
Mr. Samuel Cissell	"Caecils Chance"	60
Mr. Hugh Macklayland	"Back Meadow"	70
Mr. George Sultiner	"Loving Brother"	100
Mr. Peter Shees	"Alamangle"	100
Mr. Solomon Sparks	"Cold Fryday"	93
Mr. Michael Legett	"Dam Head"	74
Mr. Mathias Stalcop	"Poor Man's Loss" originally "Mathias"	144
Mr. Benjamin Hall (Pipe Creek)	"Halls Choice"	874
Mr. Thomas Dawson	"Resurvey on Dawson's Purchase"	215¾
Mr. Daniel Ashcraft	pt. "Skye Thorn"	135
Mr. Richard Stimpson	"Sympsons Chance"	214
Mr. Edward Sprigg s/o Col.	pt. "Happy Choice"	593
Mr. Gilbert Sprigg	pt. "Piles Delight"	400
22:1753:64 ...		
Mr. James Sprigg	pt. "Piles Delight"	400

h/o Daniel Dulany, Esq.	pt. "Conclusion"	956½
	pt. "Middle Plantation"	361
	pt. "Spring Garden"	340
	pt. "Partnership"	100
	"Good Hope"	132
	"Ocorson"	100
	"Dispatch"	100
	"Addition to Spring Garden"	436
	pt. "Dearbought"	200
	"Sasafras Bottom"	100
	"Woolfs Chance"	100
	"Sawyers Purchase"	50
	"Epenah"	100
Daniel Dulany, Esq.	pt. "Dulany's Lott"	2479½
	pt. "Taskers Chance"	850½
	"Long Headone"	550
	"Addition to Long Headone"	110
	"West Addition to Long Headone"	100
	pt. "Taskers Chance"	320
	pt. "Taskers Chance"	289¾
	pt. "Taskers Chance"	153
	pt. "Taskers Chance"	355½
	pt. "Taskers Chance" (unsold land)	40
	"Albins Choice"	300
	"Locust Levell"	3180
	"Williamsborough"	1500
Mr. Jacob Kellor	pt. "Ramshorn"	102
h/o Mr. John Charlton	"Darling's Sale Resurveyed"	420
Mr. Joseph Mayhew	"Chidley's Range Resurveyed"	100
~~Mr. Mathias Staleup~~	~~"Poor Man's Loss" originally called "Matthias Resurveyed"~~	~~144~~
Mr. George Clem	pt. "Lost Spring Resurveyed" now called "George & Margaret"	150
Mr. Allen Killough	"Three Cousens Resurveyed"	491
Mr. John Mobberly	"Mount Pleasant"	122
Mr. Martin Whetsal, Jr.	"Bonnets Resolution"	150

22:1753:65 ...		
Mr. Frederick Unselt	"Beauty"	100
Mr. Thomas Johnson	"Johnson's Lane" between elder surveys	323
	"Johnson's Levels"	50
Mr. John Stull	"Shoal Spring"	150
	"Pleasant Hill"	90
John Aldridge	"Tuckers Cultivation"	11
Jacob Keller	"Rhodes Purchase"	102
h/o Isaac Downes	pt. "Bear Bacon"	223½
Benjamin Perry	"Addition to Hensley"	50
Thomas Wilson s/o Thomas	pt. "Ridge & Knaves Dispute"	66
Solomon Turner	pt. "Ralpho"	202
22:1753:66 ...		
Hans Ulrich Wagganaer	pt. "Maidens Choice"	302
John Jacks	"Pleasant Bottom"	164
John Howard s/o Gideon	"Resurvey of Howards Range" – in addition to f. 51	653
Samuel Magruder 3rd	"Resurvey of Hensley" & "Addition to Hensley" – in addition to f. 14	806
Adam Spaugh	"Gap"	100
John Hook	"Resurvey of John & Sarah" – in addition to f. 57	288
22:1753:67-77 Index		
22:1753:78 Overcharged		
Mr. Dowden – f. 22	"Hammerhill"	10
<n/g> – f. 40	"Browns Delight"	50
John Charlton – f. 61	<n/g>	<n/g>
Peter Rench – f. 25	pt. "Spriggs Delight"	75
Peter Youngblood – f. 31	"Cattail Marsh" tbc Dr. Carrol	200
22:1753:79 Recapitulation		
22:1753:80 Shortcharged		
<n/g> – f. 62	"Thrashers Lott"	10
<n/g> – f. 63	"Damhead"	<n/g>
Hancock Lee – f. 5	<n/g>	<n/g>
Errors		
<t>	<t>	<t>
John Jackson	pt. "Jacksons Necessity"	211
Charged in this book & in PG		

William Wheat	<n/g>	<n/g>
Joshua Beall	pt. “Pritchets Purchase”	13
	pt. “Charles & William”	80
George Noble	“Addition”	24
Thomas Noble	pt. “Addition”	24

22:1754:1 ...		**Acres**
Henry Boon	pt. "Easy Comeby"	200
h/o Col. Thomas Addison	"Addisons Choice"	2300
	½ of "Whithaven"	407
	"Phillip & Jacob"	400
	pt. "Friendship"	1600
Thomas Harriss	pt. "Charles & William"	201
Robert Pottenger	pt. "Charles Purchased" a/s "Charles & William"	297
	pt. "Fenwick"	35
	"Brothers Request"	500
Samuel Williamson Brisco	pt. "Clegate Purchase"	236
Jeremiah Berry	pt. "Charles & Benjamin"	1090
	"Addition to Charles & Benjamin"	31
Hon. George Plater, Esq.	"Brightwells Hunting Quarter"	1036
	pt. "Bradford Rest"	4793
James Swann	pt. "Dann"	26
h/o Meredith Daviss	"West Tract"	100
	pt. "Good Luck"	245
	pt. "Josiah"	100
	"Best Breeches"	100
	"Meredith"	118
	"Friend Good Will"	57
22:1754:2 ...		
William Luckett	"Merrideth Hunting Quarter Resurveyed"	498
	"Kitechton Bottom"	100
Rev. John Eversfield	"Deer Park" & "Bear Garden Inlarged"	200
	"Addition"	50
	pt. "Give"	43
	pt. "Inlargment"	90
Benjan Brooke	pt. "Friendship Inlarged" now called "Upper Tract"	204
	pt. "Grove"	43
	pt. "Inlargement"	90
Nathaniel Offutt (cnp)	pt. "Cool Springs Levil"	230
	pt. "Young Brother"	200
	"Grose Pond"	100
	pt. "Bishops Island"	23

	"Addition to Grose Pond"	133
Edward Willett	"Scotland"	100
	"Poackland"	260
	"Addition to Scotland"	73
Thomas Wilson (Monky)	pt. "Poplar Thickett"	50
	"Addition to Poplar Thickett"	63
Clement Hill	pt. "Partnership"	1000
	pt. "Addition to Partnership"	200
h/o John Needham	"Forrest"	612
	pt. "Huntington"	308
	pt. "Pritchats Purchase"	45
	"Forrest"	100
22:1754:3 ...		
widow Culver	"Batchelor Forrest"	200
	"Chance"	100
	"Addition to Chance"	200
	"2nd Addition to Chance"	400
Thomas Clegatt	pt. "Dann"	250
h/o Arnold Livers	pt. "Ogles Good Will"	105
	"Arnolds Chance"	600
	pt. "Backland" a/s "Arnolds Delight"	1074
William Young	pt. "Duckers Wood"	533
William Carmack	pt. "Duckers Wood"	46
	"Lubberland"	99
John Carmack	pt. "Duckers Wood"	56
John Ash	pt. "Mill Land"	50
Benjamin Becraft	"Becrafts Delight"	50
Hon. Benedict Calvert	pt. "Hermitage"	873¼
Benjamin Boyd	"Castle Plains"	300
	"Rich Land"	200
	"Shelbys Addition"	50
John Boyd, Jr.	"Boyds Delight"	233
22:1754:4 ...		
Abraham Boyd, Jr.	"New Sore"	79
Thomas Lancaster	pt. "Easy Purchase"	350
Riggnal Odell	pt. "Three Bealls Manner"	216

John Beall, Jr.	pt. "Allisons Park"	306
	pt. "Lay Hills"	649
	pt. "Drummins Derry"	15½
	pt. "Bealls Reserve"	233
	"Cowpen"	75
Joseph Ray	"Lashmates Folly"	50
Joshua Bucey	pt. "Charles & Thomas"	60
	"Jones Slipe"	50
	pt. "Charles & Thomas" called "Gift"	70
Nathaniel Wickham, Sr.	pt. "Bury Stone"	105
Joseph Evans	pt. "Batts Hunting Quarter"	200
Col. Joseph Belt	"Senneca Hills"	200
	"Chevy Chase"	520
	"Friendship"	200
James Dooley	pt. "Chevy Chase"	40
	"Roberts Lott"	50
	"Robinson Low Ground"	10
	"Dooleys Chance"	34
22:1754:5 ...		
Peter Dent	"Falling Spring"	50
h/o John Bowie, Jr.	"Piney Thickett"	200
	"Piney Thickett Inlargd"	200
	pt. "Hermitage"	602¾
	"Allen & James"	34
John Brice, Esq.	"Wintersels Range"	400
Richard Richardson	pt. "Henry"	280
	pt. "Josiah"	100
	"Addition to Mill Lott" & "Ballingers Endeaver Resurveyed"	1003
Thomas Clayland	pt. "Hermitage"	100
	"Busheba"	5½
widow Mason (VA)	"Barbadoes"	75
Alexander Harbert	pt. "Exchanged Inlarged"	250
William Harbert	pt. "Dunghill"	197
George Frazier	pt. "4 Gallions & ½ of Rum"	350
	"Cut Knee"	315

22:1754:6 ...		
h/o John Thompson	"Thompsons Purchase"	227
	"Cool Spring"	190
	"Small Island"	12
	"Thompson Hop Yard"	110
	"Dutch Folly"	105
	"Long Island"	20
	"John Jacky Manty"	445
	"Darby Island"	70
Henry Clegate	"Addition"	200
George Scott	pt. "Hermitage"	200
	"Friendship"	600
Charles Walker	pt. "Virgins Delight"	75
Henry Allison	pt. "Allisons Adventure"	150
John Baker	pt. "Snowdens Mill"	273
John Jackson	"Jacks Improvement" & pt. "Friendship Inlarg'd"	194
William Thomas	pt. "2nd Addition to Snowdens Manor"	415
	pt. "4th Addition to Snowdens Manor"	84
h/o John Thomas	pt. "Snowdens Mannor"	549
	"Thomas's Discovery"	1480
	pt. "Charley Forrest"	318
22:1754:7 ...		
John Adamson	"Clean Shaving"	277
	"Lucas Friendship"	10
	"Bealls Good Will" originally called "Largo"	762
George Moore	"Gideon"	20
James Holemaid, Jr.	"Addition to James"	630
	"Discovery"	150
Thomas Lucas, Jr.	pt. "Plumyard"	100
	"Thomas & Nancy"	50
William Lucas	pt. "Plumyard"	100
Sarah Lucas	pt. "Plumyard"	100
Richard Snowden (cnp)	pt. "Snowdens Mannors"	451
	pt. "Addition to Snowdens Mannors"	573
	pt. "3rd Addition to Snowdens Mannors"	419
	pt. "4th Addition to Snowdens Mannors"	4111

	pt. "Bealls Mannor"	523
	"John & Sarah"	200
	pt. "Snowdens Mill Land"	153
	"Moores Rest"	185
	"Walnut Levils"	50
	pt. "Gunders Delight"	73
	"Snowdens 2nd Addition to His Mannor"	75
	"John & Katherine"	76
	"4th Addition to the Mannor"	1023
22:1754:8 ...		
Nathaniel Walker	pt. "Virgins Delight"	75
James Holmard	"James"	600
	"James's Park"	52
	pt. "Ken of Love"	100
	pt. "Widdows Might"	206
	"No Name"	38
	"Bealls Plains"	508
	"Outlet" a/s "Lamars Hills"	450
	"Mill Seat"	30
	pt. "Elizabeth"	25
Hancock Lee	"Addition"	576
William Masters	pt. "Progress"	49
Thomas Warring	pt. "Younger Brother"	200
John Darnall	pt. "Hope"	2757
	pt. "Good Luck"	155
Jeremiah Belt	"Belts Tomy Hauk"	150
David Cox	"Lubberland"	50
John Willcoxen	pt. "Accord"	200
	"Georgia"	36
	"Gleanings"	64
Caleb Letton	"Oatery"	405
	"St. Mary"	67
22:1754:9 ...		
Thomas Catterrall (cnp)	"James & Mary"	636
	"Brothers Content"	360
	pt. "Bear Garden"	206

	pt. "Prevention"	218
Alexander & Robert Beall	pt. "Batchlers Forrest"	405
John Flemming	pt. "Hemsley"	100
Jerremiah Stimpson	pt. "Hermitage"	100
h/o Bryan Kelly	pt. "Brothers"	100
	"Advantage"	135
	pt. "Discontent"	100
h/o Osborn Sprigg	pt. "Stack Quarter"	160
	"Forrest"	85
John Hepburn, Esq.	pt. "Hermitage"	400
	"Resurvey on Hanover"	2216
Charles Carroll, Esq.	"Piles Grove"	566
	"Carrolls Forrest"	500
	"Clown Core"	925
	"Carrolton"	10000
	"Stage"	228
	"Addition to Carolton" originally "Jo. Rest"	2700
	"Martins Fields"	100
	"Elkins Fields"	153
	"Carrolls Delight"	5000
	"Carrolls Burgh"	5000
	"Girls Portion"	1700
William Wallace	pt. "Brothers Industry"	500
22:1754:10 ...		
James Wallace	pt. "Brothers Industry"	929
	"Hopsons Choice"	134½
	"Discovery"	83
	"Beavers Denn"	200
	"Piney Levil"	130
h/o James Offutt	"William & James"	530
	"James's Park"	200
	"Young Mans Folly"	100
James Offutt, Jr.	pt. "Clever Will Inlarged"	1000
William Offutt	pt. "Clever Will Inlarged"	400
	pt. "Bear Denn"	200
	"Real Friendship"	10

Alexander Offutt	pt. "Clever Will Inlarged"	600
h/o John Rogers	pt. "Bealls Mannor"	230
	pt. "Snowdens Gift"	40
John Gaitthers	pt. "Bealls Mannor"	200
Mrs. Crabb	"Bowling Green"	128
	pt. "Two Brothers"	28
	"Valentines Garden"	950
	pt. "Crabbs Purchase"	100
Jeremiah Crabb	"Deer Park"	470
22:1754:11 ...		
John Phillips	"Walnut Bottom"	50
Millburn Simms (CH)	pt. "Easy Comeby"	100
John Smoot	"Cranford"	100
Thomas Fletchall	"Bealls Design"	100
	pt. "Flints Grove"	150
John Flint	pt. "Newton"	100
	pt. "Elizabeth"	25
	pt. "Partnership"	12½
Thomas Flint	pt. "Newton"	100
John Flint, Jr.	pt. "Newton"	100
William John Jackson	pt. "James & Mary"	54
	pt. "Bealls Lott"	100
Miss Elizabeth Bordley	pt. "Backland"	542
	pt. "Backland"	90
John Riggs	"Bordley Choice"	1000
Beall Bordley	"New Years Gift"	1143
Mathias Bordlley	pt. "Backland"	2030
Richard Keene	pt. "New Exchange Inlargd"	360
	pt. "Cucolds Delight"	23
22:1754:12 ...		
John Davisson (CH)	"Charles & Jane"	100
	pt. "Bealls Mannor"	234
	pt. "Bealls Mannor"	41
John Beall Taylor (cnp)	pt. "Grove"	219
	"Bealls Seat"	100
	pt. "Resurvey on James & Mary"	220

	pt. "Grove"	89
John Hoskisson	pt. "Resurvey"	50
h/o John Radford	pt. "Sennaca Landing"	52
	pt. "Long Acre"	52
	pt. "Elizabeth"	50
	pt. "Henry"	105
William Hughs	pt. "James & Mary"	130
John Madding	"Stoney Point" a/s pt. "Lybranths"	100
	"Addition to Stoney Point"	50
James Plummer	"Wickhams Good Will"	270
h/o John Vanmetre	"Pipe Meddow"	200
David Shepherd	"Pell Mell"	162
Thomas Palmer	pt. "Mitre"	158
	"Palmers Choice"	58
	pt. "Mitre"	142
	"Palmer Taner"	154
22:1754:13 ...		
Basil Adamson	"Adamsons Choice"	100
h/o Edward Crabb	"Crabbs Purchase"	356
James Lamar	pt. "Pines"	103½
Peter Butler	"Paradice"	210
	"Magruders Hazard"	100
	"Locust Thickett"	100
	"Paradice Inlarged"	100
	"Buttlers Lott"	120
Robert Lamar	pt. "Joseph & Mary"	200
	pt. "Two Brothers"	200
	pt. "Pines"	45
	"Resurvey on Mill Tract"	173
	"Boys Lott"	100
Michael Jones	pt. "Pines"	200
Thomas Lamar	"Buck Bottom"	120
	pt. "Joseph & James"	200
James Perry, Sr.	"Stroden"	220
	"Stoney Hive"	200
Thomas Beall 2nd	"Frozen Levil"	200

Richard Duckett	"Ducketts Misfortune"	200
22:1754:14 ...		
Joseph Wheat	"Wheats Choice"	53
David Trail, Jr.	"Good Will"	100
	"Locust Thickett"	72
Benjamin Hall	pt. "Halls Choice Resurveyed"	202
Joseph Hall	"Halls Choice Resurveyed"	672
James Belson of Robert	"Easter"	225
	"Farm"	128
Pharaoh Riely	pt. "Dann"	100
Hugh Riley	pt. "Dann"	250
Ninian Tannyhill	pt. "Fenwick"	265
h/o John Watkins	pt. "Paschaham"	100
	"Watkins Range"	100
	"Addition to Watkins Range"	320
h/o John Aldrige	pt. "Paschaham"	100
	pt. "Tuckers Cultivation"	111
Matthew Robinson	"Joseph Good Will"	150
22:1754:15 ...		
William Pritchett	pt. "Dunghill"	100
	"Harberts Chance"	100
	"Eleanors Green"	150
John Leech	"Rockey Spring"	100
Capt. Samuel Magruder	"Forrest"	300
William or Sarah Williams	pt. "Smiths Pasture"	100
Dr. Andrew Scott	"Fancy"	144
	"Saturn"	200
	"Venus"	200
	"Badgers Hole"	22
h/o John Abbington	"Wet Work"	700
	"Whitehaven"	350
Daniel Clary	pt. "Bradford Rest"	115
	"Buck Bottom"	100
Benjamin Brown	pt. "Bradfords Rest"	115
Benjamin Tasker, Esq.	pt. "Magruder & Bealls Honestly"	322
	pt. "Prevention"	140

Samuel Selby	pt. "Baily Crist"	200
22:1754:16 ...		
James Edmonston	pt. "Brothers Content"	360
	"Amsterdam"	80
	"Accord"	100
	pt. "Pristen March"	334
	pt. "Lubberland"	27
	"Batchlers Forrest"	405
	"Western Fields"	82
	pt. "Hermitage"	131
	pt. "Discovery"	41¼
	"Land of Ease"	40
	"Georges Delight"	20
	"Piles Delight"	500
	pt. "Piles Hall"	360
	pt. "Prevention"	159½
Alexander Magruder	pt. "Magruder & Bealls Honesty"	121
William Condon	pt. "Hermitage"	100
John Toleson	"I Never See It"	400
Thomas Thompson	pt. "Rattle Snake Denn"	150
	"Thompsons Hop Thickett"	34
Patrick Reading	pt. "Clegates Purchase"	50
John West	pt. "Two Brothers"	200
	pt. "Joseph"	200
Clement Mosely	pt. "Clegatts Purchase"	50
Stephen Hampton	pt. "Bear Denn"	100
22:1754:17 ...		
h/o Dr. John Haswell	"Allisons Foark"	153
Joseph Richardson	pt. "Charles & Benjamin"	100
	pt. "Brooks Reserve"	40
	"Rogues Harbour"	50
Grove Tomlisson	"Fletchall Good Will"	100
	pt. "Good Luck"	200
	"Addition to Fellowship"	20
	"Groves Hunting Lott"	136
Joseph West s/o Ben	"Younger Brother"	370

George Beckwith	"Beckwith Range"	250
	"Charles's Choice"	49
John Halsel	pt. "<t> Delight"	100
William Cummings	pt. "Accord"	100
	pt. "Amsterdam"	80
	pt. "Norway"	680
	pt. "Prestons March"	334
	"Drummine"	668
	"Barbers Beginning"	100
	"Sluce"	100
	"Brashears Choice"	45
John Walters	"Maidens Fancy"	430
	"Bear Neck"	151
	"Mothers Gift"	400
	"Paris"	100
	"Resurvey on Ward's Delight"	256
22:1754:18 ...		
Patrick Mockbee	"Fellowship"	200
John Nelson	pt. "Chance"	555
John Brunner	"Sweeds Folly"	100
	pt. "Taskers Chance"	232
	"Good Luck"	100
Elias Delashmete	pt. "Sweeds Folly"	100
	"Ramble"	100
	"Addition to Sweeds Folly"	25
	pt. "Childrens Chance"	50
	"Dipford"	32
	"Moreland"	41
Weaver Barnes	pt. "2nd Addition to Snowdens Mannor"	200
	pt. "2nd Addition to Snowdens Mannor"	200
	"Inspection"	<t>
George Moore (PG)	"Chance"	50
John Cramphins	"Grandmothers Good Will"	150
	"Henry & Mary"	110
George Moore	"Moors Industry"	100
Phillip Murphey	"Buck Lodge"	100

Rev. George Murdock	"Friends Good Will"	150
	"Glebe Rock" a/s "Generosity"	100
	pt. "Mill Land"	2
	pt. "Charles & William"	248
22:1754:19 ...		
Abraham Eltinge	"Abrahams Lott"	312
	pt. "Concord"	100
	"New Esopus"	100
Isaac Hite	pt. "Black Walnutt Tree Island"	142
	pt. "Forrest"	140
Abraham Fore	"Eltings Fight"	325
John Hite	pt. "Black Walnutt Tree Island"	142
	"Discord"	215
	"Discovery"	37
	pt. "Forrest"	140
h/o Dr. Samuel Stringer	"Joy Church"	1045
	pt. "Stringers Chance"	300
Col. John Culvil	"Maryland"	6300
Cornelius Eltinge	pt. "Partnership"	100
	"Suerplus"	170
	"Frog Island"	30
	"Millburn"	270
	pt. "Darby Island"	76
	"Fork Grubby Hill"	305
	"Senneca Ford"	160
	pt. "Concord"	201
	pt. "Long Acre"	52
	"Fortune"	118
	"Eltings Rest"	60
	"Addition"	50
	"Mill Roade"	240
	"Isaac Elting"	112
	"Fair Island"	172
	"Hills"	105
	"Invention"	46
22:1754:20 ...		

John Dickson, Jr.	pt. "Charley Forrest"	100
Thomas Hillary	"Pickett"	58
	"Sugar Loaf"	80
	pt. "Stock Quarter"	100
Joseph Walters	pt. "Moores Industry"	30
	"Josephs Advance"	200
Thomas Odell	pt. "Grubby Thickett"	200
h/o James Magruder, Jr.	"Lost Jackett"	200
Nathan Magruder	"Point"	30
	"Knaves Dispute & Ridge"	180
	pt. "Charles & Benjamin"	50
	"Knaves Dispute"	40
	"Addition to Turkey Thickett"	40
Zadock Magruder	"Turkey Thickett"	350
	"Robert & Sarah"	100
	"Ridge"	78½
John Magruder, Jr.	pt. "Friendship" & "Magruders Purchase"	316
	pt. "Grubby Thickett"	166
James Magruder s/o Nin	pt. "Magruder & Bealls Honesty"	300
Zachariah Magruder	pt. "Friendship"	220
	"Zachariah"	100
Charles Williams	"White Oak Valley"	100
22:1754:21 ...		
Stephen Julian	"Hedge Hog"	254
h/o Bazill Beall	"Industry"	163
	"Archibalds Lott"	100
Samuel Magruder 3rd	pt. "Friendship" & "Addition to Magruders & Bealls Purchase"	320
	"Mill Use"	25
	"As Good As We Could Get"	200
	"Samuels Delight"	200
	pt. "Magruder & Bealls Honesty"	83
	"Resurvey to Part Hensley & Addition to Hensley"	956½
Archibald Edmonston	pt. "Deer Park" & "Bear Garden"	458
	"Bealls Good Will"	50
John Garrett	pt. "Hermitage"	197

Thomas Dowden	pt. "Hermitage"	70
William Davis s/o Griffith	"Hazard"	60
h/o John James	"Dispute"	50
Edward Offutt	"Cool Springs Levils"	296
	pt. "Outlet"	520
John Delazell	pt. "Outlet"	80
Flayl Pain	"Pains Delight"	100
	"Pains Industry"	50
h/o George Noble	pt. "Wetwork"	350
	pt. "Spring Garden"	170
	pt. "Dry Work"	42½
22:1754:22 ...		
Thomas Noble	"Spring Garden"	170
	pt. "Wetwork"	350
	pt. "Dry Work"	42½
Edward Owen	"Shepherd Fortune Resurveyed"	292
	"What You Please"	120
Ninian Beall, Sr.	"Friendship Inlarged" now "Upper Tract"	322
Thomas Lucas	"Lucas Adventure"	100
John Smith Prater	pt. "Bear Garden Inlarged" & "Deer Park"	620
Ann Magruder	"Friendship"	310
	pt. "Elizabeth" & "Partnership"	10
Ezekiel Magruder	pt. "Friendship"	100
Nathaniel Magruder	pt. "Grubby Thickett"	333
h/o Charles Williams	pt. "Bealls Mannor"	73
Thomas Cuse	pt. "Bealls Mannor"	100
John Cartwright	pt. "Charles & Thomas"	150
	pt. "Lybranth"	123
James Moore	pt. "Allisons Park"	100
Charles Allison	pt. "Allisons Park"	52
22:1754:23 ...		
William Black (London)	"Partners Exchange"	700
	"Gordons Purchase"	150
	"Black Acre"	435
George Gordon, Esq.	pt. "Knaves Disapointment"	236
Richard Garthen	pt. "Allisons Park"	50

Robert Wells	"Cannoe Bottom"	50
John Dowden	"Addition to Fellowship"	49
	pt. "John & Molly"	137
	"Johnnys Poplar Spring"	42
	"John & Molly"	106
	"Dowdens Luck"	90
John Beall s/o Robert	"Snowdens Mill Land"	120
	pt. "3 Bealls Mannor" a/s "Elizabeth & John"	108
Edward Beatty	"Poplar Bottom"	52
	pt. "Dulany Lott"	166
	"Patricks Colt"	60
William Oneal	pt. "Taken of Love"	197
	"Wheel of Fortune"	100
Thomas Johnson (Kitocton)	"Johnsons Levils"	50
	"Johnsons Lane" between elder survey	323
Charles Jones (cont. f. 101)	pt. "Clean Drinking"	350
Peter Murphy	"Bear Garden"	100
22:1754:24 ...		
Joseph White or James Wallace, Jr.	"Fletchers Garden"	60
	pt. "Reeds Delight"	100
	"Robinsons Low Grounds"	10
Richard Dean	pt. "Hunting the Hare"	50
Moses Chaplain	"Joyners Fancy"	50
	"Resurvey on the 3 Springs"	739
	"Resurvey on Mount Pleasant"	217
Thomas Willett	"Lick Hill"	100
	pt. "Little Denn"	26
William Farquer	pt. "Rock Land"	74
	"Kitfadoh"	200
	pt. "Mount Pleasant"	40
	"Swamp Miserable"	60
	"Forrest in Need"	120
	"Unity"	25
	"Williams Defiance"	270
	"Chesnut Spring"	62
widow FranceWay	pt. "Nany's Delight" a/s pt. "Lybranth"	100

Samuel Blackmore	pt. "Discovery"	100
Cornelius Verney	pt. "Concord"	236
	pt. "Forrest"	142
	½ of "New Esopus"	100
22:1754:25 ...		
William Williams s/o Thomas	"Fork"	400
	"Mill Lands"	166
	"Addition to the Fork"	80
	"Haymonds Addition"	75
	pt. "New Exchange Inlargd"	73¾
James Holland	pt. "Gittings Hollow"	117
	"Panthers Range"	50
Thomas Stump	pt. "Stumps Valley"	133¼
James Lee, Jr.	pt. "Lybranth" & "Discovery"	100
John Dannyhill	pt. "Hills & Dales"	70
Samuel Beall	pt. "Lybranth"	240
Humphy Batts	pt. "Magruders & Bealls Honesty"	233
	pt. "Elizabeth Manner"	100
	pt. "Partnership"	200
Thomas Plummer, Jr.	"Sapling Hill Resurveyed"	177
h/o Col. Thomas Lee (VA)	"Morton"	165
	"Eaton"	320
	"Hill in the Middle"	315
Thomas Plummer	pt. "Plummer Island"	100
	"Greenland"	37
Thomas Kendrick	pt. "Addition to the Remains"	100
	pt. "Division of the Tythe"	29
h/o Isaac Downs a/s Edward Doran	pt. "Bear Bacon"	467
22:1754:26 ...		
Joseph Peach	pt. "Bear Bacon"	200
Peter Apple	pt. "Rockey Creeck"	150
	pt. "Arnolds Delight" a/s "Backland"	100
	pt. "Small Hope"	20

Ninian Magruder, Jr.	pt. "Friendship" & "Addition to Magruders Purchase"	300
	pt. "Pritchetts Purchase"	50
	"Magruders Lott"	100
	"Addition to Magruders Lott"	50
	"Black Oak Thickett"	150
	"Addition to Magruders Purchase"	18
	pt. "Magruders & Bealls Honesty"	83
Daniel Sing	"Breeches"	100
h/o Jacob Fout	pt. "Rockey Creek"	539
	pt. "Mill Lott"	50
	pt. "Small Hope"	10
	"Goose Nest"	30
Hon. Richard Lee, Esq.	"Angle"	300
	"Cucold Delight"	100
	"Scotts Ordinary"	100
	pt. "Forrest Green"	170
	"Bowling Green"	86
	"Thomas's" a/s "Fletchalls Last Shift"	200
	pt. "Dann"	500
Francis & Charles Pierpoint	pt. "Rockey Creek"	250
	"Small Hopes"	80
Edward Tully	"Hard Lodging"	322
Benjamin Norris s/o John	pt. "Hopewell"	125
Zachariah Lyles	pt. "Hopewell"	50
22:1754:27 ...		
William Holland	pt. "Charles & Benjamin"	137
	"Hollands Addition"	80
Francis Hall	pt. "Hope"	216
Ignatius Diggs	"Chittam Castle"	218
	"Clear Spring"	50
	"Mountain Prospect"	600
Stephen Lewis (VA)	"Strife"	500
	"Lewis's Discovery"	65
h/o Thomas Charters	pt. "Henry"	193
Holland Middleton	"Maidens Bower"	100

Thomas Conn	pt. "Lybranth"	184
	"McGilligan" pt. "Lybranth"	183¾
	"Lost Knife"	150
George Gump	"Chesnut Hill"	142
	"Four Springs"	50
	pt. "Addition to Carrolton"	167
h/o Daniel Carroll	"Batchlors Chance"	100
	"Batchelors Content"	176
	"Killman"	1300
	"Aix la Chaple"	942
	"Refused"	150
	pt. "Elizabeth Delight"	100
	pt. "Joseph Park"	1435¼
William Moore	"Spriggs Delight"	75
Daniel Carroll	pt. "New Exchange"	200
	pt. "Josephs Park"	2058½
	pt. "Aix la Chaple"	650
	"Henry"	100
	pt. "Josephs Park"	100
22:1754:28 ...		
Higginson Bell	"Spring Garden"	250
	"Rogers Chance"	200
h/o William Parks (VA)	"Park Hall"	1550
Robert Lazenby	pt. "Woolf Denn"	217
Richard Pelly & others	"Wickhams Chance"	300
Thomas Spriggs	pt. "Wood Stock"	1000
Charles Beall s/o Capt. Charles	"Pickeltons Rest"	100
Miss Rachel Beall	pt. "Grubby Thickett"	133¾
	pt. "Magruder & Bealls Honesty"	287
Samuel White, Sr.	pt. "Charles & Benjamin"	170
Samuel Richardson	pt. "Charles Forrest"	743
	"Richardsons Range"	540
Elizabeth Snowden (widow)	pt. "Charles Forrest"	409
h/o Col. Edward Sprigg (cnp)	"Three Partners"	75
	pt. "Happy Choice"	493

	pt. "Resurvey on Addition to Piles Delight"	1800
h/o Hugh Parker	"Astills Delight"	150
	"Salisbury" composed of: • "Salisbury Plain" • "Addition to Salisbury Plain" • "Vennemos Struggle" • "Salisbury Plain" • pt. "Nazareth Resurveyed"	4119
22:1754:29 ...		
Samuel Riley	pt. "Chesnut Ridge"	182
h/o William Tannyhill	"Buckingham House"	239
John Coffee	pt. "Lybranth" & "Discovery"	155
William Norris s/o John	pt. "Hopewell"	125
Robert Turner	"Nelsons Folly"	500
Thomas Pritchett	pt. "Cucolds Delight"	140
Samuel Beall, Esq.	pt. "Benjamin"	139
	"Charles & William"	330
	"Addition to Mill Seat"	325
	"White Oak Levills"	278
Joseph Glass	pt. "Dann"	93
William Callioner	pt. "Dann"	69
h/o John Beall	"Friends Delight"	100
	"Dispute or Discontent"	200
Dr. David Ross	"Poplar Thickett"	370
Josiah Beall s/o John	"Easy Purchase"	300
	pt. "Easy Purchase"	75
Joseph Belt s/o Jos.	"Plummers Delight"	50
	"Albany"	200
	"Joseph Chance"	40
22:1754:30 ...		
Samuel Plummer, Jr.	"Plummers Hunting Lott"	50
	"Plummers Delight"	50
Jacob Sinn	"No Name"	242
James Perry, Jr. (cont. f. 100)	pt. "Wickhams Park"	100
James Winders	"Medcalfs Meadows"	100
Lancelot Wilson	"Wilsons Discovery"	53¾

Mary Cramphin	"Cramphins Delight"	100
	"Grandmothers Delight"	150
h/o Edmund Castledge	"Hickory Tavern"	200
Tobias Belt	"Lost Hatchett"	192
	"Bronoko"	290
	"Belts Delight"	120
Matthew Lodge	"Deer Stone"	150
John Cook, Esq.	"Mount Pleasant"	150
Thomas Dawson	"Mothers Delight"	200
	"Addition to Mothers Delight"	200
	"Resurvey on Dawsons Purchase"	215¼
h/o Richard Parnald (AA)	pt. "Wickhams & Pottingers Discovery"	100
	"Newberry"	98
22:1754:31 ...		
George Wilson	pt. "Clegate Purchase"	50
Zachariah Lanham	"Addition to Remains"	100
William Watters	pt. "Charles & Benjamin"	152
	"Edmonstons Refuse"	67
Michael Dowden	pt. "Hermitage"	76
	"Hammor Hill"	40
	"Lucks All"	64
Ignatius Mitchell	pt. "Remains & Addition"	100
	"Mitchells Fancy"	100
William Alliburton	"Foxes Den" a/s pt. "Snowdens 2nd Addition to His Mannor"	150
John Leashear	pt. "Foxes Den" a/s pt. "Snowdens 2nd Addition to His Mannor"	126
John Vanfrees	"John Mountain"	128
John Beyne	"Hermitage"	100
	"Saterdays Work"	50
John Beyne (Andiatum)	"Any Thing"	50
John Martin, Sr.	pt. "Dulanys Lott"	100
Joseph Bonnett	pt. "Dulanys Lott"	52½
h/o Rev. Hugh Conn	pt. "Josephs Park"	200
James Conn	pt. "Joseph Park"	100
22:1754:32 ...		

h/o Samuel Chew	"No Name"	5000
h/o Hon. Daniel Dulany	pt. "Conclusion"	956
	pt. "Middle Plantation"	361
	pt. "Spring Garden"	340
	pt. "Partnership"	100
	"Good Hope"	132
	"Ocorson"	100
	"Dispatch"	100
	"Addition to Spring Gardens"	436
	pt. "Dearbought"	200
	"Sasafras Bottom"	100
	"Woofs Purchase"	100
	"Sawyers Chance"	50
	"Epanak"	100
Daniel Dulany, Esq.	"Allans Choice"	300
	"Locust Levill"	3010
	"Williamburgh"	1500
	pt. "Dulanys Lott"	2479½
	pt. "Taskers Chance"	850½
	pt. "Taskers Chance"	320
	pt. "Taskers Chance"	209¾
	pt. "Taskers Chance"	153
	pt. "Taskers Chance"	355½
	"Unsold Land" pt. "Taskers Chance"	40
	"Resurvey on Buck Forrest"	3000
	pt. "Taskers Chance"	217½
	"Long Meadow Inlarg'd" composed of: • "Addition to Long Meadow" • "West Addition to Long Meadow"	2131
Luke Barnard	"Barnards Desire"	286
22:1754:33 ...		
Walter Evans	pt. "Dunghill"	100
	pt. "Island"	32½
	"Beggars Bennison"	50
Ninian Hammilton	"Aberdeen"	100
	"Hammiltons Lott"	50

William Plummer	pt. "Bealls Pleasure"	64
Jane Wyval	"Sugar Bottom"	37
h/o Charles Friend	"Swedes Delight"	260
	"Dear Bargain"	25
John Jack	"Jacks Bottom"	175
Charles Cheney	pt. "Strife"	50
	"Rich Hill"	256
John Rutter	"Rutters Delight"	100
	"Gameing Alley"	100
Thomas Gattaret	"Farewell"	50
William Keley	"Town Hill"	50
	pt. "Kellys Delight Resurveyed"	428
James Shaw	"Brothers Chance"	223
Maj. George Beall	"Long Life to the Lord Baltimore"	150
	"Rock Donburton"	795
	"Addition to Rock Donburton"	1380
	"Pens Disappointment"	80
	"Conjures Disappointment"	46
	pt. "Lubberland"	27
	"Bealls Chance"	100
22:1754:34 ...		
h/o Miles Foy	"Hunting Bottom"	80
Enocks Enocks	"Enocksons Lott"	100
h/o Edward Charlton	"Charlstons Forrest"	275
h/o Evan Shelby	pt. "Maidens Choice"	268
	pt. "Hazard"	100
	"Long Bottom"	126
James Jack	pt. "Mouldy Pone"	50
James Gilliland	"Bigg Spring"	150
	"Bealls Tort"	50
Nicholas Vennemon	"Mouldey Pone"	100
John Williams, Jr.	pt. "Maidens Choice"	100
Isaac Baker	"Alloway"	150
	"Pleasant Bottom"	226
Michael Risoner	"Spring"	200

Peter Rench	pt. "Spriggs Delight"	75
	"Strife" – cont. f. 97	150
	"4 Springs"	200
	pt. "4 Springs Little"	50
Daniel Arnold	"Rams Horn"	392
	"Goates Horn"	50
	"Luck"	175
John Arnold	"Buck Horn"	40
22:1754:35 ...		
Samuel Arnold	"Hogg Yard"	100
	"One Horn"	26
	"Piggs Sty"	54
Col. Thomas Cressap	"Forrest of Needwood"	146
	"Scythem"	10
	"Indian Field"	150
	"Linton"	155
	"Conquest"	275
	"Three Fields"	165
	"Good Hope" originally "Indian Field"	420
	pt. "Scythom"	95
Thomas Cressap, Jr.	"Enocksons Delight"	80
	pt. "Darlings Delight"	75
	"Devils Hole"	128
	"Round Bottom"	96
Daniel Cressap	"Indian Purchase"	330
	"Little Meadow"	50
Daniel Ashcraft	"Boils Cabbin"	60
	pt. "Scythom"	65
George Pack	pt. "Scythom"	30
Barney Fore	pt. "Scythom"	40
Jacob Kellor	pt. "Ramshorn"	102
Thomas Cheney	pt. "Scythom"	120
	"Chance"	138
William Anderson	"Andersons Delight"	212
William Gilliland	pt. "Darlings Delight"	100
22:1754:36 ...		

Joseph Tomlisson	"Water Smith"	150
	pt. "Water Smith"	50
John Feltigraw	"Feltigraw"	150
	"Felts Addition"	120
	"Batchlors Delight"	818½
Andrew Hull	"Lemons Choice"	200
John Lemon	"Addition to Lemmons Choice"	40
	"Lemons Lott"	196
	"White Oak Swamp"	50
Samuel Waters	pt. "Charles & Benjamin"	4
Joseph Ogle – cont. at bottom	"Peace"	250
	"Peace & P<unr>ty"	750
	"Content"	210
	pt. "Creve"	50
	"Worleys Delight"	104
	"Grazing Ground"	100
	"Resurvey on Black Walnut Bottom"	310
Jerremiah Mullican	pt. "Charles & Benjamin"	96
h/o Isaac Simmons (Andiatum)	"Charlston Rack"	100
	"Simmons Rack"	200
	pt. "Simmons Rack"	245
Miss Susanna Beatty	pt. "Dulanys Lott" & pt. "Rockey Creek"	298
	pt. "Providence"	72
Maj. Joseph Ogle	"Farmers Delight"	440
	"Resurvey on Fountain Low"	2110
22:1754:37 ...		
Thomas Beatty	pt. "Dulanys Lott"	158
	"Well Waterd Bottom"	76
	"Mackeys Choice"	50
Peter Cripple	pt. "Beattys Venture"	100
h/o John Beatty	pt. "Dulanys Lott"	166
	pt. "Rockey Crook"	85
William Beatty	pt. "Dulanys Lott"	268
James Brooke – see at bottom (cnp)	pt. "Brook's Grove"	3142
	pt. "Brothers Content"	222
	pt. "Charleys Forrest"	1080

	"Fork"	100
	"Brooke Chance"	20
	"Crows Content"	150
	"Brooke Park Resurveyed"	1040
	pt. "Snowdens Mannor Inlargd"	394
	pt. "2nd Addition to Snowdens Mannor Inlargd"	218
	"Long Choice"	50
	"Brooks Black Meadow"	50
	"Brook Bottom"	584
	"Discovery Omitted"	119
James Brook, Jr.	pt. "Brookes Grove"	12
	"Younger Brother"	146
	"Knee Deep"	150
h/o James Beatty	pt. "Dulanys Lott" & pt. "Rockey Crook"	245
Joannes Middagh	pt. "Dulanys Lott" & pt. "Rockey Crook"	251
Agnes Beatty also John Kimbel	pt. "Dulanys Lott" & pt. "Rockey Crook"	300
Benjamin Stoddard	pt. "Friendship"	230
James Brooke	"Small Gains"	520
22:1754:38 ...		
Zachariah Maccubbin	pt. "Friendship"	380
	pt. "Pritchetts Purchase"	81½
William Ray	pt. "Charles & Thomas"	70
Robert Masters	"Thorough Fare"	100
h/o Charles Higginbottham	"Charley Mount"	300
	pt. "Piles Delight"	95
	"Aldridges Purchase", pt. "Piles Delight" & pt. "Bid. Green"	8
Richard Simmons	pt. "Gittings's Hah Hah"	200
	pt. "Wickhams & Pottingers Discovery"	100
William Flintham	"Neglect"	150
Conrad Cross	"Fouts Delight"	150
George Shersner	"Dutch Folly"	100
	"Addition to Dutch Folly"	100
Michael Kirkpatrick	"Narrow Point"	50
John Will Smith a/s Deelman Washabaw	"Smiths Field"	150

h/o Edward Fotterall	"Collers Hall"	100
Isaac Plummer	"Tradeland"	40
William Spurgion	pt. "Andiatum Bottom"	50
22:1754:39 ...		
John Shephard	pt. "Andiatum Bottom"	50
John Vandever	pt. "Andiatum Bottom"	50
James Spurgion	pt. "Andiatum"	50
	"Trenton"	120
	pt. "Stoney Hill"	50
Joseph Mayhew – cont. f. 96	"Resurvey on Chidleys Range"	100
John Moore	pt. "Andiatum Bottom"	50
Michael Cregar	"Anchor & Hope"	150
	"Batchelor Hall"	40
Amos Shanner	"Johns Bottom"	100
Mathias Stalcup	"Poor Mans Loss" originally "Matth."	144
Buttler Evans	"Evans Look Out"	20
Thomas Elder	pt. "Dann"	100
Samuel Ellis	pt. "Chance Resurveyed"	273
h/o Isaac Wells	"Low Land"	100
	pt. "Childrens Chance"	175
Henry Thomas	"Perrys Lott"	50
22:1754:40 ...		
John Henthorn	"St. Johns Resurveyed"	218
h/o Charles Polk	"Henthorns Rest"	100
William Hynes	"Polks Meadow"	100
h/o John Harding	pt. "Hardings Choice"	126
John Harding	pt. "Ganders Delight"	62
James Walling	"Dumb Hale"	50
	"Wifes Choice"	50
George Moore (Andiatum)	"Moors Delight"	50
William Elder	"Beaver Dam Levil"	100
	"Black Walnut Bottom"	100
	pt. "Ogles Good Will"	107
	pt. "Arnold Delight"	300
	"Addition to Beaver Dam Levil"	43
	"Elders Choice"	240

Jacob Mathias	"Slate Ridge"	123
Edward Diggs & others	"Brothers Agreement"	60
	"Brothers Tryal"	30
George Unkafore	pt. "Diggs's Lott"	150
22:1754:41 ...		
John Diggs	pt. "Chance"	25
	"Charles's Discovery"	100
	"Richard Hunting Ground"	366
	pt. "Justice's Delight"	150
	"Rich Levils"	352
	"Williams Intention"	246
	"Bear Garden"	568
	"Spring Plains"	348
	"Hazel Valley"	118
	"Meadows"	172
	"Disappointment"	182
	"Coder Clift"	290
	"Diggs Lott"	372
Benjamin Biggs	pt. "Diggs Lott"	25
	"Benjamins Good Luck"	100
	pt. "Good Luck"	43
John Ramsey	"Laybrynth"	100
John & Thomas Fletchall	"Two Brothers"	200
John Justice	pt. "Justices's Delight"	100
Richard Daviss (Madle Co.)	pt. "Dear Bought"	53
Charles Coates	"Flints Grove"	100
h/o Edward Gillmore	"Owens Rest"	107
John Burgess	"Stone Hill"	50
h/o John Settern	"Desire"	47
22:1754:42 ...		
Thomas Maynard	"Forrest"	60
	"Maynards Chance"	50
William Turner	"Turners Promise"	50
	"Turners Lott"	40
John Cook (Rock Creek)	"Turleys Chance"	50
	"Cooks Choice"	87½

James Turley	pt. "Rattle Snake Denn"	100
Mark Speagler	"Stulls Choice"	100
	"Hickory Bottom"	26
	"Marks Delight"	26
	"Speaglers Addition to Stulls Choice"	50
Rev. William Williams	"Green Bottom"	250
	"Williams Project"	250
Evans Jones	"Jones's Lott"	100
	"Evans Chance"	50
h/o Maj. Henry Mundy	"Truro"	844
George Read	"New Seat"	300
	"Earl Douglas's & Earl Pearcy"	73
George Swinyard	pt. "Lost Spring"	150
George Clem	"George & Clem"	150
George Hutsell	pt. "Lost Spring"	55
Edward Shippon	"Addition to Lafferdays Lott"	186
	"Addition"	52
22:1754:43 ...		
William Collier	"Stubb Hill"	100
	"Elders Delight"	50
	pt. "Dann"	67
Edmund Rutter	pt. "Strife"	50
William Bowill	"Menocon"	50
John Friend	"Hogg Hall"	66
James McCullam	"Chesnutt Levills"	50
h/o Godfrey Mong	"Delight"	100
Abraham Neighbours	"Abrahams Choice"	50
David Jones	pt. "Bakers Purchase"	100
	"Addition to Bakers Purchase"	100
Baltis Miller	pt. "Bakers Purchase"	100
Joseph Beall	pt. "Lay Hill"	649½
John Clegate, Jr.	pt. "Clegats Purchase"	286
	pt. "Pritchetts Purchase"	321½
Charles Brook	pt. "Dann"	150
John Pigman	pt. "Charley Forrest"	50
Fredrick Fiscus	"Catail Marsh"	200

22:1754:44 ...		
Henry Holland Hawkins	"Grandfathers Gift"	305
h/o Col. Thomas Lee (MD)	"Backland"	350
MM Edward & Osb. Sprigg	"Sweedland"	150
Thomas Brook	"4½ Gallons of Rum"	350
Samuel White, Jr.	pt. "Charles & Benjamin"	250
William Hardy	pt. "Addition to Remains"	100
James Docker	"Dockers Mite"	40
William Roberts (Pipe Creek)	"Broomwood"	200
James Dickson	"Matthews Lott"	100
	"Content"	112
	"Kingstonsted"	100
	"Townoloway Lick"	100
	"Chance on Beaver Creek"	100
	"Dicksons Struggle"	229
	"Whickey Alley"	115
	"Fearet Bottom"	104
Madam Lucy Brook	pt. "Dann"	947
Lucy Brook, Jr.	"Venture" from Madam Lucy Brook	32
22:1754:45 ...		
Charles Clegate s/o John & Phillip Berry	pt. "Dann"	200
Edward Birtch	pt. "Dann"	100
	pt. "Division Syth"	29
Francis Burrell, Jr.	"Burrills Choice"	50
Francis Burrill	"Burrells Bower"	50
Daniel Vears	"Rum Punch"	60
Samuel Farmer	"Jack of the Green"	100
Charles Traile	"Trails Choice"	50
William Fields	"Bedforsdshire Carrier"	108
Lewis Duvall	"Minuns Plains"	50
	"Griffiths Chance"	60
Christian Ketchindaner	"Christian Choice"	100
	"Alamangle"	50
	"Franford Resurveyed"	200
Margaret Harn	pt. "Three Cousins Resurveyed"	22

Allen Kellogh	pt. "Three Cousins Resurveyed"	469
Handle Barricdk	"Mill Place"	100
Thomas McPherson	"Dann"	100
22:1754:46 ...		
Robert Birtchfield	"Roberts Purchase"	50
	"Crooked Piece"	50
Arthur Charlton	"Charltons Purchase"	100
	"Friendship"	106
William Downey	"Walnut Point"	164
	"Downeys Contrivance"	61
James Crouch	"Pleasant Valley"	84
John Mobberly	"Mount Pleasant"	122
	"Rich Levills"	120
Benjamin Warfield	"Walnut Ridge"	278
John Jones	"Linthcums Discovery"	84
	"Mill Race"	10
David Watson	"Sarahs Delight"	90
	"Harys Grave Resurveyed"	140
	"Nicholl's Mistake"	10
Dr. James Deall	"James's Field"	100
	"Finis Coronat Opus"	290
	"Dealls Chance"	143
	"Dealls Folly"	156
	"Twenty Acres"	20
	"Hay Park"	40
	"Hunting Park"	50
	"Doulls Discovery"	123
	"Contriversy"	15
22:1754:47 ...		
Charles Hedge	"Hedges Delight"	192
	"Charles & Mary"	100
	"Whisky"	100
John Waufford	"William & John"	100
	"Cumberland"	25
Thomas Wilson (Pipe Creek)	pt. "Rockland"	100
	"Addition to Rockland"	50

Thomas Wilson (Toms Creek)	"Disappointment"	46
	"Marys Fancy"	104
James Beall s/o Nin	"Poplar Spring"	150
Charles Scaggs	"Scaggs Delight"	30
James Forde	"Turnip Patch"	60
George Lambart	"Lambart"	200
Daniel Lafeaver	pt. "Dulanys Lott"	10
Daniel Lafeaver	"Resurvey on Bennetts Resolution"	400
Martin Whetshall	"Wonie Garden"	150
Allen Farquer	pt. "Dulanys Lott"	100
	"Locust Thickett"	50
	"Chance"	118
Thomas Hargiss	"Darlings Delight"	50
Phillip Daviss	"Save All"	50
Notly Thomas	"Hazard"	150
22:1754:48 ...		
Andrew Barland	"Wood Yard"	60
	"Green Castle"	100
John Thompson	"Thompsons Adventure"	50
h/o Patrick Matthews	"Mullingah"	100
Nicholas Ridenor	"Nicholas Ridenours Ground"	100
David Candlen	"Swing A Barker"	100
h/o Mathias Rieslius	"Beaver Damm"	100
	"Ogles Good Will"	100
Richard Collyer	pt. "Token of Love"	96
Thomas Ford	"Upper Indian Bottom"	200
John Hamilton	"Hamiltons Recovery"	100
John Pritchett	pt. "Pritchetts Purchase"	38
Henry Child	"Wickhams & Potytingers Discovery"	100
Yous Cope	"Range"	420
Nathan Veach	"Round Knowl"	100
Calmore Beans	"Colmores Ramble"	66
	pt. "Addition to James"	200
Frederick Havenor	"Rich Bottom"	75
	pt. "Taskers Chance"	171
22:1754:49 ...		

John Chalmers	"Bear Denn"	100
Christopher Lownds	pt. "Hermitage"	300
	"Last Choice"	120
	"Matthews Good Will"	176
	pt. "Taskers Chance"	260
	"Bakers Ramble"	50
	"Salisbury Plains"	50
John Chambers	"Stumps Valley"	66½
Sammuel Plummer, Sr.	"Food Plenty"	167
	"Rich Hills"	198
	"Hunting Lott"	226
	"Rockey Hill"	170
	"Supply"	100
	"Hickory Plains"	454
Joseph Plummer s/o Samuel	"Pleasant Meadow"	184
Peter Mier	"Cool Spring"	188
William Morgan	"Thomas's Forrest"	100
George Honey	"Denn of Wolves"	100
Adam Spaugh	"Addition to the Sandy Elizabeth"	100
Basil Beckwith	"Garter Lost"	200
Peter Dent, Jr.	"Crabby Street"	100
Daniel Slagle	"Sinking Spring"	100
22:1754:50 ...		
Baltis Fout	"Boiling Spring"	47
William Tracey	"Traceys Desire"	60
Robert Ward	"Grubby Hill"	50
Edward Brawner	"Elders Kindness"	100
James Trail	"Rock Head"	60
William Norris, Jr.	"Rays Venture"	150
Conrad Hawersmith	"Low Mill"	100
	"Long Mill"	50
Thomas Lashear	"Square"	50
David Dealander	"Davids Choice"	100
John Reeter	"Higginsbottham Exchange"	100
Peter Stuley	"Sapling Ridge Resurveyed"	195

Robert Twigg	"Beer Range"	50
	"Jerricho"	44
Thomas Hitchcraft	"Hannahs Purchase"	55
William Hickman	"Three Springs"	100
22:1754:51 ...		
John Smith	"New Germany"	50
	"Addition to New Germany"	50
	"Come at Last"	50
Christian Kemp	"Kemps Delight"	100
	"Dispatch"	230
	"Kemps Long Meadow"	600
	"Resurvey on Good Luck"	639
	"Great Desire"	82
John Thompson	"Griffiths Park"	500
Francis Guttnak	"Graves Lott"	500
Henry Leek	pt. "Gittings Hah Hah"	200
	"Leeks Lott"	50
	pt. "Leeks Lott"	107
John Veach	pt. "Progress"	83
	"Pleasant Nest"	100
	pt. "Poplar Spring"	220
Absalom Wilson	pt. "Forrest"	100
Joseph Belt s/o Ben	pt. "Joseph Park"	326½
Wadsworth & Thomas Wilson	"St. Thomas"	150
John Young	"Backland" a/s "Arnolds Delight"	100
	"Resurvey on Switzerland"	103
William Murdock s/o Parsons	pt. "Discovery"	263
h/o Thomas Masterson	pt. "Bear Bacon"	176
22:1754:52 ...		
Benjamin Ricketts	pt. "Snowdens Addition to His Mannor"	134
	"Green Marsh"	78
John Perrins	"Perrins Adventure"	222
Michael Thomas	"Inlet"	60
Daniel Pellinger	"Reyinton Plains"	261
h/o Peter Studen Baker (cnp)	pt. "Bakers Lookout" & "Bakers Lott"	265
	"Shooemakers Purchase"	63

	"Woofs Lott"	100
John Long	pt. "Bakers Look Out"	100
Robert Brightwell	"Skythorn"	60
Nicholas Fink	"Prevention"	50
	"Arabia"	208
Peter Bemgarner	pt. "Nazareth"	100
Joseph Wellcomatt	pt. "Dutch Folly"	34
	pt. "Dutch Folly"	78
	"Free Stone"	100
	pt. "Nazareth"	100
	pt. "Dutch Folly"	66
James Bolting	pt. "Wickhams & Pottingers Discovery"	100
William Beall s/o Nin	pt. "Govib Ramble"	109
William Cummings	"Hope"	50
	"Brashears Choice"	45
22:1754:53 ...		
John Hawkins, Jr.	pt. "Magruders & Bealls Honesty"	104
	"Forrest of Needwood"	300
	"John Priscilla"	125
	"Hawkins's Island"	125
	"Contention"	499
	"Hawkins Merry Peep of Day" composed of: • "Coxens Rest" • "Chance" • "Refuse" • "Haw Meadow"	3100
	"Hawkins's Plains"	390
	"Hawkins Rich Lands"	420
	"Hawkins Tenement"	120
Nathaniel Wickham, Jr.	"Salisbury"	50
	pt. "Chance"	25
	"Paw Paw Thicket"	160
	"Turkey Thickett"	100
	"Locust Thickett"	190
	"Good Luck"	80
Ninian Beall s/o Nin (cnp)	pt. "Dispute"	200
	"Barren Hill"	100

	"Gravely Ridge"	50
h/o Arthur Nelson	pt. "Nelsons Island"	24
	pt. "Nelsons Island"	150
	"Hobsons Choice"	60
	pt. "Chance"	25
22:1754:54 ...		
John Frammell, Jr.	pt. "Nelsons Island"	136
Uriah Virgin	pt. "Dicksons Delight"	133
h/o John Dickson	"Dicksons Chance"	30
Seratt Dickson	"John & James's Choice"	150
Abell Brown	"Abells Levills"	400
John Sturrum	"Hoosers Choice"	110
Thomas Witten	"Small Hope"	60
Jacob Brunner	"Inlet"	25
	pt. "Taskers Chance"	248
	"Resurvey on Chevy Chase"	730
Jacob Clount	"Hallow Spring"	100
Stoffell Saw	"Half Moon"	108
James McCullam	"Oval"	100
John Patsull	"Blacksmiths Lott"	50
	"Smiths Lott"	50
Lodwick Daviss	"Lodwick Range"	150
	"Benjamin Squall"	50
	"Daviss Content"	50
22:1754:55 ...		
h/o John Houses	"Strife"	100
	pt. "Andiatum Bottom"	50
	"Two Wives"	33
	"Houses Addition"	70
	"Mill Place"	25
	"Walnut Point"	100
Stephen Gatterall	"Gatteralls Venture"	100
	pt. "Leeks Lott"	78
Jacob Staley, Sr.	"Switzerland"	150
	"Othersum"	423
Jacob Staley, Jr.	"Creams Quitness"	100

Adam Mayner	"White Gravil Spring"	190
James Smith (Andiatum)	"Smiths Hills"	200
George Bond	"Saw Pit"	150
	"Forrest"	100
Adam Stull	"Chesnut Hill"	150
	pt. "Chesnut Hill"	100
Robert Owens	"Horse Shoe"	96
Thomas Harris	"Pleasant Levills"	50
	"Madens Point"	100
	"Brotherly Love"	64
	"Boxes Search"	96
David Scott	"Charlstons Victory"	50
22:1754:56 ...		
Matthew Pigman	"Rich Bottom"	15
	"Very Good"	100
Martha Lakin widow of Abraham	"James & Marriots Lott"	100
Joseph Lakin	pt. "Two Brothers"	50
Abraham Lakin	"Abrahams Lott"	50
	pt. "Resurvey on Two Brothers"	146
Peter Shaver	"Palentine"	100
James Brown	"Browns Choice"	50
	"Browns Delight"	100
Nicholas Hall	"Mishees Garden"	200
Joseph Wilson	"Boys Lott"	100
	"Mill Tract"	93
	"Roberts Delight"	300
John & Benjamin Mackingley	"Benjamins Inspection"	300
John Campbell	"Johns Good Luck"	130
	"Partnership"	300
	"Johns Delight"	59
John Wollen	"Beauty"	50
22:1754:57 ...		
Jacob Weller	"Taylors Lott"	200
	"Taylors Prick Louse"	50
	"Taylors Shears"	50

Charles Davis s/o Griffith	"Daviss Forrest"	70
George Matthews	pt. "Good Luck"	212
	"Daviss Delight"	100
William Hays	"Dove Harbour"	90
William Chambers	"Chambers's Desire"	44
Ignatius Perry	"Perrys Delight" a/s "Wolf Den"	100
h/o John Perry	"Perrys Range"	100
	"Bushey Neck Hill"	100
Robert Constable	"Constables Range"	100
Lawrence Cregar	"Cregars Delight"	100
	"Langatpaugh"	140
Elias Brunner	pt. "Taskers Chance"	303
h/o Francis Wise	pt. "Taskers Chance"	206
	"Stumbling Block"	10
Casper Myer	pt. "Taskers Chance"	273
Jacob Sturrum	pt. "Tasker Chance"	202
22:1754:58 ...		
h/o Peter Huffman	pt. "Taskers Chance"	225
Christian Thomas	pt. "Taskers Chance"	209
George Loy	pt. "Taskers Chance"	213
	"Lambersons Resurveyed"	196
Henry Sinn	pt. "Taskers Chance"	145
Gilbert Kemp	pt. "Taskers Chance"	115
	"Kemps Discovery"	30
	"Above House"	150
Conrod Kemp	pt. "Taskers Chance"	220
	"Peace & Quietness"	50
	"Wilbersign"	30
	"Kemps Lott"	3
Fredrick Kemp	"Low Kempter"	150
	pt. "Kemps Lott"	7
Melchor Whorefield	pt. "Taskers Chance"	352¾
Stephens Ransberg	pt. "Taskers Chance"	465
	"Shoe Makers Choice"	100
	"Stoney Hill"	100
	"Ransberg's Chance"	190

Henry Brunner	pt. "Taskers Chance"	215
Abraham Miller	"Millers Chance"	100
	"Coopers Point"	200
22:1754:59 ...		
Conrod Keller	pt. "Taskers Chance"	159
	"Lura"	208
h/o Robert Dubutt	"Debutts's Hunting Lott"	72
	"Sun is Down & Moon is Up"	500
h/o Jacob Stoner	pt. "Taskers Chance"	571¾
	"Isaacs Inheritance"	200
	"Stoners Chance"	75
h/o Matthews Hopkins	pt. "Salop"	300
	pt. "Knaves Disappointment"	64
Henry Threlkield	pt. "Salop"	265
	pt. "Friendship"	400
Christopher Ellis	"Beginning"	50
Jacob Millier	"Meadows"	33
	"Swamp"	50
William Ridgely	"Pocoson"	13
	"Hobsons Choice"	337
	"Round About Hill"	12
	"Jones's Addition"	40
	"Ridgelys Ridges"	50
	"Meeks Delight"	50
MM Robert & Thomas Dunlop	"Hazell Thickett"	100
	"Addition to Hazell Thickett"	50
Thomas Taylor	pt. "Addition to Hazel Thickett"	50
	"Mount Pleasant"	50
h/o Henry Futney	"Dier Spring"	200
Thomas Thrasher	"Thrashers Lott"	110
22:1754:60 ...		
Alexander Warfield s/o John	"Warfield Vineyard"	270
Robert Miller	pt. "Brothers Generosity" a/s "Pork Hall"	587
Alexander Warfield s/o Richard	pt. "Stringers Chance"	195

Elisha Lawrence	pt. "Maidens Choice"	24
	"Good Luck Resurveyed"	245
	"Phillips Disappointment"	50
George Hartman	"Hartman"	100
Jacob Henry	pt. "Good Luck"	100
Leonard Decose	"Leonard Frolick"	50
Melchor Staley	"Maswander"	30
	"Onoctrandy"	7½
Oliver Matthews	pt. "Georges Discovery"	100
	"Chesnut Valley"	25
Daniel Matthews	pt. "Georges Discovery"	75
	"Daniels Addition"	25
Michael Jessuang	"Piney Neck"	100
William Durbin	pt. "Good Fellowship"	50
22:1754:61 ...		
Edward Lamb	"Lambs Choice"	150
	pt. "Good Fellowship"	100
Henry Coock	"Shear Spring"	100
	pt. "Shear Spring"	135
William Kearley	"St. Patrick Colt" originally "St. Patrick"	127
Edward Stevenson, Jr.	"Cromwells Resurvey"	213
	"Leonards Range"	100
Henry Avey	"Scotts Lott"	202
Valentine Myre	"Michael Fancy Resurveyed"	186
Phillip Stryden	"Addition to Wolfs Pit"	50
George Gue	"St. George That Slue the Wolf"	50
Jacob Peck	pt. "Addition"	100
h/o William Richardson	pt. "Snowdens 4th Addition to His Mannor"	200
	pt. "2nd Addition to Snowdens 4th Addition to His Mannor"	218
William Kersey	"Gravely Spring"	56
Mathias Ambraser	"Backland" a/s "Arnolds Delight"	125
	"Sweedland"	50
h/o Samuel Hyde (cnp)	pt. "Progress"	176
	pt. "Concord"	553
	pt. "Conclusion"	956½

	pt. "Middle Plantation"	361
	"William & Elizabeth"	150
22:1754:62 ...		
Jacob Ambroser	"Gap"	100
h/o John Stull	"Whisky"	380
	"Stulls Addition to Whisky"	160
John Stull	"Shoal Spring"	150
	"Pleasant Hill"	90
Mathias Gray	"Grays Delight"	50
	"Grays Choice"	10
	"Grays Neck"	119
Joseph Wood (Pipe Creek)	pt. "Woods Lott"	862
Matthew Jones	"Jones's Addition"	20
Mary Jones	"Fletchall"	253
Nicholas Baker	"Hazard"	300
	pt. "Knaves & Richard Dispute"	133
	"Pigg Pen"	50
	"Wolf Pit"	50
	"Lost Hammer"	104
Moses Shelby	"Hunts Cabbin"	310
John Hughs	"William & John"	50
	"Retreat"	15
William Loveday	"Exchange"	100
22:1754:63 ...		
Thomas Mills	"Conclusion"	56
	"Batchlers Hall"	100
	"Lanes Fields Resurveyed"	231
James Burgess	"Burgess's Choice"	50
	"Halseys Folly"	50
Benjamin Hiskitt	"Hiskitts Choice"	50
Owen McDonald	"Watsons Welfare"	100
~~h/o Martin Earnest~~	~~"Widdows Rest"~~	0
h/o Martin Earnest	"Martin's Intention"	31
William Matthews	"Widdows Rest"	100
William Dyal	"Dyalls Delight"	50

Richard Watts	"Susannah & Elizabeth"	50
	"Peach Tree Hill"	75
	"Addition to Susannah & Elizabeth"	150
Edward Mobberly	"I Look Many Many Places Now I Like"	100
	"Peace & Quietness"	68
Michael Ramar	"Meadow"	150
John Owens	"Rich Plains"	100
	"Owens Choice"	80
Andrew Bawlas	pt. "Delight"	50
22:1754:64 ...		
Thomas Swift	pt. "Delight"	50
	"Hunters Delight"	50
Robert French	pt. "Ridge & Kna Delight"	100
Shadrick Hyatt	pt. "Hermitage"	101
John Nicholls (Linton Hundred)	"Butter & Cheese"	80
Jeremiah Virgin	pt. "Dickensons Delight"	100
Joseph Farress	"Farress's Delight"	200
James Odell	"Ball Christ"	303
Joseph Robinett	pt. "Piles Delight"	129
	pt. "Piles Delight"	17
William Williams	"Williams Range"	132
	"Red Quarter"	21
	pt. "Conclusion"	200
Charles Tenly	"Non Such"	136
Edward Crow	"Shady Grove"	50
	"Addition to Shady Grove"	54
	"Abells Levills"	400
22:1754:65 ...		
Jacob Foy	"Foys Habitation"	80
	"Foys Addition"	50
Joseph Hains	pt. "Cromwells Resurveyed"	250
	"Addition to Cromwell"	50
	"Woolf Harbour"	100
	"Pleasant Grove"	52

Uncle Uncles	pt. "Cromwells Resurveyed"	219
	"Buck Range"	100
John Ryley	pt. "Chesnut Ridge"	219
	"Ryles Chance"	80
Daniel Spaugh	"High Spring"	100
Jacob Duckett	"Friendship"	100
	"Flag Pond"	406
John Mason	"Masons Folly"	17
Martin Hilderbridle	"Providence"	50
Nathan Maynard	"Maynards Good Will"	50
John Nash	"Ivey Reach"	40
John Simpson	"Simpsons Garden"	35
Thomas Hawkins	"Uncles Gift"	160
22:1754:66 ...		
John Ross, Esq.	"Woolf Pit"	100
	"Wingsfield Delight Resurveyed"	1300
	"Plains"	50
	"Resurvey on Ross Range"	3400
	"New London"	1360
	"Long Hope"	100
	"Ross's Town Creek Lott"	530
	"Corner"	112
	"Addition to the Discovery"	80
h/o Samuel Keley	pt. "Hunting the Hare"	50
h/o Rev. John Lang	"Inverness"	575
Joseph Chapline (cnp)	"Rush Bottom"	100
	"Josephs Chance"	100
	"Abstons Forrest"	156
	"Content"	100
	"Exchange"	100
	"Hills & Dales"	45
	"Grove"	195
	"Mindall"	66
	"Watsons Wellfare"	260
	"Batchlers Delight"	100
	"Nazarite"	100

	"Tick Neck"	54
	"Policy"	40
	"Hopewell"	104
	"Learning"	50
	"Little Good"	50
	"Frywell"	58
	"Bad Enough"	136
22:1754:67 ...		
Thomas Keley	pt. "Hunting the Hare"	50
John Woodfield	pt. "Hunting the Hare"	50
Edmund Martin	"Martins Choice"	35
George Smith	"Catail"	100
John Greenup	"Red Oak Slipe"	32
John Prather s/o William	"William & John"	100
	"Prathers Adventure"	75
	"Turky Flight"	25
George French	"Georges Adventure"	50
	"Barrens"	100
Caleb Dorsey	"Sparks Chance"	50
	"Harveys Borough"	50
	"Slate Hill"	50
	"Sparks Found"	50
	"Benjamins Folly"	50
	"Calebs Delight"	375
Josiah Darby	"Darbys Delight"	125
Jacob Rorar (PA)	"Hagurs Fancy"	507
Jacob Rorar (Marl.)	"Rorars Lott"	50
	"Addition to Rorars Lott"	100
	"Weter"	10
	"Defiance"	90
	"Rushia Corner"	50
	"Rarars Fancy"	100
	"Dry Poind"	100
22:1754:68 ...		
Frederick Rorar	pt. "Defiance"	10
Cornelius Poleson	"Polesons Chance"	50

George Winters	"Batchlors Hall"	125
	"Winters Addition to Batchlors Hall"	75
Joshua Hickman	"Elizabeth"	121
	"Barsheba"	179
Kennedy Farrell	"Fortune"	100
William Ingleman	"Carpouch"	50
Daniel Steward	"Indian Field"	50
Robert Leath	"Samuels Lott"	50
Lodowick Miller	"Toms Chance"	150
Capt. Thomas Prater	"Choice"	185
	"Richard Choice"	100
	"Dutchmans Misfortune"	100
William Rayman	"Wards Spring"	200
William Wheat	"Wheatts Purchase"	100
22:1754:69 ...		
Garah Davis	"Ganders Delight"	64¼
	"Addition to Ganders Delight"	70
	"Whisky"	282
Barnett Wymer	"Addition"	100
	"Sandy Run"	150
George Clapsaddle	"Empty Cupborde"	112
	"Addition to Empty Cupborde"	42
Valentine Skyetaker	pt. "Sandy Run"	50
John Wymer	"Wymers Cheges"	100
John Casteel	"Little Worth"	50
Matthew Sparks	pt. "Bedfordshire Carrier"	68
William May	"Dutchmans Request" originally "Maidens Choice"	148
Jacob Judith	pt. "Dutchmans Folly" originally "Maidens Choice"	3
Martin Casner	"Youngs Folly"	50
John Baily	"Fountain"	50
Daniel Moore	"Moors Delight"	100
22:1754:70 ...		
Kath. Jennings	"Good Luck"	87
	"Three Springs"	525
	"Widdows Chance"	108

John Worthington	"Whisky Rydge"	500
	pt. "Whisky Rydge"	563
John Ridgely	"Disappointment"	46
William Gibson	"Gibsons Chance"	100
Thomas Boilstone	"Boilstones Discovery"	39
Andrew Hover	"Addition to Mirry Spring"	50
	"Miery Spring"	50
Aberpart Appler	"Deope"	220
Joseph Dodings	"Andiatum Levills"	50
John Everall	"Goose Quarter"	125
Adam Miers	"Black Oak Hill"	50
	"Miers Pleasure"	175
	"White Gravel Spring"	190
Ninian Ryly	"Haly"	100
22:1754:71 ...		
Daniel Kelley	pt. "Hunting the Hare"	50
Caleb Touchstone	"Rich Thicket"	10
	pt. "Whisky Alley"	10
Philip Keilfalper	pt. "Whisky Alley"	67
Joseph Smiths	"Elswicks Dwellings"	180
	pt. "Elswicks Dwellings"	99
	"Smiths Pasture"	68
Edward Bucey	"Black Walnut Plains"	100
Charles Wood	"Charles Choice"	350
Teter Meisner	"Stoney Hill"	50
Fredrick Woolhide	"Jereusulem"	75
Henry Bitzall	"Smith Shop"	100
John Howard s/o Gideon	"Pretty Salley"	20
	"2nd Adventure"	54
	pt. "Woods Lott"	94
	"Bears Forrest"	30
	"Many Glades"	25
	"Chance"	50
	"Locust Woods"	25
	"Good Range"	125
	"Lime Stone Land"	20

22:1754:72 ...		
Michael Hains	"Meadows"	275
	"Pleasant Springs"	100
Bazil Williams	"Williams Lott"	10
Richard Watters	pt. "Charles & Benjamin"	152
	pt. "Williams Lott"	30
	"Buck Pond"	50
Edward Dorsey, Esq.	"Brandy Wine Spring Inlargd"	377
	"Brandy Wine Spring"	50
	pt. "Woods Lott"	584
	"Mount Pleasant"	50
	"Addition"	230
	"Resurvey on Pretty Salley"	1244
	"Pleast Field" originally called "Venture"	1394
	"Resurvey on Derbys Delight"	696
	"Rich Forrest"	125
	"Request"	378
	"Second Addition"	72
	"Cold Fryday Resurveyed"	2640
Basil Dorsey, Sr.	"Middleway"	295
William Purdey	"Howards Rest"	172
Michael Havenor	"Vulverspem"	50
	"Bull Frogg"	50
h/o Darby Lux	"Canton"	100
	"Hunting Lott"	159
22:1754:73 ...		
Solomon Turner	"Solomons Flower"	50
Mathias Sayler	"Misery"	50
John Wallers, Jr.	"Wards Delight"	100
	"Wards Delight"	100
Samuel Offutt	"Offutts Pasture"	613
	"Offutts Adventure"	93
	pt. "Younger Brother"	200
	"Addition to the Pasture"	19
Phillip Turner	"Turners Delight"	30
Thomas Clegate Prather	"Maidens Fancy"	100

Benjamin Pen	"Moors Delight"	100
Francis Hartley	"Hartleys Lott"	10
Rev. Samuel Hunter	"Lenards Good Luck"	100
	"Tams Stool"	100
Alexander Grant	"Alexander & John"	30
Edward Northcraft	"Molls Rattle"	25
Bigger Head	"Martha Delight"	85
	"Heads Good Luck"	19
	"Heads Industry"	19
22:1754:74 ...		
Benjamin Riddle	pt. "Creve"	50
Capt. John Dorsey	"Mount Pleasant"	400
	"Johns Good Luck"	50
	"Dorseys Search"	856
Morriss Mill House	pt. "Maidens Choice"	160
	pt. "Jemima" originally called "Maidens Choice"	235
Jacob Mier	pt. "Maidens Choice"	190
Hance Teter	pt. "Maidens Choice"	94
James McDonald	"Galloway"	175
	"McDonalds Chance"	100
	"Ile of Barren"	50
	"Bite the Biter"	144
John Barnwell	"Barnwells Choice"	50
John Brazilton	"Levill Spring"	100
Michael Millier	"Ash Swamp"	150
Miller Miller	"Skipton in Craven"	100
	pt. "Skipton in Craven"	180
Alexander Perry	"Batchlors Purchase"	100
William Porter	"Wilsons Fancy"	100
22:1754:75 ...		
Richard Clegate, Jr.	pt. "Dann"	150
	pt. "Friendship"	250
Rachel Lee	pt. "Lybranth"	50
William Biggs	pt. "Benjamins Good Luck"	168
h/o Peter Johnson	pt. "Skythorn"	85
	"Johnsons Lott"	139

Peter Johnson (PA)	"Johnsons Desire"	67
widow Wilson	pt. "Forrest"	100
	"London"	100
	"Suburbs"	90
John Cooe	"Locust Neck"	100
Jacobs Mills	"Beaver Dam Bottom"	138
Henry Rhodes	"Round Meadow"	50
James Green Martin	"Martin's Fancy"	50
Joseph Harriss	"White Oak Swamp"	50
John Grosenickle	"Resurvey on Grossnichels Delight"	201
Martin Shoap	"Mankin"	231
22:1754:76 ...		
Alexander Mackain	"Addition"	80
	"Doushitts Chance Resurveyed"	280
Henry Storey	"Storeys Grove"	50
John Martin, Jr.	"Johnsons Chance"	100
George William Lawrence	"Hoggs Delight"	55
William Johnson	"Exchange"	50
William Hallem	"Great Hall"	100
	"Look Out"	215
h/o John Dunn	"James & Elizabeth"	170
Joseph Williams	"Collins Folly"	11
William Willson	"Long Meadow"	50
	"Willsons Delight"	50
Andrew Scriver	"Wilsons Chance"	50
Mounts Justice	"Hard Quarter"	45
John Hobbs	"Hobb's Purchase" originally "Bush Creek Hill"	319
Owen David	"Neighbours Neglect"	52
Daniel Richards	"Richards Delight"	50
22:1754:77 ...		
Lawrence Heifner	"Stulls Delight"	100
Capt. William Griffith – see at the bottom	"Nipple"	53
	"Fairly Gol"	200
	"Bubby"	100
John Howard s/o Ben	"Marys Delight"	100
William Sparks	"Sparks Delight"	50

William Murdock & Rev. Henry Addison	"Friendship"	100
John Mellor	"Rockey Ridge"	50
Philip Knavel	"Shoemakers Knife"	50
Henry Funk	"Shippens Mistake"	54
	"Barne"	38
Stephen Newton Chiswick	"What You Will"	50
George Jacob Poe	"Well Taught"	100
John Helderbrand	"Chesnutt Spring"	50
Charles Harding	"Pritty Spring"	91
	pt. "Hermitage"	58½
Jacob Ganse	"Egypt"	104
Capt. William Griffith	"Black Acre"	100
22:1754:78 ...		
David Foutz	"Good Spring"	100
William Cullom	"Hogg Pen"	64
John England	"Englands Choice"	100
John Johnson	"Stoney Hill"	50
John Purdam	"Bear Garden"	10
Ann Kersner	"Widdows Last Shift"	100
Setth Hyatt	"Setths Folly"	50
Adams Pickinpaw	"Parratt Hole"	50
h/o William Fuller	"Fullers Folly"	50
h/o Thomas Sparrow	"Sparrows Request"	100
John Nicholls (Sinneca)	"Hickory Levill"	45
Robert Lamar, Jr.	"Wilsons Delay"	500
James Gore	pt. "Allisons Adventure"	150
William Summers	"Strawberry Patch"	50
John Hook – cont. f. 100	pt. "Kitocton Bottom"	50
	pt. "John & Sarah"	135
22:1754:79 ...		
Robert Kinchick or Jo. McDonald	"Kendricks Hoop"	50
George Fee	pt. "Andrews Folly & Discontent"	25
Richard Ancrum	pt. "Andrews Folly & Discontent"	25
	pt. "John & Sarah"	133

h/o Samuel Pottinger	pt. "Wickhams & Pottingers Discovery"	100
John Pottinger	"Addition to First Purchase"	200
Capt. John Stoddart	pt. "Friendship"	300
Thomas Cramphin	"Johns Delight"	100
	"Thomas & Mary"	450
	"Hermitage"	200
Solomon Whitnall	pt. "Charles & Thomas"	69
William Norris (Mountain)	"Norriss Seal"	65
h/o John Hayman	"Constant Friendship"	150
	"Haymans Delight"	225
h/o Will Norris (schoolmaster)	"Ralphe"	65
	"Sarahs Love"	100
Edward Wilson	"Wilsons Lott"	40
	pt. "Fat Oxen"	18
Thomas Johnson (Monk.)	"No Name" a/s "Sarahs Delight"	100
	pt. "Bear Den"	100
	pt. "New Exchange Inlargd"	24
William Wilkey	"William & Ann"	30
22:1754:80 ...		
Thomas Johnson (shoemaker)	"Fork"	50
	"Thomas Johnsons Chance"	50
Alexander Beall s/o William	"Jovial Ramble"	98
	pt. "Discovery"	268
	"Jacobs Cowpen"	50
	"Rubbish"	84
	"Refuse"	84
Lewis Duval, Samuel Farmar, & Edward Crow	"Beginning"	29
Jonas Brown	"Williams Neglect"	50
William Starr	"Starrs Fancy"	50
John Stinchecome	"Stinchecoms Friendship"	150
William Willburn	"Leeds"	50
William Albough	"Alboughs Choice"	50
Charles Hammond	"Charles Lott"	42
Michael Foutz	"Clear Meadow"	91

Robert Downey	"Ester"	100
	"Downinge Lott Resurveyed"	319
	"Addition to Blares Forrest"	100
	"Resurvey on Ester"	388
22:1754:81 ...		
Joshua Owens	"Joshua's Lott"	430
John Jones	"Resurvey on William & John"	224
Karles Kelly	"Kellys Range"	100
John Stoner (PA)	"Cumberland"	100
Henry Ford	"White Oak Spring"	50
Joseph Benton	"Bentons Lott"	50
Solomon Brewer	"Rattle Snake Den"	50
Christian Koonce	"Koonces Delight"	54
Westal Ridgley	"Ridgleys Rest"	100
John Harman Gurt	"Dispatch"	50
George Valentine	"Swiveing Swamp"	50
Handle Henn	"Harns Choice"	55
George Weddle	"Huckelberry Levil"	80
John Hutchinson	"Roses Delight"	50
Theobald Boone	"Boons Content"	50
22:1754:82 ...		
George Brown	"Resurvey on Browns Delight"	500
John Cryder	pt. "Browns Delight"	100
John Logsdown	"Bedford"	50
Andrew Young	"Sappling Hill"	100
Philip Key, Esq.	"Paradice Regained"	530
	"Epping Forrest"	1070
	"Friendship"	206
	"Terra Rubia"	1685
Richard Smith	"Smiths Field"	44
Joseph Hill	"Mountain Branch"	87
Charles Hammond s/o John	"Bite Me Softly"	152
Joseph Grabble	"Shippys Neglect"	54
	"Timber Wood"	50
	"Black Oak Rushes"	50

Jacob Funk	pt. "Shippys Neglect"	20
	"Good Luck"	50
Ezekiel Gosline	"Coolspring"	50
George Valentine Makgar	"Quakers Bite"	38
Dr. Henry Snavely	"Plunks Delight"	100
22:1754:83 ...		
Peter Balzel	"Turnoh"	150
Richard Cooms & Denniss Easy	"Coomes Inheritance"	203
Thomas Jones	"Jones Chance"	36
George Smith (Moky.)	"Make Shift"	150
Richard Croxall	"Mattinglys Part of Portk Hall"	490
Roger Davise	"Davis's Bargin"	50
John Banks	"Taffeys Lott"	45
John Huffman	"Bethleham"	100
Casper Devilbess	"Hunting Lott"	150
Daniel Harly	"Friends Good Advice"	30
Jacob Matthew (Intrust)	"Gift"	10
	"Resurvey on Slate Hill"	220
William Stewart	"Vineyard"	150
Dr. George Stewart	"Marshall Plains"	200
James Rimmer	pt. "Chance Resurveyed"	145
James Ellis	pt. "Chance Resurveyed"	65
h/o William West	"Two Brothers"	400
22:1754:84 ...		
Nathaniel Magruder s/o Nin	pt. "Grubby Thickett"	166½
	pt. "Friendship"	101
	pt. "Magruders & Bealls Honesty"	200
James Smith (blacksmith)	pt. "Grove"	37
Nicholas Haymand	pt. "Constant Friendship"	150
John Youngblood	"Youngbloods Choice"	100
William Brashears	"William & John"	100
Thomas Radford	pt. "Senneca Landing"	52
Hugh Tomlinson	pt. "John & Molly"	100
	"Squabble"	50
Robert Marks	"Shuttle"	50

William & Alexander McGaughy	"Rich Levill"	214
Sarah Offutt widow of James	"William & James"	82
Thomas Gilliland	"Indian Bottom"	100
	"Indian Bottom"	51
John Swaringan, Jr.	"Piney Hill Inlargd"	320
Matthew Clark	"Discontent"	100
22:1754:85 ...		
Thomas Lynthcum	"Lynthcus Chance"	50
Nicholas Martin	"Swamp of Experience"	100
Frederick Unsell	"Beauty"	100
Jeremiah Hays	"Resurvey on Jeremiahs Park"	450
Abner Lewis	"Abners Choice"	100
Jacob Hooff	"Hooffs Pigcoson"	100
	"Stone Acre"	50
William Hall	"Halls Addition"	80
James Dawson	"Point Lookout"	85
Joshua Harbin	"Harbins Lott"	50
George Shichlor	"Rooking"	50
John Beall	"Addition to Annstutor"	70
Jacob Knave	"Addition to Turkey Plains"	50
Edward Burridge	"Burridges Lott"	50
Joseph Hughes	"Trachmans Value"	35
Frederick Havenor	"Havenors Discovery"	45
Joseph Sparks	"Sparks Delight"	50
22:1754:86...		
Isaac Garrison	"Garrisons Choice"	50
Christopher Robinger	"Isles Mountain"	94
William Wheat, Jr.	"Lucks All"	50
George Williams	"Williams Chance"	150
William Cooper	"Coopers Choice"	80½
Peter Whetstone	"Hartmans Place"	50
Edward Ward	"Wards Pleasure"	50
William Waufford	"William & Mary"	56
James Young	"Bite Him Softly"	50

George Burkitt	"Debate Spring"	19
	"Georges Fancy"	31
	"Burkitts Folly"	25
Thomas Estup	"Rock Spring"	62
George Clark	"Cecils Chance"	60
Hugh Maclayland	"Buck Meadow"	70
22:1754:87...		
George Sultner	"Loving Brother"	100
Peter Shies	"Alumangle"	100
William Currance	"Peach Blossom"	50
h/o Leonard Albright	"Albrights Fancy"	50
Darley Ryan	"Mackeys Delight"	47
Stephen Richard	"Spring Garden"	50
William Dent	pt. "Dann"	150
Thomas Davis, Jr.	"Gold Branch"	257
	"Hyum"	100
	"Sapling Ridge"	72
	pt. "Benjamins Lott"	166
John Hammond s/o John	pt. "Gaithers Chance"	177½
	"Discovery"	15
Henry Gaitther	"Benjamin's Lott Resurveyed"	238
h/o Benjamin Gaither	pt. "Gathers Chance"	684½
Edward Gaitther	pt. "Gaitthers Purchase"	100
	pt. "Benjamin"	150
	"Gaitthers Chance"	200
22:1754:88 ...		
Matthew Howard	"Cold Fryday"	93
Michael Legatt	"Dam Head"	74
Jacob Gripe	"Non Such Resurveyed"	300
Clement Davis	"Hunting Hill"	300
	pt. "Pines"	78
Mrs. Lamer widow of Thomas	pt. "Two Brothers"	300
Samuel Lamer	"Anns Garden"	50
	pt. "Conclusion"	213
John Lamar s/o Thomas (cnp)	pt. "Josephs & James"	135
	pt. "Conclusion"	85

	pt. "Pines"	52¼
John Rawlins	"Lost Hatchett"	50
	"Beginning"	100
	"Hobsons Choice"	50
James Wardrope	"Partnership"	285
	"Read Oak Levil"	100
	"Wooden Platt Resurveyed"	327
	"Oxford"	54
	"Johns Delight"	104
	"Brenford"	35
	"Bloomsberry"	104
	"Coolspring"	75
	"Dearbought Resurveyed"	500
	"Resurvey on Hazard"	790
22:1754:89 ...		
Richard Simpson	"Simpsons Chance"	214
Edward Sprigg s/o Col.	pt. "Happy Choice"	593
Gilbert Sprigg	pt. "Piles Delight"	400
James Sprigg	pt. "Piles Delight"	400
John Webster	"Fountain"	100
William Beall, Sr.	"William & Elizabeth"	135
	pt. "Friendship Inlargd"	290
	pt. "Discontent"	100
	"Hill & Dale"	66
	pt. "Prevention"	11
	pt. "Fat Oxen Resurveyed"	700
John Richards	"Welsmans Purchase" originally pt. "Prevention"	122
Joseph Beall s/o Nin	"Lost & Found"	85
	pt. "Fat Oxen"	46
	"Choice Improved" originally called "Choice"	649
William Webb	"Darlings Sale Resurveyed"	420
Walter Frienderburg	pt. "Jemima" originally "Maidens Choice"	200
Hance Waggoner	"Flagger Meadow"	121
	"Long Meadow"	25
Samuel Reed (cnp)	"Nowry"	50
	"Baily's Purchase"	26

	"York" .	168
22:1754:90 ...		
Nathaniel, Ninian, James, & Samuel Magruder	"Resurvey on Part of Honesty" originally called "Magruders & Bealls Honesty"	865
Thomas Wilson s/o Thomas	pt. "Ridge & Knaves Dispute"	66
Thomas Miles	pt. "Labrinth"	150
John Jack	"Jacks Bottom"	175
William Boyd	pt. "Castle Plains"	150
	"Pleasant Bottom"	164
Benjamin Berry	pt. "Hermitage"	250
	"Addition to Hensley"	50
Charles Bussy	"Red Oak Bottom"	60
	"Self Defiance"	113
	"Cool Spring Mannor"	50
Samuel Thomas	pt. "Winexburgh"	493
	pt. "Snowdens 4th Addition to His Mannor"	1029
Arthur Lee	pt. "Clean Drinking"	350
William Tee	"Batchlors Purchase"	150
	"First Lott", "2nd Lott", "3rd Lott", & "4th Lott" originally called "Batchlors Purchase"	49½
Jacob Smith	"Jacobs Fancy"	21
John Johnson (Tuscaror)	"Johnsons Folly"	108¼
22:1754:91 ...		
Dr. Charles Carroll (cnp)	"Sluce Galleon"	50
	"Iron Hill"	31
	"Iron Mountain"	250
	"Shelbys Misfortune"	250
	"Carroles Range"	390
	"Hoyles Home"	100
	"Ittalfer Steed"	184
	"Carolina"	208
	"Chesnut Ridge"	390
	"Addition"	150
	"Addition to Chesnut Ridge"	70
	"Notch"	18
	"Bear Meadow"	325

	"Forrest"	144
	"Pines"	160
	"Spriggers Addition to Hall's Choice"	50
	"Black Oak"	225
	"Addition to Black Land"	22
	"Barren"	55
	"Addition to Strawberry Plains"	40
	"Hogles Luck"	116
	"Castle Fur"	112
	"Springhead"	96
	"Killmon"	190
	"Bear Den"	355
	"Mecoys Delight"	100
	"Turkey Hill"	110
	"Bottom"	56
	"Earnests Choice"	50
	"Long Acre"	144
	"Peters Park"	216
	"Shiers Bottom"	110
	"Holy Guns Forrest"	50
	"Addition to Bear Meadow"	70
	"Waddles Delight"	60
	"Stoney Meadow"	96
	"Adventure"	180
	"Lemons Range"	208
	"Charlton"	200
22:1754:92 ...		
Dr. Charles Carroll (continued) (cnp)	"Frys Delight"	268
	"Chance Medley"	92
	"Addition to the Pines"	264
	"High Germany" on Cat. Marsh	1254
	"Resurvey on Sarahs Delight"	500
	"Fellowship"	140
	"Resurvey on Hens Choice"	155
	"Lenards Chance"	46
	"Something"	86

	"Wadels Fancy"	48
	"Jacob Lott"	48
	"Dealy's Delight"	82
	"Saplin Valley"	53
	"Logg Cabbin"	220
	"Hazard"	140
	"Busshes Folly"	116
	"Barron Hill"	216
	"Plea's Meadow"	128
	pt. "Kellys Delight"	607
Solomon Turner (PG)	pt. "Ralpho"	202
John Lee	pt. "Lybranth"	50
Thomas Powell	"First Choice"	50
Joseph Flint	"Grassy Bottom"	66
22:1754:93 ...		
John Leatherman	"Much Grumbling"	30
Peter Youngsey	"By the Garden"	89
John Emmitt	"Emmitts Fancy"	100
Felting Shoater	"Hobsons Choice"	40
John Forrest Davis	"Charles & James"	50
John Carie	"Panmare"	50
Conrod Hogmire	"White Oak Grove"	50
	"Clayland's Contrivance"	90
	"Beaver Dam"	101
Andrew McHever	"Bethlam"	100
Archibald Beall	"Bealls Discovery"	26
Thomas Gilbert	"Gilberts Inheritance"	50
Michael Funk	"Margarets Industry"	50
Edward Chambers	"Hare Hill"	53
Hugh Green	"Pleasant Green"	50
Alexander Mackeen	"Williams Lott"	25
22:1754:94 ...		
Jonathan Hagur	"Hagurs Delight" composed of: • "Higginbotthams Exchange" • "Dicksons Rest" • "Dicksons Fatigueing Journey"	1474
John Hammond s/o Charles	"Hammond's Contrivance"	280

Thomas Awbrey	"Heartless Island"	18
Michael Hodgkiss	"Resurvey on Hawkins's Choice"	284
Thomas Sloy	"Sloys Consideration"	108
Peter Dyeser	"Mistaken Friend"	106
John Larkins	"Larkins Lott"	45
David Pierpoint	"Small Bit to David"	40
John Bombland	"Chance"	110
Zachariah Albough	"Alboughs Choice"	125
Mathias Moornet	"Hard to Find"	54
Mary Brook	"Chance"	25
	"Jones's Discovery"	60
22:1754:95 ...		
John Holland	"Holland's Delight"	50
Rebeccah Brook	"Azalon"	20
Rachel Brook	"Gibson"	20
John Spurgeon	"Fathers Good Will"	46
John Martin Whip	"Piney Grove"	50
Hance Waggoner	"Smiths Lott"	50
Alexander Gorden	"Gordens Chance"	25
Daviss Dean	"Resurvey on David's Choice"	174
William Campbell	"Resurvey on Montross"	580
John Hammond s/o Thomas John	"Strife"	1230
William Shoope	"Rogues Harbour"	110
Lawrence Cregar	"Resurvey on Middle Choice"	386
John Kennedy	"Resurvey on Dublin"	981
22:1754:96 ...		
Alexander Magruder (PG)	"Lost Pen & Ink"	150
John Kellor	"Resurvey on the Ash Swamp" & "Head of the Ash Spring"	363
Henry Piepoint	"Pierpoint Discovery"	210
Casper Smith	"Resurvey on Mount Olivert"	487
John Buxton	"Buxtons Delight the Resurvey"	860
Henry Starts	"Startmans Shears"	100
John Downey	"Nicholass Contrivance"	110
Thomas Hog	"White Oak Swamp"	93

Joseph Mayhew	"Addition to Chitchleys Range"	80
John Duttera	"Matthew's Good Will"	200
Joseph Hartman	"Four Friends"	118
George Valentine	"Volentines Garden"	50
Martin Whetsel	"Resurvey on Bonnetts Resurvey"	250
John Eason	"Discovery"	100
	"William Chance"	50
22:1754:97 ...		
James Kendrick	"Kendricks First Choice"	100
Peter Renet	"Resurvey on Hickmans Meadow"	780
	"Penny Pack Pond"	50
Henry Buttler s/o Capt. Henry Buttler	"Uncles Favour"	100
Nicholas Back	"Chesnut Hill"	64
Charles Hoskinson	"Elizabeths Delight"	32
Brice Woorley	"Worleys Choice"	50
William Douglass	"Scotts Grief"	100
Joseph Fivell	"Coursey"	30
Andrew Spowls	"Deer Spring"	58
Greenberry Cheney	"Hopewell"	100
	"Cheneys Lott"	50
John Carmack, Stephen & Daniel Richards	"Hobsons Choice"	25
John Barber	"Barbers Out Lott"	53
William Patrick	"Williams Tryal"	50
22:1754:98 ...		
Daniel Laitherman	"Pilgrims Harbour"	50
h/o Cornelius Eltinge	"Invention"	46
Thomas Kelly	"Kellys Purchase"	256
Thomas Durlin	"Fathers Advice"	50
William Littlefield	"William & John"	100
John Trenner	"Jones's Lott"	50
Conrade Miller	"Millers Desire"	100
Jacob Meek	"Kent"	50
Richard Stephenson	"Discovery"	100
John Williams, Jr.	"Table of Stone"	50

Aarron Moore	"Addition to Chenys Neck"	50
Nicholas King	"Kings Hill"	50
Philemon Barnes	"Horse Pasture"	100
22:1754:99 ...		
Jacob French	"Dry Spring Joyning to a Sharp Rock"	100
William Toyenden	"Tocarts Delight"	150
John Carr	"Hens Choice"	300
John Myers	"Boyles Fancy"	50
John Maccantire	"Smiths Choice"	50
Tobias Stansbury	"Feelfoot Inlargd" originally called "Felfoot"	210
Samuel Middleton	"Pooles Delight"	287
Joseph Cowman	"Catch as Catch Can He Thats Gets the Land is the Best Man"	540
	"Cowmans Mannor"	454
Francis Warring	"Warrington"	270
Benjamin Ryan	"First Choice"	190
Ninian Veach	"Narrow Lane"	46
Sarah Hall	"Addition to William & James"	194
Peter Ridingover	"First Snow"	190
22:1754:100 ...		
Edward Ricketts	"Mistaken Friend"	116
h/o John Cole	"Crouches Gift"	250
James Perry – continued on the other side	pt. "Wickham & Pottingers Discovery"	200
Larkin Pierpoint	"Second Addition"	42
	"Pierpoints Range"	139
Basil Dorsey, Sr.	"Resurvey on Howard's Range"	856
Adam Spaugh	"Gap"	100
Hans Ulrick Waggonear	pt. "Maidens Choice"	302
John Hooke	pt. "John & Sarah"	179
Stephen Woolbrack & Jacob Gripe	"Laffardys Lott"	100
	"Marsh Head"	100
	"Walnutt Grove"	175
John Darling	"Darlings Choice"	150
	"Deceit"	108
22:1754:101 ...		

Charles Jones	pt. "Clegate Purchase"	50
James Crow	"Resurvey on Locust Levill"	363
James Walling, Jr.	"Adventure"	50
Thomas Hinton	"Resurvey on Sapling Ridge"	290
Jacob Kellor	pt. "Rhodes Purchase"	102
George Shidelor	"Killackahall"	100
James Hook	"Kitockton Bottom"	100
	pt. "Kitockton Bottom"	50
	"Hooks Hills"	55
James Perry	pt. "Addition to Wickhams & Pottingers Discovery"	50
Jacob Fore	"Batchlor's Hall"	100
William Beall	pt. "Fat Oxen Resurveyed" – short charged on f. 89	157
22:1754:102-3 Recapitulation		
22:1754:104-121 Index		

22:1755:1 ...		Acres
Henry Boone (PG)	pt. "Easycomeby"	200
h/o Col. Thomas Addison	"Addisons Choice"	2300
	½ of "White Haven"	409
	"Phillip & Jacob"	400
	pt. "Friendship"	1600
Thomas Harris	pt. "Charles & William"	251
Robert Pottinger	pt. "Charles's Purchase" a/s "Charles & William"	297
	pt. "Fenwick"	35
	"Brothers Request"	500
Hon. George Plater, Esq.	"Brightwells Hunting Quarter"	1086
	pt. "Bradford Rest"	4795
Samuel Williamson Briscoe	pt. "Cligetts Purchase"	286
	pt. "Cligetts Purchase"	50
Jeremiah Berry (PG)	pt. "Charles & Benjamin"	1090
	"Addition to Charles & Benjamin"	31
James Swann	pt. "Dann"	26
h/o Meridith Davis	"Welch Tract"	100
	pt. "Good Luck"	245
	pt. "Josiah"	100
	"Best Breeches"	100
	"Meredith"	118
	"Friends Good Will"	57
William Luckett	"Merediths Hunting Quarter"	498
	"Kitchocton Bottom"	100
Rev. John Eversfield	pt. "Dear Park" & "Bear Garden Inlargd"	200
	"Addition"	50
	pt. "Inlargement"	90
Benjamin Brooke (PG)	pt. "Friendship Inlarged" now called "Upper Tract"	204
	pt. "Grove"	13
22:1755:2 ...		
Nathaniel Offutt	pt. "Coolspringlevel"	230
	"Goosepond"	100
	pt. "Bishops Island"	28
	"Addition to Goosepond"	133
	"Bear Denn"	200

William Offutt	pt. "Younger Brother"	200
	pt. "Cloverwell Inlargd"	400
	"Real Friendship"	10
Edward Willett	"Scotland"	100
	"Buckland"	260
	"Addition to Scotland"	73
Thomas Wilson (Monococy)	"Poplar Thickett"	50
	"Addition to Poplar Thickett"	63
Clement Hill (PG)	pt. "Partnership"	1000
	pt. "Addition to Partnership"	200
h/o John Needham	pt. "Forrest"	412
	pt. "Huntington"	308
	pt. "Pritchetts Purchase"	45
	"Forrest"	100
Andrew Hughs	pt. "Forrest"	200
widow Culver	"Batchelors Forrest"	200
	"Chance"	100
	"Addition to Chance"	200
	"Second Addition to Chance"	400
Thomas Cligett	pt. "Dann"	250
h/o Arnold Livers	pt. "Ogles Goodwill"	105
	pt. "Arnolds Chance"	100
	pt. "Buckland" a/s "Arnolds Delight"	949
Matthias Ambrosier	pt. "Arnolds Chance"	500
	pt. "Arnolds Delight"	125
	pt. "Swedeland"	50
22:1755:3 ...		
William Young (PG)	pt. "Duckers Wood"	533
William Carmack	pt. "Duckers Wood"	56
	"Lubberland"	99
John Carmack	pt. "Duckers Wood"	56
	"Hitt or Miss"	50
	"Widows Lott"	90
	"Pleasant Mount"	160
John Ash	"Mill Land"	50

Benjamin Becraft	"Becrafts Delight"	50
	pt. "Mount Pleasant"	36
Hon. Benedict Calvert, Esq.	pt. "Hermitage"	873¼
Benjamin Boyd	pt. "Castle Plains"	350
	"Rich Land"	200
	"Shelbys Addition"	50
John Boyd, Jr.	"Boyds Delight"	233
Abraham Boyd, Jr.	"Newstore"	79
Thomas Lancaster (PG)	pt. "Easy Purchase"	350
Rignal Odell	pt. "Three Bealls Mannor"	216
John Beall, Jr. (PG)	pt. "Allisons Park"	306
	pt. "Layhills"	649
	pt. "Drummonderry"	152
	pt. "Bealls Reserve"	253
	"Cowper"	70
Joseph Ray	"Lashmets Folly"	50
22:1755:4 ...		
Joshua Bucey	pt. "Charles & Thomas"	60
	"Jonas's Slip"	50
	pt. "Charles & Thomas" called "Gift"	70
Nathaniel Wickham, Sr.	pt. "Benyston"	100
Joseph Evans	pt. "Batts Hunting Quarter"	200
Col. Jos. Belt (PG)	"Senneca Hills"	200
	"Chevy Chace"	520
	"Friendship"	200
James Dooley	pt. "Chevy Chace"	40
	"Roberts Lott"	50
	"Robert Low Ground"	10
	"Dooleys Chance"	34
Peter Dent	"Falling Spring"	50
h/o John Bowie, Jr.	"Piney Thickett"	200
	"Piney Thickett Inlargd"	200
	pt. "Hermitage"	602¾
	"Allen & James"	34
	"Wickhams & Pottingers Discovery"	200
	"Addition to Wickhams & Pottingers Discovery"	50

John Brice, Esq.	"Wintersels Range"	400
Thomas Clayland	pt. "Hermitage"	100
	"Basheba"	5½
	"Dann"	250
Richard Richardson	pt. "Honey"	280
	pt. "Josiah"	100
	"Addition to Mill Lott" & "Ballingers Endeavour Resurveyed"	1033
widow Mason (VA)	"Barbadoes"	75
22:1755:5 ...		
Alexander Harbert	pt. "Exchange Enlargd"	250
William Harbert	pt. "Dunghill"	197
George Frazier	pt. "Four Gallons & ½ of Rum"	300
	"Cut Knee"	315
William Wilburn	pt. "Four Gallons & ½ of Rum"	50
	pt. "Four Gallons & ½ of Rum"	50
h/o John Thompson	"Thompsons Purchase"	227
	"Cool Spring"	190
	"Small Island"	12
	"Thompsons Hopyard"	110
	"Dutch Folly"	105
	"Long Island"	20
	"Darby Island"	70
	"John Jackamanty"	445
Henry Clegatt	"Addition"	200
John Philpot (London)	pt. "Hermitage"	200
	pt. "Friendship"	300
h/o Benjamin Young	pt. "Friendship"	300
Charles Walker	pt. "Virgins Delight"	75
Nathaniel Walker	pt. "Virgins Delight"	75
	"Lamars Generosity"	170
Henry Allison	pt. "Allisons Adventure"	150
John Baker	pt. "Snowdens Mill"	273
John Jackson	"Jacksons Improvement" & pt. "Friendship Inlargd"	194
22:1755:6 ...		

William Thomas (PG)	pt. "2nd Addition to Snowdens Mannor"	415
	pt. "4th Addition to Snowdens Mannor"	84
h/o John Thomas	pt. "Snowdens Mannor"	549
	"Thomas's Discovery"	1480
	pt. "Charly Forrest"	318
John Adamson	"Clean Shaving"	277
	"Lucus Friendship"	10
	pt. "Bealls Good Will" originally "Largo"	502
	pt. "Fenwicke"	22
	pt. "Hills & Dales"	70
John Tannyhill	pt. "Bealls Good Will" originally "Largo"	260
h/o James Holmeard, Jr.	"Addition to James"	630
	"Discovery"	100
	"James"	600
	"James Park"	52
	pt. "Token of Love"	100
	pt. "Widows Mite"	206
	"No Name"	38
	"Bealls Plains"	508
	"Outlet" also "Lamars Hill"	450
	"Mill Seat"	30
	pt. "Elizabeth"	25
George Moore	"Gideon"	20
Thomas Lucas, Jr.	pt. "Plumb Yard"	100
	"Thomas & Nancy"	50
William Lucas	pt. "Plum Yard"	100
Philip Hawker	pt. "Snowdens Mannor"	110
John Gartrell	pt. "4th Addition to Snowdens Mannor"	118
22:1755:7 ...		
Hancock Lee	"Addition"	576
William Masters	pt. "Progress"	49
Thomas Warring (PG)	pt. "Younger Brother"	200
John Darnall, Esq.	pt. "Hope"	2757
	pt. "Good Luck"	155
	pt. "Grove" & "Fellfoot Enlarg'd"	100
	"Piles Grove"	556

Jeremiah Belt (PG)	"Belts Tomahauk"	150
David Cox	"Lubberland"	50
h/o John Wilcoxon	pt. "Accord"	200
	"Georgia"	36
	"Gleanings"	64
Caleb Litton	"Oatory"	405
	"St. Mary"	67
Thomas Catteral for h/o James Beall	pt. "James & Mary"	636
	pt. "Brothers Content"	360
	pt. "Bear Garden"	206
	pt. "Prevention"	218
22:1755:8 ...		
Alexander & Robert Beall	pt. "Batchelors Forrest"	405
John Flemming	pt. "Hemsley"	100
Jeremiah Stympson	pt. "Hermitage"	100
Benjamin Kelly	pt. "Brothers"	100
	"Advantage"	135
	pt. "Discontent"	100
h/o Osborn Sprigg	pt. "Stock Quarter"	160
	"Forrest"	85
John Hepburn, Esq.	pt. "Hermitage"	400
	"Resurvey on Hanover"	2216
Charles Carroll, Esq.	"Carrolls Forrest"	500
	"Clown Close"	925
	"Carrolton"	10000
	"Stage"	228
	"Addition to Carrollton"	2533
	"Martins Fields"	100
	"Molkin Fields"	153
	"Carrolls Delight"	5000
	"Carrolls Bourgh"	5000
	"Girls Portion"	1700
William Wallace	pt. "Brothers Industry"	500
James Wallace (cnp)	pt. "Brothers Industry"	929
	"Hopsons Choice"	134½
	"Discovery"	83

	"Weavers Denn"	200
	"Piney Level"	130
h/o James Offutt	"William & James"	530
	"James Park"	200
	"Young Mans Folly"	100
22:1755:9 ...		
James Offutt, Jr.	pt. "Clever Will Enlarg'd"	1000
Alexander Offutt	pt. "Clever Will Enlarg'd"	600
h/o John Rogers	pt. "Bealls Mannor"	280
	pt. "Snowdens Gift"	40
John Gaither (AA)	pt. "Bealls Mannor"	200
Mrs. Crabb	"Bowling Green"	128
	pt. "Two Brothers"	28
	"Valentines Garden"	950
	pt. "Crabbs Purchase"	100
Jeremiah Crabb	"Deer Park"	470
John Phillips	"Walnut Bottom"	50
	"Vacancy Added to Walnut Bottom"	200
Milburn Simms (CH)	pt. "Easy Comeby"	100
John Smoott	"Cranford"	100
Thomas Fletchal	"Bealls Design"	100
	pt. "Flints Grove"	150
Thomas Flint	pt. "Newton"	100
John Flint	pt. "Newton"	100
	pt. "Elizabeth"	25
	pt. "Partnership"	12½
John Flint, Jr.	pt. "Newton"	100
22:1755:10 ...		
William John Jackson	pt. "James & Mary"	54
	pt. "Bealls Lott"	100
Miss Elizabeth Bordley	pt. "Backland"	542
	pt. "Backland"	90
John Riggs	"Bordleys Choice"	1000
Reverdy Ghiselin	pt. "Resurvey on Fountain Low"	380
Christopher Edlin 3rd	pt. "Resurvey on Fountain Low"	380

Beall Bordley	"New Years Gift"	1143
	"Peggy & Molly Delight" patented to John Bordley & Henry Chew	484
Matthias Bordley	pt. "Backland"	2030
h/o Richard Keene (PG)	pt. "New Exchange Enlarg'd"	360
	pt. "Cuckolds Delight"	23
John Davis s/o Charles	"Charles & Jane"	100
	pt. "Bealls Mannor"	234
	pt. "Bealls Mannor"	41
h/o John Beall Taylor	pt. "Grove"	18
	"Bealls Seat"	100
Thomas Talbot (PG)	pt. "Grove"	246
George & John Rose (PG)	pt. "James & Mary Resurveyed"	220
John Hoskinson	pt. "Grove"	44
	pt. "Resurvey on James & Mary"	50
22:1755:11 ...		
h/o John Radford	pt. "Senneca Landing"	52
	pt. "Long Acre"	52
	pt. "Elizabeth"	50
	pt. "Henry"	105
William Hughes	pt. "James & Mary"	130
John Madding	"Stoney Point" a/s pt. "Labyrinth"	100
	"Addition to Stoney Point"	50
James Plummer (PG)	"Wickhams Good Will"	270
h/o John Vanmetre	"Pipe Meadow"	200
David Shepherd	"Pell Mell"	162
Thomas Palmer	pt. "Palmers Choice"	15
Abraham Crum	pt. "Metre"	300
	pt. "Palmers Choice"	43
	"Palmerzana"	154
Bazil Adamson	"Adamsons Choice"	100
h/o Edward Crabb	"Crabbs Purchase"	356
James Lamar	pt. "Pines"	103½
Michael Jones	pt. "Pines"	200
Peter Butler (cnp)	"Paradice"	210
	"Magruders Hazard"	100

	"Locust Thicket"	100
	"Paradice Enlargd"	100
	"Butlers Lott"	120
	"Vacancy Added to Butlers Lott"	176
22:1755:12 ...		
Nathan Hammond	"Hammonds Desire"	192
	"Forrest Range"	480
Thomas Lamar	"Buckbottom"	120
	pt. "Joseph & James"	200
James Perry, Sr.	"Straden"	220
	"Stoney Hive"	200
Thomas Beall 2nd	"Frozen Level"	200
Richard Duckitt (PG)	"Ducketts Misfortune"	200
Joseph Wheat	"Wheats Choice"	53
David Trail, Jr.	"Good Will"	100
	"Locust Thickett"	72
Benjamin Hall	"Halls Choice Resurveyed"	672
Joseph Hall	pt. "Halls Choice Resurveyed"	202
James Beall s/o Robert	"Exeter"	225
	"Farm"	128
Pharoah Riley	pt. "Dann"	100
Hugh Riely	pt. "Dann"	250
Ninian Tannyhill	pt. "Fenwicke"	243
	pt. "Outlet"	80
h/o John Watkins (AA)	pt. "Paschaham"	100
	"Watkins Range"	100
	"Addition to Watkins Range"	320
22:1755:13 ...		
h/o John Aldridge	pt. "Paschaham"	100
Matthew Robinson	"Joseph Good Will"	150
William Pritchett	pt. "Dunghill"	100
	"Harberts Chance"	100
	"Eleanors Green"	150
	pt. "Island"	32½
John Leech	"Rocky Spring"	100
Capt. Samuel Magruder	"Forrest"	300

William & Sarah Williams	pt. "Smiths Pasture"	100
Dr. Andrew Scott	"Fancy"	144
	"Salturn"	200
	"Venus"	200
	"Badgers Hole"	22
h/o John Abington	"Wetwork"	700
	"Whitehaven"	350
Daniel Clarey	pt. "Bradfords Rest"	115
	"Buck Bottom"	100
Benjamin Brown	pt. "Bradfords Rest"	115
Hon. Benjamin Tasker, Esq.	pt. "Magruders & Bealls Honesty"	322
	pt. "Prevention"	140
Samuel Selby	pt. "Baily Crist"	200
Alexander Magruder s/o Samuel	pt. "Magruders & Bealls Honesty"	121
22:1755:14 ...		
h/o James Edmonston	pt. "Brothers Content"	360
	"Amsterdam"	80
	"Accord"	100
	pt. "Prestons March"	334
	pt. "Lubberland"	27
	pt. "Batchelors Forrest"	405
	"Westorer Fields"	82
	pt. "Hermitage"	131
	pt. "Discovery"	41½
	"Land of Ease"	40
	"Georges Delight"	20
	"Piles Delight"	500
	pt. "Piles Hall"	360
	pt. "Prevention"	159½
William Condon	pt. "Hermitage"	100
John Toleson (PG)	"I Never See It"	400
Thomas Thompson	pt. "Rattle Snake Denn"	150
	"Thompsons Hop Thickett"	34
Patrick Reading (PG)	pt. "Clegatts Purchase"	50

John West	pt. "Two Brothers"	200
	pt. "Joseph"	200
Clement Mosely (PG)	pt. "Clegatts Purchase"	50
Stephen Hampton	pt. "Bear Denn"	100
h/o Dr. John Haswell	"Allisons Part"	153
Joseph Richardson	pt. "Charles & Benjamin"	100
	pt. "Brookes Reserve"	200
	"Rogues Harbour"	50
22:1755:15 ...		
Grove Tomlinson	"Fletchalls Good Will"	100
	pt. "Good Luck"	200
	"Addition to Fellowship"	48
	"Groves Hunting Lott"	136
	"Support"	50
Joseph West s/o Benjamin	"Younger Brother"	370
George Beckwith	"Beckwiths Range"	250
	"Charles Choice"	49
John Halsel	pt. "Cuckolds Delight"	100
h/o William Cumming	pt. "Accord"	100
	pt. "Amsterdam"	80
	pt. "Norrway"	630
	pt. "Prestons March"	334
	"Drum Mines"	668
	"Sluice"	100
John Waters (PG)	pt. "Maidens Fancy"	430
	"Bear Neck"	151
	"Mothers Gift"	400
Brock Mockbee	pt. "Fellowship"	200
John Nelson	pt. "Chance"	555
John Brunner	pt. "Sweeds Folly"	100
	pt. "Taskers Chance"	232
	"Good Luck"	100
Elias Delashmoot (cnp)	pt. "Sweeds Folly"	100
	"Ramble"	100
	"Addition to Sweeds Folly"	25
	"Deptford"	32

	pt. "Childrens Chance"	52
	"Dry Spring"	50
22:1755:16 ...		
Weaver Barnes	pt. "2nd Addition to Snowdens Mannor"	200
	pt. "2nd Addition to Snowdens Mannor"	200
	"Inspection"	150
George Moore (PG)	"Chance"	50
George Moore	pt. "Moores Industry"	100
h/o Philip Murphy	"Buck Lodge"	100
Stephen Julian	"Hedge Hogg"	258
Rev. George Murdock	"Friends Good Will"	150
	"Glebe of Rock" a/s "Generosity"	100
	pt. "Mill Land"	2
	pt. "Charles & William"	248
Abraham Eltinge	"Abrahams Lott"	312
	pt. "Concord"	100
	"New Esopus"	100
Isaac Hite (VA)	"Black Walnut Tree Island"	142
	pt. "Forrest"	140
Abraham Fore (PA)	"Eltinges Right"	325
John Hite (VA)	pt. "Black Walnut Tree Island"	124
	"Discord"	215
	"Discovery"	37
	pt. "Forrest"	140
h/o Dr. Samuel Stringer	"Joy Church"	1045
	pt. "Stringers Chance"	300
22:1755:17 ...		
Col. John Colvil (VA)	"Maryland"	6300
Isaac Eltinge heir of Cornelius (cnp)	pt. "Partnership"	100
	"Overplus"	170
	"Frog Island"	30
	"Milburn"	270
	pt. "Darby Island"	76
	"Fork of Grubby Hill"	305
	"Senecca Ford"	160
	pt. "Concord"	201

	pt. "Long Acre"	52
	"Fortune"	118
	"Eltinges Rest"	60
	"Addition"	50
	"Mill Rode"	240
	"Isaac Eltinge"	112
	"Fair Island"	172
	"Hills"	105
	"Invention"	46
John Dickerson, Jr.	pt. "Charly Forrest"	100
	"Stoney Range"	54
Thomas Hillary (PG)	"Pickax"	58
	pt. "Stock Quarter"	100
William Hillary (PG)	"Sugar Loaf"	80
Joseph Waters	pt. "Moores Industry"	30
	"Joseph Advance"	200
Thomas Odell (PG)	pt. "Grubby Thickett"	200
h/o James Magruder, Jr.	"Lost Jackett"	200
Nathan Magruder	"Point"	30
	"Knaves Dispute & Ridge"	180
	pt. "Charles & Benjamin"	50
	"Knaves Dispute"	40
	"Addition to Turkey Thickett"	40
	"Rush Marsh"	63
22:1755:18 ...		
Zadock Magruder	"Turkey Thickett"	350
	"Robert & Sarah"	100
	"Ridge"	78¼
Zechariah Magruder	pt. "Friendship"	220
	"Zachariah"	100
John Magruder, Jr.	pt. "Friendship" & "Magruders Purchase"	316
	pt. "Grubby Thickett"	166
Charles Williams	"White Oak Valley"	100
h/o Basil Beall	"Industry"	163
	"Archibalds Lott"	100

Samuel Magruder 3rd	pt. "Friendship" & "Addition to Magruder & Bealls Purchase"	320
	"Mill Use"	25
	"As Good As We Could Get"	200
	"Samuels Delight"	200
	pt. "Magruders & Bealls Honesty"	365
	"Rest on Honesty" & "Addition to Rest on Honesty"	749½
Samuel Wade Magruder	pt. "Hensley Resurveyed" & "Addition to Hensley Resurveyed"	214
Archibald Edmonston	pt. "Deer Park" & "Bear Garden"	458
	"Bealls Good Will"	50
	"Addition to Deer Park"	142
John Garrett	pt. "Hermitage"	197
Thomas Dowden	pt. "Hermitage"	70
William Davis s/o Griffith	"Hazard"	60
h/o John James	"Dispute"	50
22:1755:19 ...		
Edward Offutt	pt. "Coolsprings Level"	296
	pt. "Outlet"	520
Flayl Payn	"Payns Delight"	100
	"Payns Industry"	50
h/o George Noble	pt. "Wetwork"	350
	pt. "Spring Garden"	170
	pt. "Drywork"	42½
Thomas Noble	pt. "Wet Work"	350
	pt. "Spring Garden"	170
	pt. "Dry Work"	42½
Edward Owen	"Shepherds Fortune Resurveyed"	292
	"What You Please"	120
Ninian Beall, Sr.	"Friendship Enlargd" now "Upper Tract"	322
Thomas Lucas	"Lucas's Adventure"	100
John Smith Prather	pt. "Bear Garden Enlargd" & "Deer Park"	620
Ann Magruder	"Friendship"	310
	pt. "Elizabeth" & "Partnership"	10
Ezekiel Magruder	pt. "Friendship"	100

Nathaniel Magruder	pt. "Grubby Thickett"	333
	"Vacancy Added to Grubby Thickett"	93
Charles Williams 3rd	pt. "Bealls Mannor"	73
Thomas Case	pt. "Bealls Mannor"	100
22:1755:20 ...		
John Cartwright	pt. "Charles & Thomas"	150
	pt. "Labyrinth"	123
Richard Gaither	pt. "Allisons Park"	50
	pt. "Allisons Park"	100
Charles Allison	pt. "Allisons Park"	52
William Black (London)	pt. "New Exchange"	700
	"Gordons Purchase"	150
	"Black Acre"	435
George Gordon	pt. "Knaves Disappointment"	236
Robert Wells	"Cannoe Bottom"	50
John Dowden	pt. "Addition to Fellowship"	49
	pt. "John & Molly"	137
	"Johnys Poplar Spring"	42
	"John & Molly"	106
	"Dowdens Luck"	90
John Beall s/o Robert	"Snowdens Mill Land"	120
	pt. "3 Bealls Mannor" a/s "Elizabeth & John"	108
Edward Beatty	"Poplar Bottom"	52
	pt. "Dulanys Lott"	166
	"Patricks Colt"	60
	pt. "Dulanys Lott" & pt. "Rockey Creek"	30½
William Oneal	pt. "Johen of Love"	197
	"Wheel of Fortune"	100
	"Come by Chance"	90
22:1755:21 ...		
Thomas Johnson (Kittocktin)	"Johnsons Levels"	50
	pt. "Johnsons Lands" between elder & survey	173
	"Vacancy Added to Johnsons Levels"	255
Rev. Samuel Hunter (cnp)	pt. "Resurvey on Johnsons Levels"	150
	"Leonards Good Luck"	100
	"Farris Stool"	100

	"Leeds"	50
	"Shuttle"	50
	"Pleasant Plains"	136
Charles Jones	pt. "Clean Drinking"	350
Arthur Lee (CH)	pt. "Clean Drinking"	350
Peter Murphy	"Bear Garden"	100
Richard Dean	pt. "Hunting the Hare"	50
h/o Jos. White or James Wallace, Jr.	"Fletchalls Garden"	65
	pt. "Reeds Delight"	100
Moses Chapline	"Joyners Fancy"	50
	"Resurvey on Mount Pleasant"	217
James Smith (Andicatum)	"Resurvey on 3 Springs"	739
	"Smiths Hills"	200
	"Addition to 3 Springs"	30
Thomas Willett	"Lick Hill"	100
	pt. "Little Denn"	26
22:1755:22 ...		
William Farquer	pt. "Rock Land"	74
	"Rillfudoh"	200
	pt. "Mount Pleasant"	40
	"Swamp Miserable"	60
	"Forrest in Need"	120
	"Unity"	25
	"Williams Defiance"	270
	"Chesnut Spring"	62
	"Chesnut Spring"	50
	"Fancy"	195
widow Fransway	"Nanny's Delight" a/s pt. "Labrynth"	100
Samuel Blackmore	pt. "Discovery"	100
Cornelius Vernoy	pt. "Concord"	236
	pt. "Forrest"	142
	½ of "New Esopus"	100
William Williams s/o Thomas (cnp)	"Fork"	400
	"Mill Lands"	166
	"Addition to the Fork"	80
	"Haymonds Addition"	75

	pt. "New Exchange Enlargd"	73¾
James Holland	pt. "Gittings Hollow"	117
	"Panthers"	50
Thomas Stump	pt. "Stumps Valley"	133½
James Lee, Jr.	pt. "Discovery" & "Labrynths"	100
	"James & Richard"	100
22:1755:23 ...		
Samuel Beall	pt. "Labrynth"	240
Humphrey Batts (PG)	pt. "Magruders & Bealls Industry"	233
	pt. "St. Elizabeths Mannor"	100
	pt. "Partnership"	200
Thomas Plummer, Jr.	"Sapplin Hill Resurveyed"	177
h/o Col. Thomas Lee (VA)	"Mortin"	165
	"Eden"	320
	"Hill in the Middle"	315
Thomas Plummer, Sr.	pt. "Plummers Island"	100
	"Green Land"	37
Thomas Kendrick	pt. "Additions to the Remains"	100
	"Division of the Tythe"	29
Joseph Peach (PG)	pt. "Bear Bacon"	200
Peter Apple	pt. "Rockey Creek"	150
	pt. "Arnolds Delight" a/s "Backland"	100
	"Small Hope"	20
Ninian Magruder, Jr.	pt. "Friendship" & "Addition to Magruders Purchase"	300
	pt. "Pritchetts Purchase"	50
	"Magruders Lott"	100
	"Addition to Magruders Lott"	50
	"Black Oak Thickett"	150
	"Addition to Magruders Purchase"	18
	pt. "Magruders & Bealls Honesty"	83
22:1755:24 ...		
Daniel Sing	"Breaches"	100
h/o Jacob Foutz (cnp)	pt. "Rockey Creek"	539
	pt. "Mill Lott"	50
	pt. "Small Hope"	10

	"Goose Nest"	30
Hon Richard Lee, Esq.	"Angle"	300
	"Cuckolds Delight"	100
	"Scotts Ordinary"	100
	pt. "Forrest Green"	170
	"Bowling Green"	86
	"Thomas's Last Shift"	200
	pt. "Dann"	500
Francis & Charles Pierpoint	pt. "Rockey Creek"	250
	"Small Hopes"	80
Edward Tully	"Hard Lodging"	322
Benjamin Norris s/o John	pt. "Hopewell"	125
Zachariah Lyles	pt. "Hopewell"	50
William Holland	pt. "Charles & Benjamin"	187
	"Hollands Addition"	80
Francis Hall (PG)	pt. "Hope"	216
Ignatius Diggs (PG)	"Christian Castle"	218
	"Clear Spring"	50
	"Mountain Prospect"	600
22:1755:25 ...		
Stephen Lewis (VA)	"Strife"	500
	"Lewis's Discovery"	65
h/o Thomas Charters	pt. "Henry"	193
Holland Middleton	"Maidens Bower"	100
Thomas Conn	pt. "Labrynth"	184
	"Lost Knife"	150
Richard Clagett (PG)	"Mogilligan" pt. "Lybranths"	183¾
	pt. "Dann"	150
	pt. "Friendship"	250
George Gump	"Chesnut Hill"	142
	"Four Springs"	50
	pt. "Addition to Corrolton"	167
	"Huofion Hart" originally called "Corrolton Vacancy"	599
h/o Daniel Carroll (cnp)	"Batchelors Chance"	100
	"Do's Content"	176

	"Kilman"	1300
	pt. "Aix la Chapelle"	942
	"Refuse"	150
	pt. "Elizabeth Delights"	100
	pt. "Joseph Park"	1435¼
Daniel Carroll	pt. "New Exchange"	200
	pt. "Joseph Park"	2058½
	pt. "Aix la Chapelle"	850
	"Henry"	100
	pt. "Joseph Park"	100
	"Grandmothers Good Will"	150
	"Henry & Mary"	110
William Moore	"Spriggs Delight"	75
22:1755:26 ...		
Higginson Belt	"Spring Garden"	250
	"Rogers Chance"	200
h/o William Parks (VA)	"Park Hall"	1550
Robert Lazinby	pt. "Woolf Denn"	217
Richard Pelty & others	"Wickhams Chance"	300
Thomas Sprigg (AA)	pt. "Woodstack"	1000
Charles Beall s/o Capt. Charles	"Pickeltons Rest"	100
Miss Rachel Beall	pt. "Grubby Thickett"	133¾
	pt. "Magruders & Beall Honesty"	287
Samuel White, Sr.	pt. "Charles & Benjamin"	250
Samuel Richardson	pt. "Charles Forrest"	743
	"Richardsons Range"	540
Elizabeth Snowden	pt. "Charles Forrest"	409
h/o Col. Edward Sprigg	"3 Partners"	75
	pt. "Happy Choice"	593
	pt. "Resurvey on Addition to Pyles Delight"	1800
22:1755:27 ...		
h/o Hugh Parker (cnp)	"Astills Delight"	150
	"Salisbury" composed of: • "Salisbury Plain" • "Addition to Salisbury Plain" • "Vennemons Struggle"	4119

	• "Salisbury Plain" • pt. "Nazareth Resurveyed"	
Samuel Riely	pt. "Chesnut Ridge"	182
	"Jericho Plains"	50
h/o William Tannyhill	"Buckingham House"	289
John Coffee	pt. "Lybranth" & "Discovery"	155
William Norris s/o John	pt. "Hopewell"	125
Robert Turner	"Nelsons Folly"	500
Thomas Pritchett	pt. "Cuckolds Delight"	140
Samuel Beall, Esq.	pt. "Benjamin"	139
	"Charles & William"	330
	"Addition to Mill Seat"	325
	"White Oak Levels"	278
	"Frenchmans Purchase"	2680
Joseph Glass	pt. "Dann"	93
h/o John Beall	"Friends Delight"	100
	"Dispute or Discontent"	200
22:1755:28 ...		
Dr. David Ross	pt. "Poplar Thickett"	144
Gabriel Thomas	pt. "Poplar Thickett"	326
	"Stoney Lick"	100
Josiah Beall s/o John	"Easy Purchase"	300
	pt. "Easy Purchase"	75
Joseph Belt s/o Joseph	"Plummers Delight"	50
	"Albany"	200
	"Joseph Chance"	40
Samuel Plummer, Jr.	pt. "Plummers Delight"	50
William Maclain	"Plummers Hunting Lott"	50
Jacob Sinn	"No Name" – Jacob M. Minshin's land	242
James Perry	pt. "Wickhams Park"	200
James Windor	"Medcalfs Meadows"	100
Lancellot Wilson	"Wilsons Discovery"	53¾
Mary Cramphin	"Cramphins Delight"	100
	"Grandmothers Delight"	150
22:1755:29 ...		
h/o Edmund Cartlidge	"Hickory Tavern"	200

Tobias Belt (PG)	"Lost Hatchet"	192
	"Cronoho"	290
	"Belts Delight"	120
Matthew Lodge	"Deer Stone"	150
Casper Cregar	"Mount Pleasant"	150
Thomas Dawson	"Mothers Delight"	200
	"Addition to Mothers Delight"	200
Henry Truman (PG)	"Resurvey on Dawsons Purchase"	215¾
h/o Richard Purnell (AA)	pt. "Wickhams & Pottingers Discovery"	100
	"Newbury"	98
Zachariah Lanham	"Addition to Remains"	100
William Hardey	pt. "Addition to Remains"	100
William Waters	pt. "Charles & Benjamin"	152
	"Edmonstons Refuse"	67
Michael Dowden	pt. "Hermitage"	76
	"Hammerhill"	50
	"Lucks All"	64
Ignatius Mitchel (CH)	pt. "Remains" & "Addition to the Remains"	100
	"Mitchels Fancy"	100
22:1755:30 ...		
William Allyburton	pt. "Foxes Den" a/s pt. "Snowdens 2nd Addition to His Mannor"	150
John Lashear	pt. "Foxes Denn" a/s pt. "Snowdens 2nd Addition to His Mannor"	126
John Vantrees	"John Mountain"	128
John Beyne	"Hermitage"	100
	"Saturdays Work"	50
John Bean (Andicatum)	"Any Thing"	50
John Martin, Sr.	pt. "Dulanys Lott"	100
Joseph Bonnett	pt. "Dulanys Lott"	52½
h/o Rev. Hugh Conn	pt. "Josephs Park"	100
Thomas Wilcoxon (PG)	pt. "Josephs Park"	100
James Conn	pt. "Josephs Park"	100
h/o Hon. Daniel Dulany (cnp)	pt. "Conclusion"	956½
	pt. "Middle Plantation"	361
	pt. "Spring Garden"	340

	pt. "Partnership"	100
	"Good Hope"	132
	"Bevison"	100
	"Peapatch"	100
	"Addition to Spring Garden"	436
	pt. "Deer Bought"	200
	"Sasafras Bottom"	100
	"Woolfs Purchase"	100
	"Sawyers Chance"	50
	"Epinah"	100
22:1755:31 ...		
Hon. Daniel Dulany, Esq.	"Albins Choice"	300
	"Locust Level"	3180
	"Williamsbourgh"	1500
	pt. "Dulanys Lott"	2479½
	pt. "Taskers Chance"	850½
	pt. "Taskers Chance"	320
	pt. "Taskers Chance"	290¾
	pt. "Taskers Chance"	153
	pt. "Taskers Chance"	217½
	pt. "Taskers Chance"	40
	"Long Meadow"	550
	"Resurvey on Buck Forrest"	3000
	"Long Meadow Enlargd" composed of: • "Addition to Long Meadow" • "West Addition to Long Meadow"	2131
Luke Barnard	"Bernard Desire"	236
Walter Evans	pt. "Dunghill"	100
	"Beggars Bennison"	50
Ninian Hamilton	"Aberdeen"	100
	"Hamiltons Lott"	50
	"Vacancy Added to Aberdeen"	100
William Plummer	pt. "Bealls Pleasure"	64
Jane Wyval	"Sugar Bottom"	37
Charles Friend	"Swedes Delight"	260
	"Dear Bargain"	25

22:1755:32 ...		
Charles Chaney	pt. "Strife"	50
	"Rich Hill"	60
John Rutter	"Rutters Delight"	100
	"Gaming Alley"	100
Thomas Galtard	"Farewell"	50
William Kelly	"Town Hill"	50
	pt. "Kellys Delight"	426
James Shaw	"Brothers Chance"	223
Maj. George Beall	"Long Life to the Lord Baltimore"	150
	"Rock Dunbarton"	795
	"Addition to Rock Dunbarton"	1380
	"Pens Disappointment"	80
	"Conjurors Disappointment"	46
	pt. "Lubberland"	27
	"Bealls Chance"	100
Miles Foy	"Hunting Bottom"	80
Enock Enocks	"Enocksons Lott"	100
h/o Edward Charlton	"Charltons Forrest"	275
Evan Shelbys	pt. "Maidens Choice"	268
	pt. "Hazard"	100
	"Polks Venture"	10
22:1755:33 ...		
Aaron Riely	"Long Bottom"	126
James Jack	pt. "Mouldy Pone"	50
James Gilliland	"Bigg Spring"	150
	"Bealls Fort"	50
Nicholas Vennemon	"Mouldy Pone"	100
John Williams, Jr.	pt. "Maidens Choice"	100
	"Stable of Stone"	50
Isaac Baker	"Alloway"	150
	"Pleasant Bottom"	226
Michael Risenor	"Spring"	200
Peter Rench (cnp)	"Strife"	150
	"4 Springs"	200
	pt. "Dolittle"	50

	"Resurvey on Hickmans Meadows"	730
	"Penny Pack Pound"	50
	"Resurvey on Spriggs Delight"	387
John Arnold	"Buckshorn"	40
	pt. "Luck"	104
Daniel Arnold	pt. "Rams Horn"	392
	"Goats Horn"	50
	pt. "Luck"	71
	"Friendship"	100
22:1755:34 ...		
Samuel Arnold	"Hogg Yard"	100
	"One Horn"	26
	"Pigg Sty"	54
Col. Thomas Cresap	"Forrest of Need Wood"	146
	pt. "Skythorn"	10
	"Indian Field"	250
	"Conquest"	275
	"3 Fields"	165
	"Good Hope" originally "Indian Fields"	420
	pt. "Skythorn"	95
Jacob Shees – killed by the Indians	pt. "Linton"	91
William Ervin	pt. "Linton"	64
Thomas Cresap, Jr. – killed	"Enocksons Delight"	80
	pt. "Durlings Delight"	75
	"Devils Hole"	128
	"Round Bottom"	96
Daniel Cresap	"Indian Purchase"	330
	"Little Meadow"	50
	"Limestone Rock"	63
	"Vacancy Added to Indian Purchase"	308
Daniel Ashcraft	"Boils Cabbin"	60
	pt. "Skythorn"	65
George Pack	pt. "Skythorn"	30
Barney Fore – killed	pt. "Skythorn"	40
22:1755:35 ...		

Jacob Kellor	pt. "Rams Horn"	102
Thomas Cheney	pt. "Skythorn"	120
	"Chance"	138
William Anderson	"Andersons Delight"	212
William Gilliland	pt. "Durlings Delight"	100
Joseph Tomlinson	"Water Sink"	150
	pt. "Water Sink"	50
	"Vacancy Added to Water Sink"	322
John Feltigraw	"Feltigraw"	150
	"Fats Addition"	120
	"Batchelors Delight"	818½
Andrew Hall	"Lemons Choice"	200
John Lomon	"Addition to Lomons Choice"	40
	"Lemons Lott"	196
	"White Oak Swamp"	50
Samuel Waters	pt. "Charles & Benjamin"	4
Maj. Joseph Ogle	"Peace"	250
	"Peace & Plenty"	750
	"Fountain Low"	1050
	"Content"	210
	pt. "Creve"	50
	"Worleys Delight"	104
	"Resurvey on Black Walnut Bottom"	310
	"Farmers Delight"	440
	"Kingstentad"	100
	"Vacancy Added on Content"	475
22:1755:36 ...		
John Miller	"Grazing Ground"	100
	"Clover Ground"	40
Jeremiah Mullican (PG)	pt. "Charles & Benjamin"	96
Isaac Simmons (Andicatum)	"Charltons Rack"	100
	"Simmons Rack"	200
	pt. "Simmons Rack"	245
Susannah Beatty	pt. "Dulanys Lott" & pt. "Rocky Creek"	298
	pt. "Providence"	72

Thomas Beatty	pt. "Dulanys Lott"	158
	"Well Water'd Bottom"	76
	"Mackeys Choice"	50
Peter Cripple	pt. "Beattys Venture"	100
William Beatty	pt. "Dulanys Lott"	268
h/o John Beatty	pt. "Dulanys Lott"	166
	pt. "Rocky Creek"	85
James Brookes, Jr.	pt. "Brooks Grove"	12
	"Younger Brother"	146
	"Knee Deep"	150
h/o James Beatty	pt. "Dulanys Lott" & pt. "Rocky Creek"	213½
22:1755:37 ...		
James Brookes, Sr.	pt. "Brookes Grove"	3142
	pt. "Brothers Content"	222
	pt. "Charly Forrest"	1080
	"Fork"	100
	"Brooke Chance"	20
	"Crows Content"	150
	"Brooke Park Resurveyed"	1040
	pt. "Snowdens Mannor Inlargd"	392
	pt. "2nd Addition to Snowdens Mannor Inlargd"	218
	"Long Choice"	50
	"Brookes Black Meadow"	262
	"Brookes Bottom"	584
	"Small Gams"	520
	"Discovery"	119
	"Addition to Brookes Discovery on the Rich Land"	9105½
Johannes Middaugh	pt. "Dulanys Lott" & pt. "Rocky Creek"	251
Agnes Beatty or John Kimbold	pt. "Dulanys Lott" & pt. "Rocky Creek"	300
Benjamin Stoddart	pt. "Friendship"	230
Zachariah Maccubbin	pt. "Friendship"	380
	pt. "Pritchetts Purchase"	81½
William Ray	pt. "Charles & Thomas"	70
Robert Masters	"Thorough Fare"	100

Richard Simmons (PG)	pt. "Gittings Hah Hah"	200
	pt. "Wickhams & Pottingers Discovery"	100
22:1755:38 ...		
h/o Charles Higginbotham	"Charly Mount"	300
	pt. "Pyles Delight"	95
	"Aldriges Purchase" pt. "Pyles Delight" & pt. "Bed. Green"	8
William Flintham	"Neglect"	150
Conrod Cross	"Foutz Delight"	150
George Kersner	"Dutch Folly"	100
	"Addition to Dutch Folly"	100
Michael Kirkpatrick	"Narrow Point"	50
John William Smith a/s Deelman Washabaw	"Smiths Field"	150
h/o Edward Fotterrell	"Colters Hall"	100
Isaac Plummer	"Tradeland"	40
William Spurgeon	pt. "Andicatum Bottom"	50
John Shepherd	pt. "Andicatum Bottom"	50
John Vandeaver	pt. "Andicatum Bottom"	50
James Spurgeon	"Trenton"	120
	pt. "Stoney Hill"	50
22:1755:39 ...		
Nathaniel Foster	pt. "Andicatum Bottom"	25
Margarett Foster	pt. "Andicatum Bottom"	25
Joseph Mayhew	"Chidleys Range"	100
	"Addition of Chidleys Range"	80
John Moore	pt. "Andicatum Bottom"	50
Michael Cregar	"Anchor & Hope"	150
	"Batchelors Hall"	40
Ames Thatcher	"Johns Bottom"	100
Matthias Stalkolp	"Poormans Lose" originially called "Matthias"	144
Buttler Evans	"Evans Content"	20
Thomas Elder	pt "Dann"	100
Samuel Ellis	pt. "Chance Resurveyed"	273
h/o Isaac Wells	"Low Land"	100
	pt. "Childrens Chance"	173

Henry Thomas	"Perrys Lott"	50
	"Vacancy Added"	75
22:1755:40 ...		
John Henthorn	"St. John Resurveyed"	218
h/o Charles Polk	"Henthorns Rest"	100
William Hynes	"Polks Meadow"	100
h/o John Harding	pt. "Hardins Choice"	126
John Harding	pt. "Ganders Delight"	62
James Walling	"Dumb Hall"	50
	"Wifes Choice"	50
	"Taken in Time"	100
James Walling, Jr.	"Adventure"	50
George Moore (Andicatum)	"Moores Delight"	50
William Elder, Sr.	"Black Walnut Bottom"	100
	pt. "Ogles Good Will"	107
	pt. "Arnolds Delight"	300
	"Elders Choice"	240
	"Vacancy Added to Black Walnut Bottom"	234
William Elder, Jr.	"Beaver Dam Level"	100
	"Addition to Beaver Dam Level"	43
22:1755:41 ...		
Jacob Matthias	"Slate Ridge"	123
Edward Diggs & others	"Brothers Agreement"	60
	"Brothers Tryal"	30
	"Vacancy Added to Brothers Agreement"	7840
John Digges (cnp)	pt. "Chance"	25
	"Clarks Discovery"	100
	"Richards Hunting Ground"	366
	pt. "Justices Delight"	150
	"Rich Levels"	352
	"Williams Intention"	246
	"Bear Garden"	568
	"Spring Plains"	848
	"Hazel Valley"	118
	"Meadows"	172
	"Disappointment"	182

	"Cedar Clift"	290
	pt. "Digges Choice"	222
	"Vacancy Added to Digges Lott"	973
Mark Furney	pt. "Digges Choice"	150
George Unkafore	pt. "Digges Lott"	150
Benjamin Biggs	pt. "Digges Lott"	25
	"Benjamins Good Luck"	100
	pt. "Benjamins Good Luck"	43
John Ramsey	"Labyrinth"	100
John & Thomas Fletchall	"Two Brothers"	200
22:1755:42 ...		
John Justice	pt. "Justices Delight"	100
John Davis s/o Richard	pt. "Dear Bought"	58
Charles Coates	"Flints Grove"	100
h/o Edward Gillmore	"Owens Rest"	107
John Burgiss	"Stone Hill"	50
h/o John Sittern	"Desire"	47
Thomas Maynard	"Forrest"	60
	"Maynards Chance"	50
William Turner	"Turners Promise"	50
	"Turners Lott"	40
John Cook (Rock Creek)	"Turleys Choice"	50
	"Cooks Choice"	87½
	pt. "Dublin Resurveyed"	50
James Turley	pt. "Rattle Snake Denn"	100
Mark Speagler	"Stulls Choice"	100
	"Hickory Bottom"	26
	"Marks Delight"	26
	"Speaglers Addition to Stulls Device"	50
22:1755:43 ...		
Rev. William Williams	"Green Bottom"	250
	"Williams Project"	250
h/o Maj. Henry Munday	"Truro"	844
Evan Jones	"Jones Lott"	100
	"Evans Chance"	50

George Reed	"New Seat"	300
	"Earl Douglas & Earl Piercy"	73
George Swinyard	pt. ~~"Lost Spring"~~ a/s "George & Margaret" (50 a.)	150
George Hutsell	pt. ~~"Lost Spring"~~ a/s "George & Margaret"	55
George Clem	pt. ~~"Lost Spring"~~ "George & Margaret"	50
	"George & Margaret" – not to be charged	150
Edward Shippen	"Addition to Lafferdays Lott"	186
	"Addition"	52
William Collier	"Stubb Hill"	100
	"Elders Delight"	50
	pt. "Dann"	67
Edmund Rutter	pt. "Strife"	50
William Bowill	"Monocon"	50
	"Frywoll"	58
22:1755:44 ...		
John Friend	"Hogg Hall"	66
James McCullin	"Chesnuts Levels"	50
h/o Godfrey Mong	"Delight"	100
Abraham Neighbours	"Abrahams Choice"	50
David Jones	pt. "Bakers Purchase"	100
	"Addition to Bakers Purchase"	100
Baltis Miller	pt. "Bakers Purchase"	100
Joseph Beall	pt. "Layhill"	649½
John Clegatt, Jr.	pt. "Clegatts Purchase"	286
	pt. "Pritchetts Purchase"	32½
Charles Brooke (PG)	pt. "Dann"	150
John Pigman	pt. "Charly Forrest"	50
Frederick Fiscus	"Catail Marsh"	200
Henry Holland Hawkins, Jr.	"Grandfathers Gift"	305
h/o Col. Thomas Lee (MD)	"Backland"	350
22:1755:45 ...		
h/o MM Edward & Osborn Sprigg	"Swedeland"	150
Thomas Brookes (PG)	pt. "4 Gallons & ½ of Rum"	300
James Docker	"Dockers Mite"	40
William Roberts (Pipe Creek)	"Broom Wood" a/s "Brierwood"	200

James Dickson	"Matthews Lott"	100
	"Content"	112
	"Chance on Beaver Creek"	100
	"Dicksons Struggle"	229
	"Whisky Alley"	115
	"Secret Bottom"	104
	"Stoney Range"	54
Andrew Coombs	"Town Ollaway Lick"	100
Madam Lucy Brooke (PG)	pt. "Dann"	947
Charles Clegatt s/o John & Philip Busey	pt. "Dann"	200
Edward Birtch (PG)	pt. "Dann"	100
	pt. "Division Syth"	29
Francis Burrill, Jr.	"Burrills Choice"	50
Francis Burrill, Sr.	"Burrills Bower"	50
22:1755:46 ...		
Daniel Vears	pt. "Dublin Resurveyed"	60
	"Rum Punch"	60
Samuel Farmer	"Jack of the Green"	100
	"Vacancy on Jack of the Green"	386
Charles Trayle	"Trayles Choice"	50
	pt. "Buxtons Delight Resurveyed"	102
William Fields	"Bedfordshire Carrier"	108
Lewis Duvall	"Inmans Plains"	50
	"Griffins Chance"	60
Christian Ketchindaner	"Christians Choice"	100
	"Alamangle"	50
	"Frankford Resurveyed"	200
	"Vacancy Added to Choice"	830
Margarett Harn	pt. "3 Cousins Resurveyed"	22
	pt. "3 Cousins Resurveyed"	50
	pt. "3 Cousins Resurveyed"	18
Allen Killogh	pt. "3 Cousins Resurveyed"	401
	"Sixth Addition"	52
Handle Barrick	"Mill Place"	100

Robert Birchfield	"Roberts Purchase"	50
	"Crooked Piece"	50
22:1755:47 ...		
Thomas McPherson (CH)	"Dann"	100
Arthur Charlton	"Charltons Purchase"	100
	"Friendship"	106
William Downey	"Walnut Point"	164
	"Downeys Contrivance"	61
James Crouch	"Pleasant Valley"	84
	"Vacancy Added to Pleasant Valley"	324
John Mobberly	pt. "Mount Pleasant"	86
	"Rich Levels"	120
	"Vacancy Added to Mount Pleasant"	50
Benjamin Warfield	"Walnut Ridge"	278
John Pool	"Pools Delight"	100
John Jones	"Mill Race"	10
David Watson	"Sarah's Delight"	90
	"Sarah's Delight"	500
	"Harrys Grave"	140
	"Nicholls Mistake"	10
22:1755:48 ...		
Dr. James Doull	"James Field"	100
	"Finus Coronat Opus"	290
	"Doulls Chance"	143
	"Doulls Folly"	166
	"20 Acres"	20
	"Hay Park"	40
	"Hunting Park"	50
	"Doulls Discovery"	123
	"Controversy"	15
Charles Hedge	"Hedges Delight"	192
	"Charles & Mary"	100
	"Whisky"	100
John Wauford	pt. "William & John"	15
	"Cumberland"	25

Edward Northcraft	pt. "William & John"	85
	"Molls Rattle"	25
Thomas Wilson (Pipe Creek)	pt. "Rock Land"	100
	"Addition to Rock Land"	50
	"Vacancy Added to Rock Land" now "Susans Fancy"	400
Thomas Wilson (Toms Creek)	"Disappointment"	46
	"Marys Fancy"	104
James Beall s/o Ninian	"Poplar Spring"	150
h/o Charles Scaggs	"Scaggs Delight"	30
James Ford	"Turnip Patch"	60
22:1755:49 ...		
George Lambert	"Lambert"	200
Daniel Lafever	"Resurvey on Bonnets Resolution"	400
Martin Whetsal	"Wine Garden" – not to be charged	150
	"Resurvey on Bonnets Resolution"	250
Allen Farquer	pt. "Dulanys Lott"	100
	"Chance"	118
Uler Misler	"Locust Thickett"	50
Joseph Flint	pt. "Darlings Delight"	50
	"Grassy Bottom"	66
	"Morgans Choice"	50
	"Morriss Chase"	100
Philip Davis	"Save All"	50
Notley Thomas	"Hazard"	150
	"London Beginning"	60
Andrew Barland	"Woodyard"	60
	"Green Castle"	100
John Thompson	"Thompson's Adventure"	50
h/o Patrick Matthews	"Mullingate"	100
22:1755:50 ...		
Nicholas Ridenour	"Nicholas Ridenours Pound"	100
David Candler	"Swingabarker"	100
h/o Matthias Reeslin	"Beaver Dam"	100
	"Ogles Good Will"	100
Richard Collyer	pt. "Token of Love"	96

Thomas Ford	"Upper Indian Bottom"	200
John Hamilton	"Hamiltons Recovery"	100
Henry Child (AA)	"Wickhams & Pottingers Discovery"	100
Youth Cope	"Range"	420
Nathan Veatch	"Round Knowl"	100
Colmore Beans (PG)	"Colmore Ramble"	66
	pt. "Addition to James"	200
Frederick Havenor	"Rich Bottom"	75
	pt. "Taskers Chance"	171
John Chambers (Annapolis)	"Bear Denn"	100
22:1755:51 ...		
Christopher Lowndes	pt. "Hermitage"	300
	"Last Choice"	120
	"Matthews Good Will"	176
	pt. "Taskers Chance"	260
	"Bakers Ramble"	50
	"Salisbury Plains"	50
John Chambers	pt. "Stumps Valley"	66½
Samuel Plummer, Sr.	"Food Plenty"	167
	"Rich Hills"	198
	"Hunting Lott"	226
	"Rocky Hill"	170
	"Supply"	100
	"Hickory Plains"	454
Joseph Plummer s/o Samuel	"Pleasant Meadow"	184
Peter Mier	"Cool Spring"	188
William Morgan	"Thomas Forrest"	100
Adam Spaugh	"Addition to the Sandy Elizabeth"	100
Bazil Beckwith	"Garter Lost"	200
Peter Dent, Jr.	"Crabby Street"	100
Daniel Slagle	"Sinking Spring"	100
22:1755:52 ...		
h/o Baltis Foutz	"Boiling Spring"	47
William Tracey	"Tracey's Desire"	60
Robert Ward	"Grubby Hill"	50
Edward Brawner	"Elders Kindness"	100

James Trayle	"Rock Head"	60
William Norris, Jr.	"Rays Venture"	150
Conrod Hawkersmith	"Low Mill"	100
	"Long Mill"	50
Thomas Lazure	"Square"	50
David Delander	"David's Choice"	100
John Reeter	"Higginbothams Exchange" – not to be charged	100
<t> Stilley	"Sapling Ridge Resurveyed"	195
	"Sapling Ridge"	100
Robert Twigg	"Bear Range"	50
	"Jericho"	44
22:1755:53 ...		
Samuel Yeaman	"Hannahs Purchase"	50
William Hickman	"Three Springs"	100
John Smith	"New Germany"	50
	"Addition to New Germany"	50
	"Come at Last"	50
Christian Kemp	"Kemps Delight"	100
	"Dispatch"	230
	"Kemps Long Meadow"	600
	"Resurvey on Good Luck"	639
	"Great Desire"	82
	pt. "Delight"	50
	"Hunters Delight"	50
h/o John Thompson	"Griffiths Park"	500
Francis Gatteral	"Grave Lott"	50
Henry Leek	pt. "Gittings Hah Hah"	200
	"Leeks Lott"	50
	pt. "Leeks Lott"	107
John Veach	pt. "Progress"	83
	"Pheasant Nest"	100
	pt. "Poplar Spring"	220
Absalom Wilson	pt. "Forrest"	100
22:1755:54 ...		
Joseph Belt s/o Ben	pt. "Joseph Park"	326½
Wadworth & Thomas Wilson	"St. Thomas"	150

John Young	"Backland" a/s "Arnolds Delight"	100
	"Resurvey on Switzerland"	103
William Murdock s/o Parson	pt. "Discovery"	268
h/o John Masterson	pt. "Bear Bacon"	176
Benjamin Ricketts	pt. "Snowdens Addition to His Mannor"	134
	"Green Marsh"	78
John Perrins	"Perrins Adventure"	222
Michael Thomas	"Inlet"	60
Daniel Pettenger	"Reyington Plains"	261
h/o Peter Studybaker	pt. "Bakers Lookout" & "Bakers Lott"	265
	"Shoemakers Purchase"	63
	"Woolfs Lott"	100
John Long	pt. "Bakers Lookout"	100
Robert Brightwell	pt. "Skythorn"	60
22:1755:55 ...		
Nicholas Fink	"Prevention"	50
	"Vacancy Added to Prevention"	184
	"Arabia"	208
Peter Bomgarner	pt. "Nazareth" – not to be charged	100
Joseph Wellcomott	pt. "Dutch Folly"	34
	pt. "Dutch Folly"	78
	"Free Stone"	100
	pt. "Nazareth"	100
	pt. "Dutch Folly"	66
James Balding	pt. "Wickhams & Pottingers Discovery"	100
John Hawkins, Jr.	pt. "Magruders & Bealls Honesty"	101
	"Forrest of Need Wood"	300
	"John Priscilla"	125
	"Hawkins Island"	125
	"Hawkins Merry Peep of Day" composed of: • "Coxons Rest" • "Chance the Refuse" • "Haw Meadow"	3100
William Beall s/o Nin	pt. "Jovial Ramble"	109
Nathaniel Wickham (cnp)	"Salisbury Plains"	50
	pt. "Chance"	25
	"Pawpaw Thickett"	160

	"Turkey Thickett"	100
	"Locust Thickett"	190
	pt. "Fountain Low"	300
	"Good Luck"	80
	"Butlers Gift"	50
22:1755:56 ...		
Nin Beall s/o Nin	pt. "Dispute"	200
	"Barren Hill"	100
	"Gravely Ridge"	50
Arthur Nelson	pt. "Nelsons Island"	56
	"Nelsons Adventure"	97
	pt. "Nelsons Island"	24
	pt. "Nelsons Island"	150
	"Hobsons Choice"	60
	pt. "Chance"	25
	"Huckleberry Levels"	38
Josiah Clapham	"Broken Island"	45
John Tramel, Jr. (VA)	pt. "Nelsons Island"	136
Uriah Virgin	pt. "Dickisons Delight"	133
h/o John Dickison	"Dickisons Chance"	30
Serratt Dickison	"John & James Choice"	150
Abell Brown	"Abells Levells" – not to be charged	400
John Sturrum	"Hoosers Choice"	110
Thomas Witten	"Small Hope"	60
	"Vacancy Added"	142
Jacob Brunner	"Inlet"	25
	pt. "Taskers Chance"	248
	"Resurvey"	730
22:1755:57 ...		
William Fee	2nd, 3rd, & 4th Lott originally called "Batchelors Purchase" or "Burridges Lott"	49½
Jacob Clount	"Hollow Spring"	100
Steffell Shagh	"Half Moon"	108
John Patsall	"Blacksmiths Lott"	50
	"Smiths Lott"	50
John Hamilton (BA)	"Oval"	100

Lodowicke Davis	"Lodowicks Range"	150
	"Benjamin's Square"	50
	"Davis's Content"	50
h/o John House	"Strife"	100
	pt. "Andicatum Bottom"	50
	"Two Wives"	33
	"Houses Addition"	70
	"Mill Place"	25
	"Walnut Point"	100
Stephen Gatteral	"Gatterals Venture"	100
	pt. "Leeks Lott"	78
	"Vacancy Added to Leeks Lott"	238
Jacob Staley, Sr.	"Switzerland"	150
	"Othersum"	423
	"Good Wife"	87
Jacob Staley, Jr.	"Creams Quietness"	100
22:1755:58 ...		
Adam Mayner	"White Gravel Spring" – not to be charged	190
George Bond	"Sawpit"	150
	"Forrest"	100
Adam Stull	pt. "Chesnut Hill"	175
John Stull (near Frederick Town)	pt. "Chesnut Hill"	75
Robert Owens	"Horse Shoe"	96
Thomas Harris (Monococy)	"Pleasant Levells"	50
	"Maidens Point"	100
	"Boxes Search"	96
	"Vacancy Added to Boxes Search"	490
George Buckhannan	"Brotherly Love"	64
David Scott	"Charltons Victory"	50
Matthew Pigman	"Rich Bottom"	15
	"Very Good"	100
	"Timber Point"	10
	"Good Soil"	78
Martha Lakin w/o Abraham	"James & Marriots Lott"	100
Joseph Lakin	pt. "Two Brothers"	50

22:1755:59 ...		
Abraham Lakin	"Lakins Lott"	50
	"Resurvey on Two Brothers"	196
Peter Shaver	"Palatine"	100
h/o John Kennedy	"Resurvey on Dublin" – not to be charged	981
James Brown	"Browns Desire"	50
	"Browns Delight"	100
George Bond, Jr.	"Meshahear's Garden"	200
Joseph Wilson (Monococy)	"Boys Lott" – not to be charged	100
	"Mill Trace" – not to be charged	93
	"Roberts Delight"	300
John & Benjamin Maccinely	"Benjamins Inspection"	300
John Campbell (AA)	"Johns Good Luck"	130
	"Partnership"	300
	"Johns Delight"	59
Jacob Wellor	"Taylors Lott"	200
	"Taylors Prick Louse"	50
	"Taylors Sheers"	50
John Wellor	"Beauty"	50
Charles Davis s/o Griffin	"Daviss Forrest"	70
George Matthews	pt. "Good Luck"	212
	"Davis's Delight"	100
William Hays	"Dove Harbour"	90
22:1755:60 ...		
William Chambers	"Chambers Desire"	44
Ignatius Perry	"Perrys Delight" a/s "Woolfs Denn"	100
h/o John Parr	"Parrs Range"	100
	"Bushes Creek Hill" – not to be charged	100
Robert Constable	"Constables Range"	100
Lawrence Cregar	"Cregars Delight"	100
	"Longapow"	240
	"Resurvey on Middle Choice"	380
	"Vacancy Added to Cregars Delight"	275
Elias Brunner	pt. "Taskers Chance"	303
h/o Francis Wise	pt. "Taskers Chance"	206
	"Stumbling Block"	10

Casper Myer	pt. "Taskers Chance"	273
Jacob Sturrum	pt. "Taskers Chance"	202
h/o Peter Hufman	pt. "Taskers Chance"	225
Christian Thomas	pt. "Taskers Chance"	209½
George Loy	pt. "Taskers Chance"	213
	"Lambson Resurveyed"	196
22:1755:61 ...		
Henry Sinn	pt. "Taskers Chance"	145
Gilbert Kemp	pt. "Taskers Chance"	220
	"Peace & Quietness"	50
	"Willbersign"	30
	"Kemps Lott"	3
Frederick Kemp	"Lowkemper"	150
	pts. "Kemps Lott"	7
	"Kemps Bottom"	55
Melcor Wharfield	pt. "Taskers Chance"	352¾
Henry Brunner	pt. "Taskers Chance"	215
	pt. "Georges Discovery"	100
	"Chesnut Valley"	25
Stephens Ransberger	pt. "Taskers Chance"	465
	"Shoemakers Choice"	100
	"Stony Hill"	100
	"Ransbergs Chance"	190
	"Vacancy Added to Stony Hill" & "Shoemakers Choice"	282½
Conrod Kellor	pt. "Taskers Chance"	159
	"Zara"	208
h/o Abraham Miller	"Millers Chance"	100
	"Coopers Point"	200
22:1755:62 ...		
h/o Robert Debutts	"Debutts Hunting Lott"	72
	"Sun is Down & Moon is Up"	500
h/o Jacob Stoner	pt. "Taskers Chance"	571¾
	"Isaacs Inheritance"	200
	"Stoners Chance"	75

Henry Threlkeld	pt. "Salop"	300
	pt. "Salop"	265
	pt. "Knaves Disappointment"	64
	pt. "Friendship"	400
Christopher Ellis	"Beginning"	50
Jacob Mellor	"Meadows"	33
	"Swamp"	50
William Ridgley (AA)	"Pocoson"	13
	"Hobsons Choice"	337
	"Round About Hill"	12
	"Jones Addition"	40
	"Ridgelys Ridge"	50
	"Macks Delight"	50
MM Robert & Thomas Dunlop	"Hazell Thickett"	100
	"Addition to Hazell Thickett"	50
Thomas Taylor	pt. "Addition to Hazell Thickett"	50
	"Mount Pleasant"	50
	"Vacancy Added to Hazell Thickett"	386
22:1755:63 ...		
Thomas Trasher	"Thrashers Lott"	110
h/o Henry Futney	"Deer Spring"	200
Alexander Warfield s/o John	"Warfields Vineyard"	270
Robert Miller	pt. "Brothers Generosity" a/s "Pork Hall"	587
Alexander Warfield s/o Richard	pt. "Stringers Chance"	195
John Booser	pt. "Maidens Choice"	24
	"Good Luck Resurveyed"	245
David Davis	"Phillips Disappointment"	50
George Hartman	"Hartman"	100
Jacob Henry	pt. "Good Luck"	100
Leonard Decose	"Leonards Frolick"	50
Melcor Staley	"Masswander"	30
	"Onodrandy"	7½
Daniel Matthews	pt. "Georges Discovery"	75
	"Daniels Addition"	25
22:1755:64 ...		

Michael Jesserangs	"Piney Neck"	100
	"Vacancy Added to Piney Neck"	115
Edward Lamb	"Lambs Choice"	150
	pt. "Good Fellowship"	100
	"Vacancy Added to Good Fellowship"	1212
William Durbin	pt. "Good Fellowship"	50
Henry Coocus	"Shear Spring"	100
	pt. "Shear Spring"	135
	"Vacancy Added to Shear Spring"	960
William Kerly	"St. Patricks Colt" originally "St. Patrick" – not to be charged	127
Edward Stevenson, Jr.	"Cromwells Resurvey"	213
	"Leonards Range"	100
Henry Avey	"Scotts Lott"	202
Valentine Myre	"St. Michaels Fancy Resurveyed"	186
John Nicholas	"Addition to Woolf Pit"	50
George Gew	"St. George That Slew the Woolf"	50
22:1755:65 ...		
Jacob Peck	pt. "Addition"	100
	"Pecks Resolution"	50
h/o William Richardson	pt. "4th Snowdens Addition to His Mannor"	200
William Richardson	pt. "2nd Addition to Snowdens Mannor"	218
William Kersey	"Gravely Spring"	56
Jacob Ambrosier	"Gap"	100
h/o Samuel Hyde	pt. "Progress"	176
	pt. "Concord"	553
	pt. "Conclusion"	956½
	pt. "Middle Plantation"	361
	"William & Elizabeth"	150
John Stull	"Shoal Spring" a/s "Sher Spring"	150
	"Pleasant Hill"	90
h/o John Stull	"Whiskey"	380
	"Stulls Addition to Whiskey"	160
Matthias Gray	"Grays Delight"	50
	"Grays Choice"	10
	"Grays Neck"	119

Joseph Wood (Pipe Creek)	pt. "Woods Lott"	587
Matthew Jones	"Jones Addition"	20
22:1755:66 ...		
Mary Jones	"Fletchall"	253
Nicholas Baker	"Hazard"	300
	pt. "Knaves & Richards Dispute"	133
	"Pig Pen"	50
	"Woolf Pit"	50
	"Lost Hammer"	104
Moses Shelby – David Brown	"Hunts Cabbin"	310
John Hughes	"William & John"	50
	"Retreat"	15
William Loveday	"Exchange"	100
Thomas Mills	pt. "Batchelors Hall"	50
	"Lanes Fields Resurveyed"	231
	"Conclusion"	56
Michael Mills	pt. "Batchelors Hall"	50
	"Turkey Hill"	87
James Burgiss	"Burgiss Choice"	50
	"Halseys Folly"	50
Benjamin Hiskitt	"Hiskitts Choice"	50
Owen McDonald	"Watsons Welfare" – not to be charged	100
22:1755:67 ...		
h/o Martin Earnest	"Martins Intention"	31
William Matthews	"Widows Rest"	100
William Dyal	"Dyals Delight"	50
Richard Watts	"Susannah & Elizabeth"	50
	"Addition to Susannah & Elizabeth"	150
	pt. "Burtons Delight Resurveyed"	188
Edward Mobberly	"I Lookt Many Places Now I Like"	100
	"Peace & Quietness"	68
Michael Ramar	"Meadows"	150
John Owens	"Rich Plains"	100
	"Owens Choice"	80
Andrew Bawler	pt. "Delight"	50
Robert French (CV)	pt. "Ridge & Knaves Delight"	100

Shadrach Hiatt	pt. "Hermitage"	101
John Nichols (Linton Hundred)	"Butter & Cheese"	80
Jeremiah Virgin	pt. "Dicksons Delight"	100
22:1755:68 ...		
Jonathan Hagar	"Hagers Delight" composed of: • "Higgenbothoms Exchange" • "Dicksons Rest" • "Dicksons Fatiguing Journey"	1474
Joseph Farress	"Farress Delight"	200
James Odell	"Bally Cristie"	303
Joseph Robinett	pt. "Pyles Delight"	129
	pt. "Pyles Delight"	17
William Williams	"Williams Range"	132
	"Red Quarter"	21
	pt. "Conclusion"	200
	"Pretty Botty"	30
	"All I Can Get"	40
Charles Fenly	"Nonsuch" – not to be charged	136
Edward Crow	"Shady Grove"	50
	"Addition to Shady Grove"	54
	"Abells Levells"	400
Jacob Fry	"Frys Habitation"	80
	"Frys Addition"	50
Uncle Uncles	pt. "Cromwells Resurvey"	219
	"Buck Range"	100
22:1755:69 ...		
Joseph Haines	pt. "Cromwells Resurvey"	250
	"Addition to Cromwell"	50
	"Pleasant Grove"	52
	"Haines Chance"	54
John Ryley	pt. "Chesnut Ridge"	219
	"Ryleys Chance"	80
Daniel Spangle	"High Spring"	100
Jacob Ducatt	"Flag Pond"	406
John Mason	"Masons Folly"	17
Martin Hilderbridle	"Providence"	50

Nathan Manyard	"Maynards Good Will"	50
John Nash	"Joy Reach"	40
John Simpson	"Simpsons Garden"	35
	"Vacancy Added to Simpsons Garden"	104
Thomas Hawkins	"Uncles Gift"	160
22:1755:70 ...		
John Ross, Esq. (AA)	"Woolf Pit"	100
	"Wingfields Delight Resurveyed"	1300
	"Plains"	50
	"Resurvey on Ross's Range"	3271
	"New London"	1360
	"Long Hope"	100
	"Ross Town Creek Lott"	530
	"Corner"	112
	"Addition to the Discovery"	80
	"Resurvey on Black Oak Hill"	647
Andrew Young	"Sapplin Hill"	100
	pt. "Ross's Range"	129
Samuel Kelly	pt. "Hunting the Hare"	50
Daniel Kelly	pt. "Hunting the Hare"	50
h/o Rev. John Lang	"Inverness"	575
Joseph Chapline (cnp)	"Rush Bottom"	100
	"Josephs Chance"	100
	"Abstons Forrest"	156
	"Content"	100
	pt. "Exchange"	25
	"Hills & Dales"	45
	"Watsons Welfare"	260
	"Batchelors Delight"	100
	"Nazarite"	100
	"Ticknack"	54
	"Policy"	40
	"Hopewell"	104
	"Little Good"	50
	"Bad Enough"	136
	"Addition to Toms Gift"	50

	"Learning"	50
22:1755:71 ...		
Casper Schaff	pt. "Exchange"	75
Bartholomew Booker	"Mondall"	66
Thomas Kelly	pt. "Hunting the Hare"	50
	pt. "Kellys Purchase"	206
John Mcfaden	pt. "Kellys Purchase"	50
John Woodfield	pt. "Hunting the Hare"	50
Edmund Martin	"Martins Choice"	35
George Smith	"Catail Branch"	100
	"Vacancy on Catail Branch"	398
John Greenup	"Red Oak Slipe"	32
John Prather s/o William	"William & John"	100
	"Prathers Adventure"	75
	"Turkey Delight"	25
George French	"Georges Venture"	50
	"Barren"	100
Josiah Darby	"Darbys Delight"	125
Jacob Roarer (PA)	"Hagars Fancy"	507
22:1755:72 ...		
Caleb Dorsey (AA)	"Sparks Chance"	50
	"Harveysborough"	50
	"Slate Hill"	50
	"Sparkes Round"	50
	"Benjamins Folly"	50
	"Calebs Delight"	375
	"Vacancy Added to Calebs Delight"	1465
Jacob Roarer (MD)	"Roarers Lott"	50
	"Addition to Roarers Lott"	100
	"Wetor"	10
	"Defiance"	90
	"Rushia Corner"	50
	"Rorars Fancy"	100
	"Dry Pond"	100
Frederick Roarer	pt. "Defiance"	10

Cornelius Poleson	"Polsons Chance"	50
	"Vacancy Added to Polsons Chance"	56
George Winters	"Batchelors Hall"	125
	"Winters Addition to Batchelors Hall"	75
Joshua Hickman	"Elizabeth"	121
	"Beersheba"	179
Kennedy Farrell	"Fortune"	100
William Ingleman	"Carpouch"	50
22:1755:73 ...		
Daniel Steuart	"Indianfield"	50
Robert Leath	"Samuells Lott"	50
Lodowicke Miller	"Toms Chance"	150
Capt. Thomas Prather	"Choice"	185
	"Richards Choice"	100
	"Dutchmans Misfortune"	100
William Raymon	"Wards Spring"	200
William Wheat	"Wheats Purchase"	100
Garah Davis	"Ganders Delight"	64¼
	"Addition to Ganders Delight"	70
	"Whiskey"	282
Barnard Wymer	"Addition"	100
	"Sandy Run"	150
George Clapsadle	"Empty Cupboard"	112
	"Addition to Empty Cupboard"	42
Valentine Skydaker	pt. "Sandy Run"	50
John Wymer	"Weymer Chages"	100
John Casteel	"Little Worth"	50
22:1755:74 ...		
Matthew Sparks	pt. "Bedfordshire Carrier"	68
William McCoy	"Dutchmans Request" originally "Maidens Choice"	148
Jacob Judith	pt. "Dutchmans Request" originally "Maidens Choice"	3
Martin Casner	"Youngs Folly"	50
John Bailey	"Mountain"	50
Catherine Jennings (Annapolis) (cnp)	"Good Luck"	87
	"Three Springs"	525

	"Widows Chance"	108
John Worthington (AA)	"Whiskey Ridge"	500
	pt. "Whiskey Ridge"	563
John Ridgley	"Disappointment"	46
William Gibson	"Gibsons Chance"	100
Thomas Boilstone	"Boilstones Discovery"	39
Andrew Hoover	"Addition to Misery Spring"	50
	"Misery Spring"	50
Abberhart Appler	"Deeps"	220
22:1755:75 ...		
Joseph Dodderidge	"Andicatum Levells"	50
John Everatt	"Goose Quarter"	125
Adam Miers	"Black Oak Hill"	50
	"Miers Pleasure"	175
	"White Gravel Spring"	190
Ninian Ryley	"Haly"	100
Caleb Touchstone	"Rich Thickett"	10
	"Whiskey Alley"	10
Philip Kiefalper	pt. "Whiskey Alley"	67
Joseph Smith	"Elswicks Dwelling"	180
	pt. "Elswicks Dwelling"	99
	"Smiths Purchase"	63
Edward Bucey	"Black Walnuts Plains"	100
Charles Wood	"Charles Choice"	350
Teter Meisner	"Stoney Hill"	50
Frederick Woolhide	"Jerusalem"	75
Henry Bitzall	"Smiths Hap"	100
Michael Haines	"Meadows"	75
	"Pleasant Springs"	100
22:1755:76 ...		
John Howard s/o Gideon (cnp)	"Pretty Sally"	20
	"2nd Adventure"	54
	pt. "Woods Lott"	94
	"Bears Forrest" a/s "Parrs Forest"	30
	"Many Glades"	25
	"Chance"	50

	"Locut Woods"	25
	"Good Range"	125
	"Lime Stone Land"	20
Dr. Charles Carroll (Annapolis) (cnp)	"Sluce Gallon"	50
	"Iron Hill"	31
	"Iron Mountain"	250
	"Shelbys Misfortune"	250
	"Carrolls Range"	390
	"Hoyles Home"	100
	"Halferstood"	184
	"Carolina"	208
	"Chesnut Ridge"	390
	"Addition"	150
	"Addition to Chesnut Ridge"	70
	"Notch"	18
	"Bear Meadow"	325
	"Forrest"	144
	"Pines"	160
	"Spiglers Addition to Hulls Choice"	50
	"Black Oak"	225
	"Addition to Back Land"	22
	"Barrnes Hills"	55
	"Addition to Strawberry Plains"	40
	"Hoyles Luck"	116
	"Castle Fur"	112
	"Springhead"	96
	"Killmore"	190
	"Bear Den"	355
	"McCoys Delight"	100
	"Turkey Hill"	110
	"Bottom"	56
	"Earnests Choice"	50
	"Long Acre"	144
	"Peters Park"	216
	"Shiers Bottom"	110
	"Holy Gun Forrest"	50

	"Addition to Bear Den"	70
	"Waddels Delight"	60
	"Stoney Meadow"	96
22:1755:77 ...		
Dr. Charles Carroll (Annapolis) (cont.)	"Adventure"	180
	"Lemons Range"	208
	"Charlton"	200
	"Frys Delight"	268
	"Chance Medley"	92
	"Addition to the Pines"	264
	"High Germany" originally called "Catail Marsh"	1254
	"Fellowship"	140
	"Leonards Chance"	46
	"Something"	86
	"Waddells Fancy"	48
	"Jacobs Lott"	48
	"Delays Delight"	82
	"Saplin Valley"	53
	"Logg Cabbin"	220
	"Hazard"	140
	"Trustry Folly"	116
	"Barren Hill"	216
	"Pleasant Meadow"	128
	pt. "Kellys Delight"	607
	"Deep Bottom"	96
	"Kindness"	175
	"Crosbourgh"	50
	"Landstool"	140
	"Michaels Luck"	46
	"Mount Pleasant"	120
	"Escape"	96
	"Watsons Delight"	120
	"Something"	250
	"Wine Garden"	150
Bazil Williams	"Williams Lott"	10
William Purdy	"Howards Rest"	172

22:1755:78 ...		
Richard Waters	pt. "Charles & Benjamin"	152
	pt. "Williams Lott"	30
	"Buck Pond"	50
	"Collins Folly"	11
	"Lucky Range"	14
Edward Dorsey, Esq.	"Brandy Wine Spring Enlarged"	377
	"Brandy Wine Spring"	50
	pt. "Woods Lott"	584
	pt. "Woods Lott"	275
	"Mount Pleasant"	50
	"Addition"	230
	"Resurvey on Pretty Sally"	1244
	"Pleasant Fields" originally called "2nd Adventure"	1394
	"Resurvey on Darbys Delight"	696
	"Rich Forrest"	125
	"Request"	378
	"Second Addition"	72
	"Cold Friday Resurveyed"	2640
	"Resurvey on Millers Chance"	1289
Bazil Dorsey, Sr. (AA)	"Resurvey on Howards Range"	856¼
Michael Havenor	"Vulversham"	50
	"Bull Frog"	50
h/o Darby Lux (BA)	"Canton"	100
	"Hunting Lott"	159
22:1755:79 ...		
Solomon Turner (PG)	pt. "Ralpho"	202
Solomon Turner	"Solomons Flower"	50
Matthias Sayler	"Misery"	50
John Waters, Jr.	"Wards Delight" – wrong	100
	"Wards Delight" – wrong	100
	"Paris" – wrong	100
Samuel Offutt (cnp)	"Offutts Pasture"	613
	"Offutts Adventure"	93
	pt. "Younger Brother"	200
	"Addition to the Pasture"	19

	"Outlet"	8
Phillip Turner	"Turners Delight"	30
Thomas Clegatt Prather	"Maidens Fancy"	100
Benjamin Penn	"Moores Delight"	100
Aquilla Duvall	"Hartleys Delight"	10
Alexander Grant	"Alexander & John"	30
Benjamin Riddle	pt. "Crave"	50
22:1755:80 ...		
Bigger Head	"Matthews Delight"	85
	"Heads Good Luck"	19
	"Heads Industry"	19
Capt. John Dorsey (AA)	pt. "Dorseys Search"	456
	"Mount Pleasant"	400
	"Johns Good Luck"	50
Bazil Dorsey, Jr. s/o Capt. John	pt. "Dorseys Search"	400
Morris Millhouse	pt. "Maidens Choice" a/s "Flaggy Meadow"	160
	pt. "Maidens Choice" a/s "Jamaica"	125
	"Vacancy Added to Flaggy Meadow"	205
Jacob Mier	pt. "Maidens Choice"	190
	pt. "Jamaica" originally "Maidens Choice"	10
William Rivert	pt. "Jamaica" originally "Maidens Choice"	100
Hance Teter	pt. "Maidens Choice"	94
James McDonald	"Galloway"	175
	"McDonalds Chance"	100
	"Isle Aaron"	50
	"Bite the Biter"	144
	"Vacancy Added to Galloway"	140
John Barnwell	"Barwalls Choice"	50
22:1755:81 ...		
John Brazilton	"Levell Spring"	100
	"Exchange"	50
Phillip Jacob Miller	"Ash Swamp"	150
	"Ash Swamp Resurveyed"	140
Michael Miller (cnp)	"Skipton in Craven"	100
	pt. "Skipton in Craven"	180

	"Millers Fancy"	36
Alexander Perry	"Batchelors Purchase"	100
William Porter	"Wilsons Fancy"	100
Rachel Lee	pt. "Lybranth"	50
John Lee	pt. "Lybranth"	50
William Biggs	pt. "Benjamins Good Luck"	168
h/o Peter Johnson	pt. "Skythorn"	35
	pt. "Johnsons Lott"	40
MM Jacob & Peter Kline	pt. "Skythorn"	50
	pt. "Johnsons Lott"	99
Peter Johnson (PA)	"Johnsons Desire"	67
22:1755:82 ...		
widow Wilson	"London"	100
Josiah Wilson	pt. "Forrest"	100
William Wilson s/o Thomas	"Suburbs"	90
John Cooe	"Locust Neck"	100
Jacob Mills	"Beaver Dam Bottom"	138
Henry Rhodes	"Round Meadow"	50
James Green Martin	"Martins Fancy"	50
Joseph Harris	"White Oak Swamp"	50
John Grosenickle	"Resurvey on Grosenickle Delight"	201
Martin Shoap	"Mankine"	231
Alexander McKain	"Addition"	80
	"Don't Hits Chance Resurveyed"	280
Henry Storey	"Storeys Grove"	50
John Martin, Jr.	"Johnsons Chance"	100
	"My Home"	50
22:1755:83 ...		
George William Lawrence	"Hoggs Delight"	55
William Johnson	"Exchange"	50
William Hallom	"Great Hall"	100
	"Lookout"	215
h/o John Dunn	"James & Elizabeth"	170
William Wilson	"Long Meadow"	50
	"Wilsons Delight"	50
Andrew Scriver	"Wilsons Chance"	50

Mounts Justice	"Hard Quarter"	45
John Hobbs	"Hobbs Purchase" originally called "Bush Creek Hill"	319
Owen David	"Neighbours Neglect"	52
Daniel Richards	"Richards Delight"	50
Lawrence Heifner	"Stulls Delight"	100
Capt. William Griffeth	"Nipple"	53
	"Fairly Got"	200
	"Bubby"	100
	"Black Acre"	100
John Howard s/o Benjamin	"Marys Delight"	100
22:1755:84 ...		
William Sparks	"Sparkes Delight"	50
Rev. Henry Addison	pt. "Friendship"	500
Joseph Simms (PG)	pt. "Friendship"	500
John Millor	"Rocky Ridge"	50
Philip Knavill	"Shoemakers Knife"	50
Henry Funk	"Shippens Mistake"	54
	"Barne"	38
	"Good Luck"	50
Stephen Newton Chiswell	"What You Will"	50
George Jacob Poe	"Well Taught"	100
	"Vacancy Added to Well Taught"	1200
John Hilderbrand	"Chesnut Spring"	50
Charles Harding	"Pretty Spring"	91
	pt. "Hermitage"	58½
Elias Harding	pt. "Hermitage"	58½
Jacob Gans	"Egypt"	104
David Foutz	"Good Spring"	100
22:1755:85 ...		
William Cullom	"Hogg Pen"	64
John England	"England Choice"	100
John Johnson	"Stoney Hill"	50
	"Burnt House"	50
Ann Kersner	"Widows Last Shift"	100
George Scott (taylor)	"Setths Folly"	50

Adam Pickinpaw	"Parrott Hole"	50
	"Cross Stone"	50
h/o William Fuller	"Fullers Folly"	50
h/o Thomas Sparrow	"Sparrows Request"	100
John Nichols (Senecca)	"Hickory Levell"	45
Robert Lamar, Jr.	"Wilsons Delay"	500
	"Wells Invention"	2017
James Gore	pt. "Allisons Adventure"	150
William Summers	"Strawberry Patch"	50
22:1755:86 ...		
John Hook	"John & Sarah"	133
James Hook	"Kittocktin Bottom"	100
	pt. "Kittocktin Bottom"	50
	"Hooks Hills"	55
Robert Kindrick or Isaac McDonald	"Kendericks Hap"	50
George Fee	pt. "Andrews Folly & Discontent"	25
Richard Ancrum	pt. "Andrews Folly & Discontent"	
h/o Samuel Pottinger (PG)	pt. "Wickhams & Pottingers Discovery"	100
John Pottinger	"Addition to First Purchase"	200
Capt. John Stoddart (CH)	pt. "Friendship"	300
Thomas Cramphin	"Johns Delight"	100
	"Thomas & Mary"	450
	"Hermitage"	200
Solomon Whetnall	pt. "Charles & Thomas"	69
William Norris (Mountain)	"Norris's Seal"	65
h/o John Hayman	"Constant Friendship"	150
	"Haymans Delight"	225
h/o William Norris (schoolmaster)	"Ralpho"	65
	"Sarahs Love"	100
22:1755:87 ...		
Edward Wilson	"Wilsons Lott"	40
	pt. "Fat Oxen"	18
Thomas Johnson (Monococy) (cnp)	"No Name" a/s "Sarah Delight" a/s pt. "Two Brothers"	100
	pt. "Bear Den"	100

	pt. "New Exchange Enlargd"	24
Thomas Johnson (shoemaker)	"Fork"	50
	"Thomas Johnsons Chance"	50
Alexander Beall s/o William	"Jovial Ramble"	98
	pt. "Discovery"	268
	"Jacobs Cowpen"	50
	"Rubbish"	84
	"Refuse"	84
William Willkey	"William & Ann"	30
Lewis Duvall, Edward Crow, & Samuel Farmer	"Beginning"	29
Jonas Brown	"Williams Neglect"	50
William Starr	"Starrs Fancy"	50
John Stinchicum	"Stinchicums Friendship"	150
William Campbell	"Resurvey on Mon Ross"	580
William Albough	"Alboughs Choice"	50
Henry Cassell	"Clear Meadow"	91
22:1755:88 ...		
Robert Downey	"Downeys Lott Resurveyed"	319
	"Addition to Blanes Forrest"	100
	"Resurvey on Chester"	385
Joshua Owens (BA)	"Joshua's Lott"	430
John Jones	"Resurvey on William & John"	224
Charles Kelly	"Kellys Range"	100
John Stoner (PA)	"Cumberland"	100
	"Resurvey on Egypt"	161
Henry Forde	"White Oak Spring"	50
Joseph Benton	"Bentons Lott"	50
Solomon Brewer	"Rattle Snake Den"	50
Christian Koone	"Koones Delight"	54
Westal Ridgely	"Ridgelys Rest"	100
John Harmongart	"Dispatch"	50
George Valentine	"Swiving Swamp"	50
	"Valentines Garden"	50
22:1755:89 ...		
Handle Henn	"Henns Choice Resurveyed"	165

George Weddle	"Huckleberry Levells"	80
John Hutchinson	"Roses Delight"	50
Theobald Boon	"Boons Content"	50
George Brown	"Resurvey on Browns Delight"	500
John Cryder	pt. "Browns Delight"	100
John Logsdon	"Bedford"	50
Phillip Key, Esq. (SM)	"Paradice Regained"	530
	"Epping Forrest"	1070
	"Friendship"	206
	"Terra Rubra"	1685
Richard Smith	"Smithfield"	44
	"Christys Folly"	200
Joseph Hill	"Mountain Branch"	87
Charles Hammond s/o John	"Bite Me Softly"	152
	"Charles Lott"	42
22:1755:90 ...		
Joseph Grabble	"Shipys Neglect"	54
	"Timber Wood"	50
	"Black Oak Rushes"	50
Jacob Funk	pt. "Shippys Neglect"	20
Ezekiel Gosling	"Cool Spring"	50
George Valentine Matsgar	"Quakers Bite"	38
Dr. Henry Snavely	"Plunks Delight"	100
	"Vacancy Added to Plunks Delight"	1450
Peter Balsell	"Turnoh"	150
	"Vacancy Added to Turnoh"	630
Dennis Ensey	pt. "Coomes Inheritance"	101½
George Smith (Monococy)	"Make A Shift"	150
Richard Croxall	"Mattingsleys Part of Pork Hall"	490
Roger Davis	"Davis's Bargain"	50
	"Vacancy Added to Davis's Bargain"	72
22:1755:91 ...		
John Banks	"Taffeys Lott"	45
John Huffman	"Bethlehem"	100
	"Vacancy Added to Bethlehem"	150
Casper Devilbess	"Hunting Lott"	150

Daniel Hurley	"Friends Good Advice"	30
Jacob Matthews	"Gift"	10
	"Resurvey on Slate Hill"	220
William Stewart or Benjamin Tasker, Esq.	"Vineyard"	154
	"Vacancy Added"	352
Dr. George Stewart	"Marshal Plains"	200
James Rimmer	pt. "Chance Resurveyed"	145
h/o William West	"Two Brothers"	400
Nathaniel Magruder	"Resurvey on Grubby Thickett"	426
	pt. "Friendship"	101
	"Vacancy Added"	<n/g>
	pt. "Magruders & Bealls Honesty"	200
James Smith (blacksmith)	pt. "Grove"	37
22:1755:92 ...		
Nicholas Haymond	pt. "Constant Friendship"	150
John Youngblood	"Youngbloods Choice"	100
William Bashears	"William & John"	100
Thomas Radford	pt. "Senneca's Landing"	52
Hugh Tomlinson	pt. "John & Molly"	100
	"Squabble"	50
William & Alexander McGauhy	"Rich Levill"	214
Sarah Offutt widow of James	"William & James"	82
Thomas Gilliland	"Indian Bottom"	51
Nicholas Johnson	"Indian Bottom"	100
John Swearingen, Jr.	"Piney Hill Enlarged"	320
Matthew Clark	"Discontent"	100
	"Vacancy Added"	950
Thomas Lynthicum	"Lynthicums Chance"	50
Jeremiah Hays	"Resurvey on Jeremiah's Park"	450
22:1755:93 ...		
Nicholas Martin	"Swamp of Experience"	100
	"Vacancy Added to Swamp of Experience"	64
Frederick Unsell	"Beauty"	100
	"Vacancy Added to Beauty"	174½
Abner Lewis	"Abners Choice"	100

Jacob Hooff	"Hooffs Pigeon"	100
	"Stone Acre"	50
William Hall	"Halls Addition"	80
James Dawson	"Point Lookout"	85
Joshua Harbin	"Harbins Lott"	50
	"Vacancy Added to Harbins Lott"	50
Powell Marker	"Rooking"	50
John Beale	"Addition to Annstater"	70
Jacob Knave	"Addition to Turkey Plains"	50
	"Maitetancy"	50
Edward Burridge	"Burridges Lott"	50
22:1755:94 ...		
Joseph Hughes	"Tradesmans Value"	35
Frederick Havenor	"Havesnor Discovery"	45
Joseph Sparkes	"Sparkes Delight"	50
Isaac Garrison	"Garrisons Choice"	50
Christopher Robinger	"Isles Mountain"	94
William Wheat, Jr.	"Lucks All"	50
George Williams	"Williams Chance"	150
William Cooper	"Coopers Choice"	80½
Peter Whetstone	"Hartsmans Place"	50
Edward Ward	"Wards Pleasure"	50
Lawrence Owens	"William & Mary"	56
James Younger	"Bite Him Softly"	50
George Burkitt	"Debate Spring"	19
	"Georges Fancy"	31
	"Burkitts Folly"	25
22:1755:95 ...		
Thomas Eastup	"Rock Spring"	62
George Clark	"Cecils Chance"	60
Hugh Macclayland	"Back Meadow"	70
George Sattner	"Loving Brother"	100
Peter Shees	"Alamangle"	100
William Currance	"Peach Blossom"	50
George Sweagler	"Albrights Fancy"	50
Darby Ryan	"Mackeys Delight"	47

Stephen Richards	"Spring Garden"	50
William Dent	pt. "Dann"	150
Elizabeth Brown widow of Mark	"Golds Branch"	257
	"Hyam"	100
	"Saplin Ridge"	72
	pt. "Benjamins Lott"	166
	pt. "Gaithers Chance"	150
	pt. "Gaithers Chance"	200
22:1755:96 ...		
h/o Benjamin Gaither	pt. "Gaithers Chance"	534½
Edward Gaither (AA)	pt. "Gaithers Purchase"	100
	pt. "Benjamin"	150
John Hammond s/o Thomas John (AA)	pt. "Gaithers Chance"	177½
	"Strife"	1230
John Hammond s/o Charles (AA)	"Discovery"	15
	"Hammons Contrivance"	280
Henry Gaitther (AA)	"Benjamin's Lott Resurveyed"	238
Matthew Howard	"Cold Friday"	93
Michael Legatt	"Dam Head"	74
	"Vacancy Added to Dam Head"	240
Jacob Gripe	"Nonsuch Resurveyed"	300
Clement Davis	"Hunting Hill"	300
	pt. "Pines"	78
Mrs. Lemar widow of Thomas	pt. "Two Brothers"	300
Samuel Lamar	"Anns Garden"	50
	"Conclusion"	213
John Lamar s/o Thomas	pt. "Joseph & James"	135
	pt. "Conclusion"	85
	pt. "Pines"	52½
22:1755:97 ...		
John Rawlins	"Lost Hatchett"	50
	"Beginning"	100
	"Hobsons Choice"	50
Richard Simpson	"Simpsons Choice"	214
	"Vacancy Added to Simpsons Choice"	279

James Wardrop (PG)	"Partnership"	285
	"Red Oak Levill"	100
	"Wooden Platter Resurveyed"	327
	"Oxford"	54
	"Johns Delight"	104
	"Brentford"	35
	"Bloomsbury"	104
	"Coolspring"	75
	"Dear Bought Resurveyed"	500
	"Resurvey on Hazard"	690
Jonathan Wilson	pt. "Happy Choice"	593
Gilbert Sprigg (PG)	pt. "Piles Delight"	400
James Sprigg	pt. "Piles Delight"	400
John Webster (BA)	"Fountain"	100
William Beall, Sr.	"William & Elizabeth"	135
	pt. "Friendship Enlarg'd"	290
	pt. "Discontent"	100
	"Hill & Dale"	66
	pt. "Prevention"	11
Richard Beall	pt. "Fat Oxen"	55
22:1755:98 ...		
Nathaniel Beall	pt. "Fat Oxen"	262
William Magruder Selby	pt. "Fat Oxen"	98
John Richards	"Welshmans Purchase" originally pt. "Prevention"	122
Joseph Beall s/o Ninian	"Lost & Found"	85
	pt. "Fat Oxen"	46
	"Choice Improved"	649
William Webb	"Darlings Sale"	420
Walter Frienderburgh	pt. "Jamaica" originally "Maidens Choice"	200
Hance Waggoner	"Flaggy Meadow"	121
	"Long Meadow"	25
	"Smiths Lott"	50
Samuel Reed	"Nowry"	50
	"Baileys Purchase"	26
	"York"	168

Larkin Pierpoint	"Second Addition"	42
	"Peirpoints Range"	139
Jacob Smith	"Jacobs Fancy"	21
John Johnson (Tuscaroror)	"Johnsons Folly"	108½
Thomas Powell	"First Choice"	50
22:1755:99 ...		
John Leatherman	"Much Grumbling"	30
Peter Youngsey	"By the Garden"	89
John Emmitt	"Emmitts Fancy"	100
Felting Shoutacre	"Hobsons Choice"	40
John Forrest Davis	"Charles & James"	50
Conrod Hogmire	"White Oak Grove"	50
	"Beaver Dam"	101
Jacob Broombagh	"Claylands Contrivance"	90
	"Ill Will"	100
John Carie	"Panmure"	50
Andrew McHiver	"Bethlehem"	100
Archibald Beall	"Bealls Discovery"	26
Thomas Gilbert	"Gilberts Inheritance"	50
Michael Funk	"Margaretts Industry"	50
Edward Chambers	"Hare Hill"	53
22:1755:100 ...		
Hugh Green	"Pleasant Spring"	50
Alexander Mackeon	"Williams Lott"	25
Thomas Awbrrey (VA)	"Heartsless Island"	18
Michael Hodgkiss	"Resurvey on Hawkins Chance"	284
Thomas Sloy	"Sloys Consideration"	108
Peter Dyesar	"Mistaken Friend"	106
John Larkins	"Larkins Lott"	45
Zachariah Albough	"Alboughs Choice"	125
	"Alboughs Delight"	125
John Bombland	"Chance"	110
Matthias Morrnett	"Hard to Find"	54
Mary Brooke (PG)	"Chance"	25
	"Jonas's Discovery"	60
John Holland	"Hollands Delight"	50

Rebecca Brooke (PG)	"Azalon"	20
22:1755:101 ...		
Rachel Brooke	"Gibson"	20
John Spurgeon	"Fathers Good Will"	46
John Martin Whip	"Piney Grove"	50
Alexander Gordon	"Gordon's Chance"	25
David Dean	"Resurvey on Davids Choice"	174
John Waters s/o John	"Resurvey on Wards Delight"	256
	"Paris"	100
William Shoope	"Rogues Harbour"	110
h/o John Kennedy	pt. "Resurvey on Dublin"	821
Daniel Vears, Jr.	pt. "Dublin Resurveyed"	50
Alexander Magruder (PG)	"Lost Pen & Ink"	150
John Kellor	"Resurvey on Ash Swamp" & "Head of the Ash Swamp"	363
Henry Peirpoint (AA)	"Peirpoint Discovery"	210
Casper Smith	"Resurvey on Mount Olivet"	487
22:1755:102 ...		
John Buxton	"Buxtons Delight Resurveyed"	570
Henry Starts	"Startmans Shears"	100
James Downey	"Nicholas's Contrivance"	110
	"Nicholas's Contrivance"	75
	"All I Could Get"	28
Thomas Hog	"White Oak Swamp"	93
John Dutteraer	"Matthews Good Will"	200
Joseph Hartman	"Four Friends"	118
John Eason	"Discovery"	100
William Kirk	"Williams Chance"	50
James Kendrick	"Kendricks First Choice"	100
Henry Butler 3rd s/o Capt. Henry	"Uncles Favour"	100
Nicholas Back	"Chesnut Hill"	64
22:1755:103 ...		
Charles Hoskinson	"Elizabeth Delight"	32
Brice Worley	"Worleys Choice"	50
William Douglass	"Scotts Grief"	100

Joseph Frivell	"Coursey"	30
Andrew Spowles	"Deer Spring"	58
Greenberry Cheney	"Hopewell"	100
	"Cheneys Lott"	50
John Carmack, Stephen & Daniel Richards	"Hobsons Choice"	25
John Barber	"Barbers Outlett"	53
William Patrick	"Williams Tryal"	50
Daniel Leatherman	"Pilgrims Harbour"	50
Thomas Durbin	"Fathers Advice"	50
William Littlefield	"William & John"	100
22:1755:104 ...		
John Trennor	"Jones's Lott"	50
Conrod Miller	"Millers Desire"	100
Jacob Meek	"Kent"	50
Richard Stevenson	"Discovery"	100
Aaron Moore	"Addition to Chenys Neck"	50
Nicholas King	"Kings Hill"	50
Philemon Barnes	"Horse Pasture"	100
Paul Rhode	"Dry Spring Joyning to a Sharp Rock"	100
William Tegarden	"Tocarts Delight"	150
John Carr	"Hurns Choice"	300
John Myers	"Boyles Fancy"	50
John Maccantire	"Smiths Choice"	50
22:1755:105 ...		
Tobias Stansbury (BA)	"Fellfoot Enlarged"	2100
	"Cumberland"	50
	"Lott"	50
Samuel Middleton (Annapolis)	"Pools Delight"	287
h/o Joseph Cowman (AA)	"Catch As Catch Can He That Gets the Land is the Best Man"	540
	"Cowmans Mannor"	454
Francis Warring (PC)	"Warrington"	270
Lucy Brooke (PG)	"Venture"	32
Ninian Veach	"Narrow Lane"	46
Peter Ridingover	"First Snow"	190

Edward Ricketts	"Mistaken Friend"	116
James Crow	"Resurvey on Locust Levill"	363
Thomas Wilson s/o Thomas	pt. "Ridge & Knaves Disappointment"	66
John Jack	"Jacks Bottom"	175
William Boyd	pt. "Castle Plains"	150
	"Pleasant Bottom"	164
22:1755:106 ...		
Benjamin Perry	pt. "Hermitage"	250
	"Addition to Honsley"	50
Charles Bussey	"Red Oak Bottom"	60
	"Self de Fence"	113
	"Coop Spring Mannor"	50
	"Exchange"	40
	"Unexpected"	100
Samuel Thomas	pt. "Winexburgh"	493
	pt. "Snowdens 4th Addition to His Mannor"	1029
Thomas Hinton	"Resurvey on Sapling Ridge"	290
	"Pleasant Plain"	100
Phillip Hammond (AA)	"First Choice"	190
Stephen George Woolbrack & Jacob Gripe	"Laffodays Lott"	100
	"Marsh Head"	100
	"Walnut Grove"	175
John Darling	"Darlings Choice"	150
Joseph Perry	"Doccot"	108
David Peirpoint (AA)	"Small Bit to David"	40
22:1755:107 ...		
Edward Doran	pt. "Bear Bacon"	233½
Isaac Downs	pt. "Bear Bacon"	233½
Charles Graham (CV) & John Cook, Esq.	"Hope"	50
	"Barbers Beginning"	100
	"Breshears Choice"	45
Philip Loyd Chew & Bennet Chew	"Chews Farm Resurveyed"	5000
Hartman Vertrees	"Blew Spring"	100
George Atkinson for the benefit of h/o Chris. Grindall	"Shadracks Lott" surveyed for Nicholas Hail	262
	"Abednegoe's Pasture" surveyed for Nicholas Hail	70

William Mackey	"Ship"	25
Michael Tanner	"White Oak Woods"	46
Matthias Purget	"Wifes Fancy"	51
Ulrick Ekler	"New Sitzerland"	200
22:1755:108 ...		
William Lux	"By Chance"	108
	"Long Bottom"	120
Andrew Grim	"Rod Liquor"	50
Samuel Paughley	"Samuel Rackt"	50
Margarett Decartee	"Second Tryal"	50
Peter Hufman	"Peters Rum"	64
William Beall	"Long Lookt for"	42
Solomon Miller	"Its Hard to Find Out"	34
Thomas Stoddart	"Hog Park"	43
	"Tryal"	25
Johannes Leather	"Man Felt"	50
22:1755:109 ...		
Peter French	"French's Vineyard"	50
Patrick Murphy	"Addition to Smithfield"	13
Lodowicke Young	"Addition to Simons Neck"	16
Thomas Meek	"Mullins Delight"	60
John Ellison	"Part Purchase"	9½
Johannes Vandlestem	"Turkeys Range"	100
Daniel Ullick	"Stoney Hill"	16
Abraham Wise	"Looking Land"	103
Chris. Michael	"Small Meadow"	100
John Avey	"Johns Delight"	83
Jacob Sideman	"Sidemans Delight"	40
22:1755:110 ...		
George Ridingover	"Ridingover Place"	50
Andrew Bostian	"Turkless"	50
Richard Burrill	"What You Please"	25
Robert Rheinhart	"Rheinharts First Choice"	50
Hance Terig Croney	"Croneys Chance"	100
Jacob Weist	"Charming Beauty"	25
George Nahel	"Narrow Hollow"	100

Abraham Lingarfield	"Grindstone Rock"	100
John Kent	"Chance"	142
	"Kent Chance"	70
William House	"Long Bottom"	72
22:1755:111 ...		
Isaac Houser	"Resurvey on St. Patricks Lott"	587
John Rowe	"Rich Meadow"	100
Samuel Glaze	"Dry Spring"	158
John Williams	"Breeches Resurveyed" – originally 100 a.	238
John Gardner	"Gardners Discovery"	25
Jacob Rik	"Benjaner Penry"	100
Deval Coonce	"Devals Lott"	70
MM Edward & Jacob Sprigg	"Vacancy Added to Happy Choice"	1634
Moses Pigman	"Locust Bottom"	88
Henry W. Crabb & John Needham	"Lapland"	450
	"Toband"	130
22:1755:112 ...		
Henry Beall	pt. "Fat Oxen"	285
Jacob Keller	pt. "Den of Wolves"	100
Robert Lemar	pt. "Joseph & James"	200
	pt. "Two Brothers"	200
	pt. "Pines"	45
	"Resurvey on Mill Tract"	173
	"Coys Lott"	100
	"Mill Tract"	93
Richard Snowden (cnp)	"Snowdens Mannor Enlargd" composed of: • "Snowdens Mannor" • "Addition to Snowdens Mannor" • "Third Addition to His Mannor" • "Snowdens Fourth Addition to His Mannor"	9265
	pt. "Beals Mannor"	523
	"John & Sarah"	200
	pt. "Snowdens Mill Land"	153
	"Moores Rest"	185
	"Walnut Levils"	50
	pt. "Ganders Delight"	73

	"John & Catherine"	76
James Ellis	pt. "Chance Resurveyed"	64
22:1755:113 <blank>		
22:1755:114-5 Recapitulation		
22:1755:116-7 <blank>		
22:1755:118 Short Paid		
David Cox	"Lubberland"	50
Cornelius Vernoy	pt. "Concord"	236
Adam Stull	pt. "Chesnut Hills"	175
22:1755:119 Doubly Charged & Overpayments		
James Edmonson	"Piles Hall"	<n/g>
Abraham Eltinge	"Abrahams Lott"	<n/g>
James Dickson	"Stoney Range" – not to be charged	<n/g>
John Magruder, Jr.	pt. "Grubby Thickett" – not to be charged	166
Thomas Johnson (Kittochtin)	"Johnsons Levels Resurveyed"	158
Ninian Magruder	pt. "Magruder & Beals Honesty"	83
Francis Pierpoint	"Small Hopes" – overcharged	30
John Chambers	"Bear Den" – not to be charged	100
John Parr	"Parrs Range" – not to be charged	100
<n/g>	"Millers Chance" – overcast	100
John Waters, Jr.	<n/g> – twice charged	300
Benjamin Berry	"Addition to Hensley"	50
Nathaniel Magruder	pt. "Grubby Thickett"	93
Richard Snowden	<n/g>	892
Thomas Wilson	pt. "Ridge & Knaves Dispute"	<n/g>
William Plummer	<n/g>	<n/g>
Robert Lamar	"Mill Tract" – included in resurvey	93
Samuel Plummer	<n/g> – overcast	<n/g>
Samuel Beal	"Addition to Mil Seat" – overcharged	<n/g>
22:1755:120 ...		
George Clem	"Lost Spring" – not to be charged	150
h/o John Kennaday	"Resurvey on Dublin" – not to be charged	981
John Pool	"Pools Delight" – not to be charged	100
Martin Wetsall	"Resurvey on Bonnets Resolution"	250
Jacob Gans	<n/g> – not to be charged	104
22:1755:121 Adjustments		

John Flint	"Newton"	245
<n/g>	"Lost Spring" is the same as "George & Margaret"	150
h/o John Kennady	"Resurvey on Dublin" – twice charged	981
Pool & Middleton	"Pools Delight"	100
<n/g>	"Bonnets Resolution"	250
John Reeter	"Higginbothams Exchange" resurveyed into "Hagars Delight" – not to be charged	100
Peter Bomgarner	pt. "Nazareth" – twice charged	100
Adam Mayner	"White Gravel Spring" – twice charged	190
Jos. Wilson	"Boys Lott" – twice charged	100
	"Mill Tract" – twice charged	93
William Kirley	"St. Patricks" – twice charged	127
Charles Finlay	"Nonsuch" – twice charged	136
(N) McDonald	"Watsons Welfare" – twice charged	100
John Howard	"Pretty Sally" – resurveyed by E. Dorsey	20
	"2nd Adventure" – resurveyed by E. Dorsey	54
John Parr	"Bush Creek Hill" – twice charged	100
Isaac Downes	pt. "Bear Bacon" – twice charged	233½
Abel Brown	"Abels Levels" – twice charged	400
John Beall	pt. "Grove" – twice charged	18
John Hoskinson	pt. "Grove" – twice charged	44
Richard Clagett	pt. "Labyrinth" – twice charged	183¾
	pt. "Pritchets Purchase" – twice charged	38
Martin Whetsall	"Wine Garden" – twice charged	150
M. Milhouse	"Flaggy Meadow" – overcharged	60
Jacob Gans & John Stoner	"Resurvey on Egypt"	104
<n/g>	"Calebs Delight" – overcharged	200
J. Ross	"Resurvey of Black Oak Hall" – overcharged	50
(N) Snowden	"2nd Addition" – not to be left out	70
John Thomas	"Snowdens Manor Enlarged" & "Snowdens 3rd Addition"	549
James Brooke	"Snowdens Manor Enlarged" & "Snowdens 3rd Addition"	392
William Richardson	"Snowdens Manor Enlarged" & "Snowdens 3rd Addition"	200
Benjamin Rickets	"Snowdens Manor Enlarged" & "Snowdens 3rd Addition"	134

22:1755:122 Additions		
Charles Cheney	"Cheneys Neck"	52
Charles Walker	"Long Lookt for"	46
Fielder Gant	"Swedes Marsh"	300
Thomas Miles	pt. "Labyrinth"	150
George Valentine	"Valentines Garden"	50
Col. Lee (f. 23)	<n/g>	<n/g>
(N) Pierpoint (f. 24)	<n/g>	<n/g>
Dr. Carrol (f. 76)	<n/g>	<n/g>
22:1755:123 ...		
Col. Cresap (f. 34)	<n/g>	<n/g>
(N) Plummer (f. 51)	<n/g>	<n/g>
(N) Brown (f. 95)	<n/g>	<n/g>
22:1755:124 To be Deducted		
James Swann	pt. "Dan"	26
<n/g>	pt. "Moores Industry"	30
<n/g>	"Breeches"	100
Col. Cresap	"Indian Field"	250
	pt. "Skythorn"	40
<n/g>	"Batchelors Delight"	100
<n/g>	"Slate Ridge"	123
<n/g>	"Dickinsons Delight"	133
<n/g>	pt. "Progress"	44
<n/g>	"Elswicks Dwelling"	9
<n/g>	"Resurvey on Davids Choice"	174
<n/g>	"Long Meadow"	<n/g>
h/o John Bowie	"Wickham & Pottingers Discovery"	200
James Magruder, Jr.	"Addition to Wickham & Pottingers Discovery"	50
In Prince George's Co.		
John Brice	"Wintersells"	400
George Moore	pt. "Gideon"	20
William Hughs	pt. "James & Mary"	130
John Moore	pt. "Elizabeths Manor"	100
Solomon Turner	pt. "Ralpho"	202
James Green Martin	"Martins Fancy"	50
John Halsell	pt. "Cuckolds Delight"	100

Stephen Lannum	pt. "William & Elizabeth"	118
William Shaw	pt. "William & Elizabeth"	14
John Thompson	"Thompsons Hoop Thickett"	34
George Moore	"Mores Industry"	100

www.ingramcontent.com/pod-product-compliance
Lightning Source LLC
Chambersburg PA
CBHW070544270326
41926CB00013B/2201

* 9 7 8 0 8 0 6 3 5 7 2 0 1 *